WHEN INFORMATION CAME OF AGE

WHEN INFORMATION
CAME OF AGE

❧

Technologies of Knowledge
in the Age of Reason and Revolution,
1700–1850

DANIEL R. HEADRICK

UNIVERSITY PRESS

2000

OXFORD
UNIVERSITY PRESS

Oxford   New York
Athens   Auckland   Bangkok   Bogotá   Buenos Aires   Calcutta
Cape Town   Chennai   Dar es Salaam   Delhi   Florence   Hong Kong   Istanbul
Karachi   Kuala Lumpur   Madrid   Melbourne   Mexico City   Mumbai
Nairobi   Paris   São Paulo   Shanghai   Singapore   Taipei   Tokyo   Toronto   Warsaw

and associated companies in
Berlin   Ibadan

Published by Oxford University Press, Inc.
198 Madison Avenue, New York, New York 10016

Oxford is a registered trademark of Oxford University Press.

Library of Congress Cataloging-in-Publication Data
Headrick, Daniel R.
When information came of age : technologies of knowledge in the age of reason and
revolution, 1700–1850 / Daniel R. Headrick.
    p.   cm.
Includes bibliographical references and index.
ISBN 0-19-513597-0
1. Europe—Intellectual life—18th century.   2. Europe—Intellectual life—
19th century.   3. Learning and scholarship—Europe—History—18th century.
4. Learning and scholarship—Europe—History—19th century.   5. Information
resources—Europe—History—18th century.   6. Information resources—
Europe—History—19th century.   7. Enlightenment.   I. Title.
CB203 .H39 1999
306.4'2—dc21   99-050103

9 8 7 6 5 4 3 2 1

Printed in the United States of America
on acid-free paper

PREFACE

This book is an essay on the development of efficient information systems before the great push to mechanize information in the nineteenth century. Some of the systems discussed here—maps, dictionaries, botanical nomenclatures—had their origin in the distant past but were rationalized and improved in the period studied here. Others, such as statistics, graphs, and the telegraph, were truly new.

The chapters are arranged according to the purposes that systems serve: organizing, transforming, displaying, storing, and communicating information. Each chapter presents a few case studies to illustrate that particular function. This does not mean that there is a one-to-one correspondence between function and system. On the contrary, every system performs several functions; thus, cartography involves gathering information, naming and organizing that information in words and numbers, and transforming words or numbers into a graphical representation, the map, which then serves to store that information and communicate it to others. A book like this is not a replica of the real world; like a map, a graph, or a statistic, it is a lens through which to see the world.

Chapter 1 sets out the two goals of this book. One is to define the idea of information and to show that the "information revolution" is not a recent phenomenon (as some would have it) but has deep historical roots. The other is to trace the origin of some important information systems, and the flowering of others, to the eighteenth and early nineteenth centuries, the Age of Reason and Revolution.

Chapter 2 deals with systems for *organizing and classifying information,* using as its case study the language of science. The major contributions of the eighteenth and early nineteenth centuries to science revolved less around conceptual breakthroughs (Newton came before our period, and Darwin after) than in producing a flood of new observations and developing systems for handling them. Large quantities of information could be processed and understood only if there were means of classifying and organizing them. Hence, the important advances in science in this period were accompanied by new vocabularies that allowed an efficient classification of scientific findings and clarified the relationship between observed phenomena. In the life sciences, this was a product of Linnaeus's taxonomy; in chemistry, it was the work of Lavoisier's nomenclature of elements and compounds; and in all the sciences that involved measurement, it was the result of the metric system.

Chapter 3 deals with statistics as means of *transforming information*. Turning an accumulation of facts or anecdotes into numbers not only compresses them but also allows patterns to emerge that would remain hidden in narratives; thus, to the early practitioners of "political arithmetick," mortality tables (the numbers of deaths by parish every week) revealed the incidence of various diseases. From this small beginning arose the idea of demographic surveys, of censuses, and of sociological inquiries. The mania for counting and quantifying and for analyzing the resulting numbers, so characteristic of our own times, dates back to the eighteenth and early nineteenth centuries.

Chapter 4 also deals with systems used to transform and display information, namely, maps and graphs, but with the emphasis on their *display function*. While the information contained in maps and graphs differs, as systems they have much in common, for they translate narrative descriptions or tables of numbers (e.g., the depth of the sea, imports and exports) into a graphical form that can be grasped more quickly, and sometimes more accurately, than with lists of words or verbal descriptions.

Maps are an ancient form of expression, and historians of cartography have properly focused their attention on the dramatic increase in geographic knowledge represented in the cartography of the fifteenth through seventeenth centuries. By the eighteenth century, there were still blank spots to fill on the map of the world, but fewer than before. Consequently, the focus shifted from discovery and description to accuracy and precision. In a word, cartography became scientific.

Scientific cartography stimulated a growing interest in depicting other phenomena graphically. In particular, the compilation of statistics led to attempts to make such information more accessible to the public. Whereas statistics represented a means of processing information, graphs were a means of displaying and communicating it. Meanwhile, new information about the earth—geological formations, the altitude of mountains, the distribution of population or economic activities—posed similar challenges to cartographers. In their attempts to make such information visible, they developed various hybrids between graphs and traditional maps.

Chapter 5 looks at two familiar *information storage and retrieval* systems: dictionaries and encyclopedias. Although each has a long history, the eighteenth century saw a sharp increase in the number of new works, editions, and copies sold, reflecting the growing demand for general knowledge among the educated public. In addition to an increase in the amount of information compiled and disseminated in dictionaries and encyclopedias, there were also significant changes in how their information was presented—in particular the vernacular languages and the alphabetical order—aimed at making them easier and more practical to use.

Chapter 6 deals with two systems of *communicating information*. One of them—the postal service—underwent dramatic changes that transformed it from the slow, costly, and unreliable service of the seventeenth century into a fast, inexpensive, and reliable service open to the general public. The other was radically new: the creation of the semaphore telegraph and naval flag-signaling system, ways to send messages faster than any person or object could travel. Both responded to the growing needs of business, government, and the military for information about distant events, a need that was greatly accelerated by the revolutions and wars of the turn of the century.

The information systems discussed in this book, though numerous, constitute a small sampling, not a comprehensive list. Readers familiar with the period will immediately spot glaring omissions. The chapter on nomenclatures discusses biology, chemistry, and metrology but not physics or geology; also missing are the innovations in mathematical and musical notation systems. The chapter on quantification fails to discuss the evolution of accounting and bookkeeping systems, both of enormous importance to commerce and government. Graphical representation includes not only the maps and graphs represented in chapter 4 but also land registers and cadastral surveys, technical and scientific illustrations, pattern books, and engineering drawings. The chapter on compendia of information deals with dictionaries and encyclopedias because they were popular and useful to a broad spectrum of the population. But there were dozens of other compendia: law codes, calendars, almanacs, stagecoach schedules, lists of the peerage and nobility, astronomical ephemerides, cookbooks, and technical manuals of all sorts. Organizations such as museums, libraries, herbaria, and botanical gardens were also compendia of information, albeit not in print. Governments and businesses developed various filing methods to keep track of their information. Finally, under communications, the press disseminated not only political news and gossip but also information on financial matters (stock, bond, and commodity price quotations) and ships' arrivals and departures.

Clearly, this book only dips its toe into a very large sea. My purpose in writing it was not to offer an encyclopedia of information systems in the Age of Reason and Revolution but to introduce the concept of information systems as a tool of historical analysis and to demonstrate, through a few examples, that the culture of information systems—knowledge presented efficiently—existed long before the computer, even before the electric telegraph.

It is my hope that other historians will find the concept of information systems useful and will be tempted to extend the analysis and fill in the gaps. There is still so much to do.

Many people generously gave of their time to help me in organizing my thoughts, finding information, and writing this book. For over twenty years, William H. McNeill has been a friend, a mentor, and a role model. Joel Mokyr has long been an enthusiastic supporter and perceptive critic. Richard R. John helped me refine my thinking and avoid glaring errors. I would also like to thank Geoffrey Bowker and several anonymous readers for their valuable comments. Thomas LeBien and Susan Ferber of Oxford University Press have followed this project over a period of many years. Will Moore and Susan Ecklund did a superb job of copyediting and producing this book. David Robyak wrote a fine index. All of these individuals have offered me good advice that I sometimes took to heart, but too often ignored.

A book like this one could not have come of age without the encouragement and generous support of several institutions. A fellowship from the John Simon Guggenheim Foundation allowed me to spend the 1994–1995 academic year reading and broadening my understanding of information systems. I am deeply indebted to the foundation for its generosity. I am also indebted to the Alfred P. Sloan Foundation and its program officer, Jesse Ausubel, for a fellowship in 1998 that enabled me to begin writing this book. I am most grateful to Roosevelt University for awarding me a faculty research leave in 1993 and permitting me to absent myself on several other occasions. I also wish to thank the Regenstein and John Crerar Libraries of the University of Chicago, the Newberry Library, the Murray Green Library of Roosevelt University, and the New York Public Library for allowing me to use their collections, and their patient and skillful staffs for helping locate the material I needed.

I dedicate this book to my wife, Kate, and to my grandsons Zel and Avram, who make me happy when skies are gray.

Chicago, Illinois   D. R. H.
Spring 2000

CONTENTS

WHEN INFORMATION CAME OF AGE

I

INFORMATION AND ITS HISTORY

November 16, 1992—the day the Information Age began in America.... Most computer folks would place the beginning of the Information Age well before this year—maybe 10, 25, or even 50 years ago.

BOB METCALFE, *"ISDN Is the Information Age Infrastructure,"*
INFOWORLD, December 7, 1992

OF THE MANY LABELS PUNDITS HAVE SUGGESTED TO IDENTIFY THE AGE WE live in—the atomic age, the Postindustrial era, the space age—the expression *information age* has become the standard cliché.[1] Why this label? Why now?

No doubt because we have all sorts of new devices designed to keep us informed and in touch with anyone, anywhere, and at any time: beepers, cellular telephones, computers, "personal digital assistants," and all their peripherals. We access more media of more varied sorts than ever before: dozens of television channels, soon to be hundreds; electronic networks turning into global information superhighways; and the imminent promise of cyberspace and virtual reality for everyone.

In the business world, purveyors of software have dethroned computer makers, while manufacturers of audio and video equipment are turning into entertainment companies. In the wealthier countries, an ever-growing proportion of the gross domestic product comes from the information sector rather than from manufacturing, as more and more people work with computers and relax with electronic entertainment.

Most of all, we face an ever-swelling tide of information in the form of Web sites, CDs, and DVDs, videotapes and video games, docudramas, databases, hypertexts, and infomercials, not to mention old-fashioned books, magazines, and newspapers.

Information and Knowledge

What, then, is this "information" that defines our epoch? To mathematicians and scientists, the term *information* means the reduction of uncertainty in a communication system.[2] In that sense, any pattern of energy or matter in nature—tree rings, bits of DNA, light from a distant star, the spoor of an animal—contains information.

Like the tree that falls in the forest, however, such patterns become *human* information only if there is a human being present who understands them. So let us leave undeciphered patterns to the scientists and think of information as patterns of energy and matter that humans understand.

Information is not the same thing as knowledge, though the two concepts overlap. Knowledge refers to ideas and facts that a human mind has internalized and understood: how to fix a flat tire, the name of a really good dentist, speaking French. Acquiring knowledge means absorbing a lot of information—for example, how to use French irregular verbs correctly. Often, the mind acquires and organizes such information in a spontaneous and even subconscious fashion, the way a child learns to speak or a taxi driver knows her way around town. At other times, the acquisition of knowledge requires studying, a slow and difficult process.

The amount of knowledge that a human mind can hold is truly extraordinary, but it is not infinite, nor is the mind reliable. Hence the need for information. As society becomes more complex and its interactions speed up, access to information becomes increasingly important. Education was once focused on learning, that is, on acquiring knowledge; it now stresses research skills. What matters is not knowing the answer but knowing where to look it up. And that means the information is (one hopes) out there, readily accessible.

Information Systems

Information implies an assemblage of data, such as a telephone book, a map, a dictionary, or a database—not random data, however, but data organized in a systematic fashion. If we were to undertake the study of information, our task would be unending. Instead, let us focus on a more manageable concept, the study of information *systems*. By systems, I mean the methods and techniques by which people organize and manage information, rather than the content of the information itself. Information systems were created to supplement the mental functions of thought, memory, and speech. They are, if you will, the technologies of knowledge. Let us consider a few examples.

In a first category, we can put the many systems used to gather information. This includes the methods used by journalists, researchers, and spies; and, more elaborately, the activities of research organizations, laboratories, surveys, and censuses, to name only a few.

A second category includes systems for naming, classifying, and organizing pieces of information to make them comparable and accessible in an efficient manner. Libraries classify books according to the Library of Congress or the Dewey decimal system; medicine classifies diseases into nosologies; colleges classify students by year and by major; the armed forces classify their members by rank and unit; biologists have their taxonomies of plants and animals; and so on. The need to classify grows in proportion to the amount of information, so classification systems are naturally associated with organizations that handle vast amounts of information, such as the police, the patent office, or the telephone companies. There is even a bureau that registers comets.

Since information can come in many forms, a third category includes all the systems used to transform information from one form into another and to display it in a new way. Examples of such transformations might include turning narrative descriptions into lists, lists into statistical tables, statistics into graphs, or graphs into three-dimensional objects. There are dozens of systems that transform and display information, from engineering drawing to polling to mapmaking, and many organizations that do this sort of work. The analysis of such transformations constitutes a large part of the study of information systems in general.

In a fourth category we can put the many systems designed for storing and retrieving information. Here are found such historical artifacts as dictionaries and encyclopedias, schedules and calendars, telephone books and directories, and such organizations as museums, archives, libraries, and botanical gardens. More recently, databases have been proliferating like daffodils in the springtime.

Finally, a fifth category includes systems for communicating information. Within this category, some, such as the postal service, messengers, the telegraph, the telephone, or electronic mail, transmit information from point to point, while others, like newspapers, radio, television, and the World Wide Web, broadcast information from one point to many.

This little taxonomy is clearly incomplete. In particular, many systems serve several functions at once. Newspapers, for example, are both a communications medium (for recent news) and a storage and information system (for old news); museums and botanical gardens not only store and retrieve but also display and communicate. Thus, we must be careful to distinguish the *forms* that information can take from the *systems* with which it is handled. What is astonishing about the current information age is not only the amount of information available but also the proliferation of systems needed to handle it and of organizations that employ these systems.

Efficiency and Data

Individuals and organizations acquire and use information for a variety of purposes. One purpose is simply possession and the satisfaction it gives; witness the pride some people take in their phenomenal memory for trivia, their extensive libraries, their collections of compact disks, maps, or computer programs. Possessing information also confers prestige. Erudition and especially initiation into the esoteric knowledge of a small sect or secret society—Freemasons, cosmologists, and the like—have conferred prestige and awed the ignorant throughout history.

These are, however, static uses of knowledge. When information is used in an active situation—in business, in law, in medicine, in war, or even in catching a plane or making a telephone call—time enters into the equation. The time it takes to obtain and use the relevant information puts a premium on the efficiency with which it is organized.

Memory and narrative serve well enough in many situations, as they have throughout history. As the pace of life has quickened and as society, organizations, and personal lives have become more complex, however, memory has proved too unreliable and written narratives too haphazard to satisfy people's needs. Hence people have sought improvements in the efficiency of information systems—in other words, ways of handling information more rapidly, more reliably, and at lower cost than before.

To classify, process, store, retrieve, or transmit information quickly or with less cost and effort, it must be compressed, codified, and organized in a systematic fashion. In the process, narrative, descriptive, or decorative information is turned into *data*. Data can be expressed in words (as in a dictionary), in numbers (as in grade point averages and baseball statistics), in an alphanumeric code (as in telephone numbers), in symbols (as in mathematical or musical notation), in graphics (as in maps, statistical graphs, or scientific illustrations), and in many other ways. Data can be stored in and transmitted through many different media: by speech and memory, albeit not very well; more efficiently, by writing and printing; and most efficiently of all, in the newer electrical and electronic media.

We live in a world of data. On an average day, we need to unravel myriad cryptograms: sports statistics ("Knicks 27 11 .711"), stock market quotations ("NtwkEq 406 9 1/2 +7/8 +10.1"), e-mail addresses ("STOE2G@ UNI-BOCCONI.IT"), legal citations ("*Greenman v. Yuba Power Products, Inc.*, 59 Cal 2d 57, 377 P2d 897, 27 Cal Rptr 697 (1963)"), test scores ("720 on the SAT"), and media jargon ("20 percent probability of precipitation"), to name just a few.

Consider how we identify a book. We can describe its contents or its cover with a brief narrative ("that book about the post office, you know, the one with the picture of Mercury on the dust jacket"). Better yet, we can use its bibliographic citation, a verbal description that is short and precise but not narrative ("John, Richard R. *Spreading the News: The American Postal System from Franklin to Morse.* Cambridge, Mass.: Harvard University Press, 1995"). Even shorter is the call number ("HE6185.U5J640"), a code that identifies not only the book but also its subject matter and its location in a library. Even more compressed is the ISBN number ("0-674-83338-4"), designed for computers rather than people. Finally, bar codes identify books to computers but not to humans. In the process of becoming data, the identification of the book is increasingly removed from the verbal, narrative form common in oral language.

The Start of the Information Age

Living in the midst of an "information revolution," surrounded by an explosion of systems, it is fair to ask: When did this revolution begin?

Two historians of science, Michael Riordan and Lillian Hoddeson, attribute the birth of the information age to the invention of the transistor.[3] Bill Gates, CEO of Microsoft Corporation and self-appointed wizard of the Information Age, agrees: "My first stop on this time-travel expedition would be the Bell Labs in December 1947 to witness the invention of the transistor. . . . It was a key transitional event in the advent of the Information Age."[4]

Historians for whom information systems are a fruitful analytical concept are likely to ask when the information age began and how it has developed. For them, the year 1992, or even 1947, seems too recent to explain such a significant change in our culture as the information age. Yet in seeking a more plausible origin of this revolution, each historian has a different date in mind. Some trace the information age back to the late nineteenth century, with the rise of railroads and other large business enterprises spread across a continent.[5] Others go back to the introduction of the telegraph and steam-powered newspaper presses in the first half of the nineteenth century.[6] Still others have analyzed the impact of the printing press on European civilization, between the fifteenth and the eighteenth century.[7]

When scholars disagree, what is a reader to think? When, in fact, did the information age *really* begin? The short answer is: the Information Age has no beginning, for it is as old as humankind. Nonetheless, in the course of history there have been periods of sharp *acceleration* (revolutions, if your prefer) in the amount of information that people had access to and in the creation of information systems to deal with it. The appearance of writing, the alphabet, double-entry bookkeeping, the printing press, the telegraph, the transistor, and the computer—each has contributed mightily to the acceleration of information in their time. In short, there have been many information revolutions.

With few exceptions, most historians who have tried to explain the "information revolution" of the period they have studied have attributed great significance to certain favored machines: the printing press, the telegraph, the computer. For example, Steven Lubar explains:

> . I call this new world of information, communications, and entertainment machines an information culture. I use the term "information culture" because these machines, and the social structures that they are part of, have come to define our culture, at least as much as ethnicity, race, or geography. How we feel about the world around us, about one another, even about ourselves has been changed by these machines and the way we've chosen to use them.[8]

Both the printing revolution of the early modern period and the information culture of the nineteenth and twentieth centuries have been defined mainly by their machines and material technologies. To be sure, machines are important in explaining the acceleration of information in certain periods of history, but they are not the only possible causes. Between the printing revolution and the nineteenth century lies a period that was less significant for its information-handling *machines* but just as fertile in new information *systems*. This was the Age of Reason (the late seventeenth century and most of the eighteenth), followed by the Age of Revolution, from 1776 to the mid–nineteenth century. This is the period that this book covers, because it sets the stage for the electromechanical processing of information in the nineteenth century and its electronic processing in the twentieth. In other words, the cultural revolution in information systems (the "software," if you like) preceded its material ("hardware") revolution.

The Age of Reason and Revolution

The eighteenth and early nineteenth centuries are known for three dramatic upheavals: the cultural revolutions of the Enlightenment and romanticism, the political revolutions that swept through Europe and the

Americas, and the Industrial Revolution that spread from England to western Europe and eastern North America.

Historians of the Enlightenment, by and large, have followed the lead of the philosophes in stressing the fundamental ideas of that era: reason and science against religion and superstition, tolerance against prejudice, justice against the abuse of power, a social contract instead of absolutism. To stress important ideas means to exalt the cultural giants of that age: Voltaire, Kant, Diderot, Mozart, Rousseau, Lavoisier, and others of similar caliber and fame. In short, intellectual historians have written about the Enlightenment as the history of intellectuals and their ideas.[9]

Another kind of intellectual transformation, however, has received far less attention because it was less dramatic and controversial, hence more easily taken for granted. That is the demand for information, its supply, and its organization.

The Demand for Information Systems

Why did new information systems appear in the period 1700–1850? The development of information systems in these years cannot be blamed on machines that people had to find ways to use, as in our own computer-driven age. Instead, it was a cultural change driven by social, economic, and political upheavals. To understand it, let us borrow two well-known concepts from economics: demand and supply.

The rising demand for information was stimulated by the growth of population, production, and trade on both sides of the Atlantic. Although the figures are very approximate, the population of Europe (including Russia) grew from approximately 167 million to 284 million (i.e., by 70 percent) between 1750 and 1850, while the white population of North America multiplied thirteen times, from some 2 to about 26 million, in that same period.[10] The growing population was accompanied by a growing economy; it was slow by today's standards and did not benefit the poor much, but it stimulated commerce, not only the traditional trade in grain, wool, timber, and luxury goods but also long-distance trade in once rare commodities like sugar and cotton. In every way, the North Atlantic world was much wealthier and more developed in 1850 than it had been a century and a half earlier.

How did demographic and economic growth lead to new and better information systems? One source of demand came from merchants eager to know about production, prices, and risks. For them, the arrival of a ship could mean the difference between wealth and failure, and a distant war could mean profits or disaster. Then, as now, information was money.

The swelling demand for information also characterized officialdom. The political systems of the eighteenth century are often described as moving from absolutism to enlightened despotism. *Absolutism* refers to the divine right of monarchs to rule in their own personal or dynastic interests, as though these were the only interests they had to consider. In contrast, *enlightened despotism* implied that monarchs ruled for the benefit of their subjects. Knowing what was in the interest of one's subjects, however, required a lot more information than knowing one's own personal or family interests.

Government officials needed information to forestall challenges to their authority, such as food riots and local sedition. Controlling a country required good maps, enumerations of population, and reports on grain supplies, business conditions, political movements, and other such factors. Officials who dealt with foreign affairs needed information about other countries not just that obtained through espionage (a long-standing tradition) but also more general information about wealth, population, and military preparedness.

Military and naval officers were big consumers of information. Armies needed maps of the terrain on which they might have to fight. Navies needed reliable means of identifying their location on the ocean, as well as maps showing coasts and islands and the depth of the sea.

Members of different professions needed specialized information; with a growing economy, skills and knowledge could not be handed down from mother to daughter or father to son but instead required new and more complex information. Lawyers needed compilations of laws, pharmacists needed formularies, craftsmen needed instructions and diagrams, travelers needed schedules, farmers needed almanacs, and seamstresses needed patterns.

And let us not forget curiosity. This period saw a substantial increase in the number of educated people, professionals, and businesspeople and their families, who judged one another by their conversations, their wit, their knowledge of the world and of the latest news. Encyclopedias became best-sellers not just as sources of information on specific topics but as symbols of gentility and proof that their owners valued learning. People bought books, maps, and newspapers for much the same reasons as they do today, but even more avidly, for they lacked our electronic amusements.

The Age of Revolution, beginning with the troubles in the North American colonies in 1776, stimulated the demand for information even further. Revolutionaries not only claimed to act in the interest of the people but also believed that the people should be represented in political life. This meant gathering information about citizens and disseminating it broadly. The French revolutionaries, in particular, had a voracious appetite for data, for they wanted to reorganize the territory, change all the laws, introduce new taxes and finances, reform the systems of weights and measures, and bring everything else up to date. Speed mattered, for the Age of Revolution was a time of war, and they were in a hurry.

After 1815, Europe and North America entered a period of relative peace. It was not, however, a restoration of the Old Regime. Rather, governments, both despotic and liberal, remained "enlightened" in the sense that they claimed to protect and enhance the nation, not just the sovereign. To this end, they added effective administrations that could actually count populations, survey land, distribute the mail, and subsidize science in ways that had never been done before.

The Supply of Information Systems

The supply of information never "satisfies" the demand. In the first place, even when new information answers one question, it often only whets the appetite for more information. Furthermore, a great deal of information is too valuable to disseminate, and those who possess it make great efforts to keep it to themselves; think of alchemists—or modern corporations— with proprietary formulas, or of government officials inclined by nature to keep everything classified.

Yet the increase in the demand for information did lead to a concomitant increase in supply. Monarchs and their ministers who thought of themselves as enlightened gathered information about their realms through cartographic projects, population enumerations, and trade and agricultural surveys. Official investigations and private research projects brought forth plentiful data about tropical plants, yields and harvests, the shape of the earth, deaths from smallpox, and much else. Secret or hermetic knowledge, such as alchemy, Latin texts, and craft secrets, was challenged by open and accessible knowledge provided by newspapers, encyclopedias, and public lectures in vernacular languages.

The increasing amount of information, in turn, elicited innovations in the methods of handling it—in other words, in information systems.[11] Hence the development of scientific taxonomy, cartography, lexicography, statistics, and postal services that characterized the Age of Reason and Revolution.

The Age of Reason and Revolution was not a thing in itself, however. It is only a shorthand expression for the work of a great number of people, both famous and obscure. Readers will readily recognize many of the famous people of the age: the botanist Carl Linnaeus; the chemist Antoine de Lavoisier; Thomas Malthus, the demographic pessimist; John Harrison, the clockmaker; Denis Diderot and Jean d'Alembert, who wrote the

Encyclopédie; Samuel Johnson of the *Dictionary;* Samuel Morse, the inventor of the telegraph; and George Everest, who gave his name to a mountain and received fame in return. Even political figures appear in the story: Jean-Baptiste Colbert (minister to Louis XIV), Thomas Jefferson, Benjamin Franklin, and Napoleon Bonaparte, to mention a few.

Most of the protagonists of this book are known only to specialists: statisticians remember Adolphe Quetelet; astronomers know the Cassini family; botanists recognize Joseph Banks; and chemists remember Joseph Priestley. And the French know that Claude Chappe invented the telegraph fifty years before Morse.

But there are others, such as Vincenzo Marco Coronelli (an encyclopedist), Tobias Mayer (a mathematician), and William Playfair, who invented graphs—long-forgotten thinkers who deserve to be recognized for their contributions to the information revolution. It is they, and many others like them, who made information come of age.

The Spirit of Progress

French historians use the word *mentalité* (Germans would say *Zeitgeist,* or spirit of the age) to characterize the culture of the eighteenth century, the interest of educated people in applying knowledge and reason to politics and business. Even though this term lumps together many different sources of demand, it is still a useful concept. The eighteenth and nineteenth centuries were characterized not only by a growing thirst for knowledge but also by a strong faith that more knowledge would lead to the betterment of humankind.

One of the favorite words of that era was *progress.* This was the mantra of the philosophes, the enlightened despots, the educated people on both sides of the Atlantic in the Age of Enlightenment. Two hundred years later, since Hiroshima, the Holocaust, and much else, we have become cynical about progress. We have so much information, and yet the "betterment of humankind" still escapes us. Nevertheless, we still want information—more than ever, faster than ever.

If this seems like a conundrum, it is because we confuse two meanings of progress: the instrumental and the moral. Instrumental progress relates to the *means* of achieving a given goal: getting from place to place, communicating with someone far away, destroying a city. Moral progress judges the goal. In ethical terms, the human race has made little or no progress in the past three centuries. But the instrumental progress in information systems (which is how I use the term in this book) has been phenomenal. And no one would want it otherwise.

Notes

1. Some pundits, like John Naisbitt (*Megatrends* [New York: Warner Books, 1982]), Alvin Toffler (*The Third Wave* [New York: Morrow, 1980]), and Walter Wriston (*The Twilight of Sovereignty: How the Information Revolution Is Transforming Our World* [New York: Scribner's, 1992]), celebrate the information age. Others, like Theodore Roszak (*The Cult of Information*, 2d ed. [Berkeley: University of California Press, 1994]), denounce it. Yet all are mesmerized by its present and near-future effects.

2. The classic expression of this definition of information is found in Claude E. Shannon, "A Mathematical Theory of Communication," *Bell System Technical Journal* 27 (1948): 379–423, 625–56.

3. Michael Riordan and Lillian Hoddeson, *Crystal Fire: The Birth of the Information Age* (New York: Norton, 1997).

4. Quoted in *Smithsonian*, August 1996, 25.

5. See, for example, James Beniger, *The Control Revolution: Technological and Economic Origins of the Information Society* (Cambridge, Mass.: Harvard University Press, 1986); and JoAnne Yates, *Control through Communication: The Rise of System in American Management* (Baltimore: Johns Hopkins University Press, 1989).

6. For example, *InfoCulture: The Smithsonian Book of Information Age Inventions* (Boston: Houghton Mifflin, 1993), by Steven Lubar, the curator of the InfoCulture exhibition at the Smithsonian Institution's Museum of American History. See also Peter G. Hall and Paschal Preston, *The Carrier Wave: New Information Technology and the Geography of Innovation, 1846–2003* (Boston: Unwin Hyman, 1988).

7. Elizabeth L. Eisenstein, *The Printing Press as an Agent of Change: Communications and Cultural Transformations in Early-Modern Europe* (Cambridge: Cambridge University Press, 1979); Eisenstein, *The Printing Revolution in Early Modern Europe* (Cambridge: Cambridge University Press, 1983); Lucien Fèbvre and Henri-Jean Martin, *L'apparition du livre* (Paris: Albin Michel, 1958), translated by David Gerard as *The Coming of the Book: The Impact of Printing, 1450–1800* (London: Routledge, 1976).

8. Lubar, *InfoCulture*, 4.

9. Examples of intellectual histories of the Enlightenment include Ernst Cassirer, *The Philosophy of the Enlightenment*, trans. Fritz Koelin and James Pettegrove (Princeton, N.J.: Princeton University Press, 1951); Frank E. Manuel, ed., *The Enlightenment* (Englewood Cliffs, N.J.: Prentice-Hall, 1965); Jack Lively, ed., *The Enlightenment* (New York: Barnes and Noble, 1966); and Peter Gay, *The Enlightenment: An Interpretation*, 2 vols. (New York: Knopf, 1966–1969). For a broader, more social, interpretation of the Enlightenment, see Norman Hampson, *The Enlightenment* (Harmondsworth: Penguin, 1976); Ulrich Im Hof, *The Enlightenment*, trans. William E. Yuill (Oxford: Blackwell, 1994); and Dorinda Outram, *The Enlightenment* (Cambridge: Cambridge University Press, 1995).

10. E. A. Wrigley, *Population and History* (New York: McGraw-Hill, 1969), 205.

11. Readers familiar with Enlightenment ideas will recognize the idea of "systems" in the works of d'Alembert and Condillac. In the *Preliminary Discourse* to the *Encyclopédie*, d'Alembert denigrates "the spirit of system," by which he means the deductive approach to knowledge typical of Descartes, "today almost entirely banished from works of merit." In its place he praises "the systematic spirit," meaning

the combination of empiricism and rationalism characteristic of Newton. These expressions deal only with the systematic acquisition of knowledge about nature, and not with other aspects of information handling. Jean Le Rond d'Alembert, *Discours préliminaire de l'Encyclopédie* (Paris: Goutier, 1966), 33–34, 110. See also Etienne Bonnot de Condillac, *Traité des systèmes, où l'on en démèle les inconvénients et les avantages* (The Hague: Neaulme, 1749).

2

ORGANIZING INFORMATION

The Language of Science

What's in a name? That which we call a rose
By any other word would smell as sweet.
WILLIAM SHAKESPEARE, *Romeo and Juliet*

IN JUNE 1735, THE TWENTY-EIGHT-YEAR-OLD CARL VON LINNÉ, KNOWN TO US as Linnaeus (1707–1778), arrived in the Netherlands to obtain a doctorate. He headed for Harderwijk, a little university town known for its instant degrees. After a few formalities, he presented his thesis, which he had brought with him from Sweden. Six days after arriving, he was awarded a doctor of medicine degree.[1]

Though Linnaeus was undoubtedly eager to get his degree, the real purpose of his trip was to meet other botanists. Before arriving, he had already lectured at the University of Uppsala in Sweden and had traveled to Lapland—then as remote and exotic as Siberia or North America—to seek plants unknown to botanists. He chose Holland because it was the home of the great naturalist Hermann Boerhaave (1668–1738), superintendent of the botanical garden at Leiden. With colonies in Brazil, the Caribbean, South Africa, and the East Indies, Holland was the European center for botanical studies.

Linnaeus did not arrive empty-handed; he carried a short manuscript entitled *Systema naturae* (The system of nature), containing his ideas on the reformation of botany. Boerhaave was so impressed that he urged Linnaeus to join an expedition to southern Africa and the Americas, promising him a professorship at Leiden on his return.

Linnaeus declined the offer but accepted another that was even better. George Clifford, a wealthy merchant, had filled his estate with the most extensive collection of plants in Holland and even a zoo. He invited young Linnaeus to become his personal physician and superintendent of his garden, with a large salary, a huge budget, and luxurious living accommodations.

In the three years he spent in Holland, Linnaeus not only reorganized Clifford's garden but also published fourteen works in quick succession. The first were *Fundamenta botanica* and *Bibliotheca botanica,* dealing with the history of botany up to that time. *Systema naturae,* also published in 1735, divided nature into three kingdoms—animal, vegetable, and mineral—and presented a method of classifying the plant kingdom by class, order, genus, and species. In 1737 he published *Hortus Cliffortianus,* an illustrated catalog of the thousands of plants in Clifford's garden and herbarium, and *Flora Lapponica,* a travelogue of his botanizing expedition to Lapland. Having set out his organizing scheme in *Systema naturae,* he proceeded to publish *Genera plantarum* in 1737 and *Classes plantarum* in 1738—all this by the time he was thirty-one years old. In his own words, Linnaeus had "written more, discovered more, and made a greater reform in botany than anyone before him had done in an entire lifetime."[2]

These works, though extraordinarily important, were not books but outlines of books, which he intended to fill in later. The 1737 edition of *Systema naturae* was twelve folio (10 × 17–inch) pages long; by the twelfth edition in 1766–1768 (the last one he supervised), it had grown to twenty-four hundred octavo (5 × 8–inch) pages in three volumes, a fiftyfold increase.

To round out his system of nature, Linnaeus planned to include every species he could find in *Species plantarum.* It took him many years to accumulate the necessary information from personal observation and from dried plants sent to him by friends and students. By the time the first edition came out in 1753, he was a professor of medicine and botany at Uppsala University and the first president of the Royal Academy of Sciences of Sweden, a hero to his countrymen and to botanists everywhere.

What did Linnaeus do that so impressed his contemporaries and posterity? It was not just that he added to the list of known plants, for other botanists had done the same. Instead, he found a simple, effective way to classify plants and a language in which to express his classification. In doing so, he turned botany from a field of erudition into a system for managing information efficiently. As his biographer Frans Stafleu put it, "His contribution to systematics was the greatest by any single author. To start an information system and coding device which is still fully accepted after more than two centuries is a feat which finds no counterpart in any of the other sciences."[3] That information system was to have repercussions in other sciences and, from there, in how people have classified large quantities of data from that time on.

The Age of Classification

Organized research accumulates information faster than any person can absorb and process mentally. Hence the need for systems to organize existing information so that individual items can be retrieved efficiently; to place new pieces of information where they can be located again when needed; and to discern patterns in this body of knowledge.

In order to capture a new piece of information and place it in the existing body of knowledge, one must identify it with precision, in other words, give it a distinct name. To avoid ambiguity and confusion, a one-to-one correspondence must exist between every term and the object it represents.

In science, however, it is not enough to name objects with precision. The names must also indicate relations between objects—for instance, between *Panthera leo* and *Panthera tigris,* between carbon dioxide on the one hand and carbon and oxygen on the other, or between meters and kilometers. *Nomenclatures,* or systems of names, are designed to express the underlying *taxonomies,* or systems of things.

This process carries a risk, however. A nomenclature, being a construct of the mind, may impose on the objects that it names a pattern that distorts their underlying reality; do we know for a fact that *leo* and *tigris* belong to the same genus *Panthera?* In the natural sciences, there is a constant tension between the artificial classifications imposed by a system of names and the natural classification systems that reveal the patterns that exist in nature.

The eighteenth century witnessed three innovations in the language of science that have given expression to scientific discourse ever since: the binomial nomenclature of Linnaeus put order into the profusion of plants and animals; the chemical nomenclature of Lavoisier not only named known chemical substances but also identified their main characteristics and the relations among them; and the metric system expressed the connections between units of weight, length, area, volume, and others. It is the aim of this chapter to investigate the languages in which the sciences found expression.

The advances in scientific language in the eighteenth century had many causes. One was the prestige of Newtonian physics and astronomy, which identified the sciences as achievements of reason rather than as esoteric crafts. Simultaneously, educated people developed a thirst for knowledge about the natural world, its lands and peoples, its animals, plants, and minerals. Finally, naturalists and explorers made important discoveries about nature—discoveries that stimulated, but never satisfied, this rising curiosity.

The new taxonomies and nomenclatures in botany, zoology, and chemistry were not isolated developments but a reflection of the spirit of the Enlightenment. The French philosophe and mathematician Marie-Jean Condorcet (1743–1794) carried this spirit to its logical conclusion when he wrote in 1784:

When the alphabetical language will no longer be fast or rich or precise enough to meet the needs of the sciences and follow their progress; they will come to a stop, unless we create for each one a language in which invariably determined signs express the objects of our knowledge, the diverse combinations of our ideas, the operations to which we will submit the productions of nature and those which we will perform on our own ideas, languages which will be for every science what the language of algebra is for mathematical analysis.[4]

Science and Language

In the Middle Ages and well after, understanding nature was often justified as a means of understanding God, since God created nature to serve mankind. In practice, many investigators saw the mysteries of nature as secrets to be appropriated and hoarded rather than as information to be disseminated; in other words, what we call science was still closely intertwined with the cryptosciences: chemistry with alchemy, biology with medical quackery, astronomy with astrology.

By the eighteenth century, investigators no longer deemed theological justifications necessary: like virtue, understanding nature was its own reward, and the goal of science was not to hoard secrets but to spread reason and knowledge. The sciences were not yet professions but still were associated with philosophy and with "natural history." The idea that science could be used to control nature by creating new technologies originated with the English philosopher Francis Bacon (1561–1626), but the general public was not convinced of this until the nineteenth century.

The role of science was reflected in its language. Alchemists, astrologers, and other cryptoscientists of earlier ages had created their own hermetic vocabularies, designed to confuse the uninitiated rather than to advance knowledge. One reason for the interest in nomenclatures in the eighteenth century was precisely to break away from secret vocabularies and instead present nature in a clear, logical, and easily understandable language.

This created two dilemmas. First of all, which language? Latin was the traditional language of clergymen and academics. French was the language of aristocrats throughout Europe and of educated Frenchmen, but not of French peasants, who spoke various dialects. Among the educated, the trend was away from Latin and toward those dialects that were already becoming national languages: English for Great Britain, Parisian for France, Castilian for Spain, Tuscan for Italy, Hochdeutsch for the German states. Not everyone applauded this trend. Linnaeus spent years in Holland, but he never learned Dutch.[5] He wrote in Latin and rejected the use of modern languages—even his native Swedish—on the grounds that "the novice might grow old over his literary studies ere he is competent to study the sciences."[6] More surprisingly, Jean d'Alembert wrote in the preface to the *Encyclopédie:*

> The use of the Latin language can be very useful in works of philosophy [i.e., science]. . . . Before the end of the eighteenth century, a philosopher wishing to study in depth the discoveries of his predecessors will have to load up his memory with seven or eight different languages and, after having consumed in learning them the most precious years of his life, he will die before starting to learn.[7]

Yet the reading public rejected Latin. Salon society, fascinated with science, expected to learn about it in the vernacular. Whatever d'Alembert might have thought, the *Encyclopédie* had to be in French.

The second dilemma concerned not languages but vocabularies. People interested in science could not simply adopt words from everyday languages because they were imprecise, full of gaps and contradictions, and often regional. The result was a series of compromises between everyday words and scientific neologisms, a tension between a familiar but imprecise vocabulary and a precise but specialized, hence esoteric, one.

Throughout the century, we find three distinct linguistic traditions in science. The first was Latin, fast losing ground as the language of intellectuals. The second was the national languages using everyday vocabularies. The third consisted of vernacular languages used as frameworks for specialized scientific vocabularies based on Latin or Greek roots. Eventually the specialized vocabularies won out, but as the role of the sciences changed over the course of the century, so did their languages and vocabularies.

Max Fuchs analyzed this process in French, but the same holds true for English, since the two languages share the same scientific vocabulary.[8] The transition may be discerned in the progression of titles of books about insects, starting with Swammerdam's *Historia insectorum generalis,* published in Dutch in 1669 and in Latin in 1693. The next important work was Réamur's six-volume *Histoire des insectes* (1734–1742). Réamur avoided scientific terms, instead using circumlocutions, analogies with human anatomy, and long descriptions that ended up being more confusing than specific technical neologisms would have been. The vocabulary of modern entomology finally came into its own in Bonnet's *Traité d'insectologie* (1745) and Olivier's six-volume *Entomologie* (1789–1808).[9]

Writing a few years after Réaumur, Abbé Nollet took a bolder approach in his *Leçons de physique expérimentale,* an influential textbook that went through eight editions between 1743 and 1775. Nollet used numerous technical terms, including *baromètre, planétaire, siphon, télescope, apogée, ellipse, balistique, parabole, révolution, densité, élasticité, amalgame,* and *cataracte.* If these words seem familiar to us, it is because Nollet popularized them. In doing so, he consciously distinguished between everyday vernacular and scientific language, recognizing the tensions between a vocabulary that made science accessible to a larger public and one that was precise and succinct enough to convey meaning efficiently to the initiated.

The adoption of new terminologies accelerated over the course of the eighteenth century. Some words came from regional vernaculars, such as the Alpine terms *glacier* and *moraine* and the German or Scandinavian *quartz* (1749), *cobalt* (1782), and *tungstène* (1784). Most new words, however, had Greek or Latin roots. The French were willing to adopt Latin-based words such as *aberration* (1737), *convergence* (1743), and *accrétion* (1751). Greek-based words were not so popular in France, yet the ease with which they could be combined to express complex ideas succinctly made them irresistible to scientists. Thus the eighteenth century gave us *anthropologie* (1707), *minéralogie* (1732), *zoologie* (1762), *lithographie* (1771), *entomologie* (1789), and hundreds of others, many of which are still in use. By the end of the century, several sciences could boast of having their own vocabulary, reflecting their own knowledge. It was the beginning of specialization and professionalization.

To understand the development of scientific language, nomenclatures, and classification systems, I will consider the cases of botany, zoology, and chemistry.

Linnaeus and the Classification of Living Things

The strongest motivation for classifying plants and animals was the growth in the number of known species. The ancient botanists Theophrastus (371–287 B.C.) and Dioscorides (c. A.D. 20) had counted several hundred plant species. In 1623 the Swiss Kaspar Bauhin listed 6,000. The Englishman John Ray, writing in 1682, listed 18,655 species.[10] By 1758, Linnaeus had named 7,700 flowering plants. Similarly, the number of known and classified bird species rose from 564 in 1758 to 3,779 in 1812.

Estimates of the number of species, including those not yet discovered, ran much higher: 40,000 to 45,000 plant and animal species according to John Ray in 1691; 13,000 plant and 145,000 animal species according to Pieter van Musschenbroek in the 1720s; 175,000 plant and over 7 million animal species according to Eberhard Zimmermann in 1778–1783. (By the late twentieth century, taxonomists had identified 300,000 plant species and over a million animal species, with no end in sight.)[11]

To cope with the profusion of living things, naturalists classified them into categories.[12] Theophrastus had divided the plant kingdom into trees, shrubs, undershrubs, and herbs, subdividing the latter into annuals, biennials, and perennials, a system still used by gardeners. Dioscorides, a physician, divided them according to their medicinal properties.

To observant botanists of the Age of Reason, such simple empiricism no longer satisfied, for it was inconsistent.[13] John Ray (1627–1705) introduced the concept of sexual reproduction into botany in his three-volume *Historia generalis plantarum* (1686–1704), but the descriptions of the myriad plants he studied were long and confusing. His contemporary Joseph Pitton de Tournefort (1656–1708), in his *Institutionis rei herbariae* (1700), classified plants by their flowers because "these parts attract the sight more pleasantly and strike the imagination more vividly."[14] He identified some plants by descriptive adjectives (*monopétales, ombellifères*); some by their outward appearance (e.g., *papillonacée:* like a butterfly); and some by negatives (e.g., *herbes sans fleurs ni fruits:* herbs without flowers or fruits). He confused naming with describing; thus he used the phrase "Gramen Xerampelinum, Miliacea praetenui, ramosaque sparsa panicula, sive Xerampelino congener, arvense, aestivum, Gramen minutissimo semine" for the plant Linnaeus was later to call *Poa bulbosa.*[15] In naming species by such long, elaborate diagnostic phrases, botanists only accentuated the disparity between data and knowledge. As historian of biology Ernst Mayr points out, "Pre-Linnaean botanists largely split on national lines. The British followed Ray, the Germans Rivinius (Bachmann), and the French Tournefort."[16]

The trouble lay not in a lack of erudition but in a confusion between natural and artificial systems of classification. A natural system is one that seeks to classify objects on the basis of most, if not all, of their characteristics. Natural systems convey a great deal of information and have a high predictive value, but they work well only when there is a clear discontinuity between categories—for example, between plants or animals of different species, which cannot interbreed or which produce only sterile offspring.

Unlike natural systems, an artificial one starts with one predetermined characteristic and classifies objects according to that criterion alone. Within a species, for instance, there can be many varieties (cultivars, breeds, races) but no clear discontinuities; in such cases, artificial systems work better. They are easier to learn and use for practical purposes, such as dividing plants into fruits, vegetables, and flowers, or into annuals, biennials, and perennials. They are, however, less reliable and hence are considered "unscientific."[17]

Linnaeus had two passions. The first was to know every plant; in his words, "The more species a botanist knows, the greater his excellence."[18] The second was to name, classify, and organize everything in sight; he even classified plant lovers into phytologists, botanophiles, collectors, orators, taxonomists, and so on. The historian of botany Julius von Sachs called Linnaeus "a classifying, co-ordinating, and subordinating machine."[19]

The system of classification that Linnaeus devised was artificial, but it was simple and effective.[20] Following Aristotelian logic, he divided the vegetable kingdom into five levels of classification (or *taxa*): classes, orders, genera, species, and varieties.[21]

> Examples taken from other sciences make this clear: Geography: Kingdom, province, territory, parish, village, Military: Regiment, company, platoon, squad, soldier, Philosophy: Genus summum, genus intermedium, genus proximum, species, individuum, Botany: Classis, ordo, genus, species, varietas.[22]

Linnaeus made it clear that two of these five taxa—classes and orders—were cultural constructs reflecting human ignorance. They were not inherent in nature but were merely ways of identifying plants quickly and efficiently. Eventually, he wrote, "The more plants we know the more the gaps will be filled, and the boundaries between the orders and classes will disappear."[23]

In contrast, the two middle taxa—genera and species—were "natural," that is, God-given and immutable, and separated from one another by clear-cut discontinuities. Varieties—the lowest level of classification—were changeable but of little interest to Linnaeus.[24]

To classify plants, Linnaeus used a method called the *sexual system*, based on the number, size, shape, and relative position of the stamens (male organs) and pistils (female organs) of plants. He defined twenty-three classes of plants by their stamens, with a twenty-fourth class for flowerless plants such as mosses. Each class was then subdivided into orders by the number and position of the pistils. Thus within the class *Hexandria* (six stamens), plants with one pistil formed the order *Monogynia*. His system ignored all the other characteristics of plants, such as their parts, functions, physiology, and ecology.[25]

Linnaeus had described and classified all previous classification schemes in *Classes plantarum* (1738) and in *Philosophia botanica* (1750). He was well aware that his was a quintessentially artificial classification scheme. Yet he was certain that his scheme, artificial though it was, captured the true essence of plants, for the sexual organs were the means whereby plants reproduced themselves, fully and without variation. For Linnaeus, the fact that many different species of plants possessed the same number, size, shape, and relative positions of stamens and pistils proved the existence of genera: "All species with the same geometrical disposition of the parts of the flower and fruit belong to one genus."[26] For him, genera, like species, were natural and eternal: "Every genus is natural, and created as such in the beginning: genera and species are confirmed by revelation, discovery and observation."[27]

He did not explain the resemblance of different species within each genus by any biological affinity; the idea of evolution still lay far in the future. Linnaeus's simple creationism may have led him to ignore the biological meaning of affinities, but it is anachronistic to blame him for what he did not see. His purpose was not to advance biology as the understanding of life but to advance botany as a body of knowledge. In Stafleu's words,

> The great merit of the sexual system was evidently that it provided a simple, easily comprehended structure for storage and retrieval of information. It standardized usage. In combination with the code designations for species afforded by the binomial system it provided a highly useful and simple framework which was indeed internationally acceptable and which led different people to the same result.[28]

What Linnaeus is remembered and admired for is not the sexual system of classification, which was already under attack in his day and has long since been abandoned, but his nomenclature. In his mind, classification and nomenclature were inseparable:

> Botany has a double basis: classification and nomenclature. . . . Classification is the basis for nomenclature. Botanical science hinges upon these two points: within a year, at first sight, without teacher, without figures or descriptions, all plants are learned and constantly remembered: he who knows how to do this is a botanist, no one else is.[29]

Linnaeus's nomenclature is known as the *binomial system,* for it characterized every species by two Latin words, such as *Homo sapiens* or *Pisum sativum* (the garden pea). Unlike the sexual system, he developed the binomial nomenclature gradually. In *Critica botanica* (1737) he laid out the ground rules: all plants in the same genus should have the same generic name; all names should be in Latin or Greek; words implying a resemblance between one genus and another should be avoided (thus, *Bellidioides* became *Chrysanthemum* and *Chamaerhododendron* became *Azalea*); finally, botanists should avoid sentimental and spiritual names such as *Noli me tangere* or *Pater noster.*[30]

The starting point of the nomenclature was the Aristotelian or Scholastic method of defining things *per genus et differentiam,* that is, by naming the genus and describing, in a phrase, what differentiated one particular species from others in its genus.

For genus names, Linnaeus sought words that were simple and identified some characteristic shared by all its members. Thus *Triopteris* (three wings) was a plant with three "wings" around its six petals, *Convolvulus* had a twining stem, and *Heliocarpus* had a sunlike fruit. He accepted genera named after persons, such as *Cliffortiana,* after his patron George Clifford, or *Linnaeia,* of which he wrote: "*Linnaeia* was named by the celebrated Gronovius, and is a plant of Lapland, lowly, insignificant, disregarded, flowering but a brief space, from Linné who resembles it."[31]

The differentia, in the Aristotelian system, was a descriptive phrase that identified one species among others in its genus. Linnaeus tried to make his descriptive phrases as succinct as possible, for he wanted names that would be complete enough to distinguish a species from all other members of its genus, yet short enough to be easily memorized. He used just 71 words to describe the common nettle, *Urtica,* for which John Ray had needed 218 words and Joseph de Tournefort 98.[32] Linnaeus's Latin was not the Latin of his predecessors, let alone that of Cicero; it was "botanical Latin," a language reduced to pure information, without verbs or grammar.[33] For example, he described the stone pink in ten words: "Dianthus caulibus unifloris, squamis, calycinis ovatis, corollis multifidis, foliis linearibus" (Dianthus with stalks that have one flower, the scales of the calyx ovate and obtuse, the corolla many-cleft, and the leaves linear).[34]

Although he wrote much more tersely than his predecessors, Linnaeus was still not satisfied with descriptive differentia, for in genera with many species, the differentia tended to be very long to distinguish each species from all others. In other words, his two goals, brevity and completeness, were incompatible.

In the 1740s, he came up with a solution to this dilemma: a simple reference code. In *Oländska och gothländska resa* (1745), a report on his trip to the islands of Oland and Gotland, he referred to the numbers he had assigned to plants in his *Flora svecica* (1745) or to animals in *Fauna svecica* (1746); for instance, when he cited a plant as "Pyrola staminibus adscendentibus pistillo declinato Fl. Suec. 330," he meant "plant number 330 in *Flora svecica.*"[35]

This was helpful to those who brought the works of Linnaeus along when they went out botanizing. But numbers, Linnaeus knew, are very hard to remember, and the whole point of his nomenclature was to enable botanists to identify plants by name. Thus he began adding, in the margin, an epithet or "trivial name." Thus, to "Tiopteris *Hort. Cliff.* 169" (plant number 169 in his book *Hortus Cliffortianus*), he gave the epithet *jamaicensis* (from Jamaica).[36]

Trivial names were not definitions but mnemonic devices that referred to easily remembered characteristics: the purple *Gentiana purpurea,* the sweet-smelling *Jasminum odoratissimum,* the ordinary *Beta vulgaris,* and so on. Trivial names were especially useful to distinguish members of the same genus, for instance, *Pinguicula vulgaris,* 23, and *Pinguicula alba,* 23.

By the early 1750s, Linnaeus realized that the trivial names not only were easy to remember but also were just as efficient a reference code as the numbers he had started with. He therefore dropped the bibliographic reference numbers; thus, *Achillea* 705 became *Achillea millefolium.* In *Species plantarum* (1753) and in the tenth edition of *Systema naturae* (1758), he used two nomenclatures. The first consisted of the genus plus a diagnostic phrase describing the species, for example, *Potamogeton foliis oblongo-ovatis petiolatis natantibus.* The second—the true binomial nomenclature—consisted of the genus name plus a trivial name designating, but not describing, the species, as in *Potamogeton natans.*[37]

The connection between botanical nomenclature and bibliographic references was no coincidence. As John Heller has pointed out, Linnaeus had studied and classified the botanical literature of his day. In *Hortus Cliffortianus,* he cataloged Clifford's books, using a number, the author's name, the title, the place and date of publication, the size and number of pages, and comments on the contents. In *Critica botanica* (1737), he explained how to cite books:

> In every citation the author's name should be given in an abbreviated form, corresponding to the generic name of a plant, and his works, corresponding to the scientific [i.e., species] name, since a particular author often owes his fame to more than one work in the form *Dillen. elth., Dill. gissens., Dill. gener.*—the name of a book should be abbreviated into a single word.[38]

In other words, Linnaeus was using a binomial nomenclature for books as early as 1737. Thus, says Heller: "It does not seem too bold to suggest that Linnaeus' experience with his binomial system of reference to books led to his trying it for reference to other things."[39]

What made the Linnaean system so popular was its practical applications. As Ernst Mayr explains:

> Any botanist using the sexual system would come to the same result as Linnaeus. All he had to do was to learn a rather limited number of names of the parts of the flower and fruit and then he could identify any plant. No wonder nearly everybody adopted the Linnaean system.[40]

Gardeners could arrange their plantings in an orderly fashion, like books on a shelf. Amateurs, whom Linnaeus had classified as "botanophiles," could press flowers and arrange the pages neatly into their own herbaria. The Linnaean method appealed both to the orderly minds of mid-eighteenth-century rationalists and, as the century wore on, to increasing numbers of sentimental nature lovers. For the fine ladies and gentlemen who strolled the royal gardens of Paris and Kew and for the country parsons who collected wildflowers, botanizing was a fashion and a proof of their gentility. Even celebrated writers like Johann Wolfgang von Goethe and Jean-Jacques Rousseau fancied themselves botanists.[41]

The Linnaean system quickly conquered professional botanists as well as botanophiles. It became popular in the Netherlands in the 1750s. In France, Montpellier was the first botanical garden to adopt it in the early 1760s.[42] The Jardin du Roi in Paris reorganized its plants along Linnaean lines in 1774.[43] In Spain, it was first used by Miguel Barnades, a professor at the Madrid botanical garden, in his *Principios de botánica* (1767); by the early 1780s, it was enshrined in the arrangement of plants in the garden and in the examinations for students in botany.[44] In Mexico, the Linnaean system was adopted in 1787.[45] It reached Peru in 1778 when the Spanish botanical explorers Hipólito Ruiz and José Pavón arrived with copies of Linnaeus's works in their luggage; by the 1790s, it was taught at San Marcos University, and it was used to arrange the botanical garden of Lima in 1808.[46]

Nowhere was the victory of Linnaeanism more complete than in Britain. When William Hudson's *Flora Anglica,* organized in the Linnaean manner, appeared in 1762, it displaced all previous floras. Several of Linnaeus's students traveled to Britain and its colonies and participated in the great expeditions of the day. Among them were Peter Kalm, who visited North America in 1747–1751 and wrote a three-volume work full of natural history;[47] Daniel Solander, librarian to Joseph Banks and naturalist on Captain James Cook's first voyage to the Pacific on the *Endeavour* (1768–1771); and Jonas Dryander, Solander's successor and bibliographer of Banks's collection.[48]

Sir Joseph Banks (1743–1820) and the voyages of Captain James Cook (1728–1779) to the Pacific have attracted much well-deserved interest.[49] Two aspects are interesting in the present context. One is the flood of new plants that they found. By the time Banks died in 1820, his herbarium contained 23,500 "arranged" species, plus another 5,000 "unarranged" and 1,700 parcels of unsorted material. In addition, both Clifford's and Linnaeus's own herbaria ended up in London. To the delight of visiting scholars, the materials were arranged in the Linnaean way.[50]

Botanical gardens helped spread the new system in England. The first to be organized along Linnaean principles was the Chelsey Physic Garden under the direction of Philip Miller, whose *Gardener's Dictionary* (seventh edition, 1759) brought Linnaean taxonomy into the English language.[51] Much more important was Princess Augusta's garden at Kew, near London, where the gardener William Aiton laid out 3,400 species on nine acres of land between 1760 and 1767. In 1771, King George III put the garden under the charge of Joseph Banks, who made it "the great exchange house of the Empire," sending "Kew collectors" out to India, North America, the Pacific, and Australia and exchanging plant material with collectors from other countries. Seven thousand new plants were introduced into England this way between 1772 and 1820. With Dryander's help, Aiton published *Hortus kewensis* (1789), a book that Frans Stafleu called

> the greatest contribution of its time toward creating order in the
> nomenclature and taxonomy of plants cultivated in British gardens. . . .
> The arrangement is of course that of Linnaeus, and the book is therefore
> not so much a contribution to the principles of taxonomy as a compendium of taxonomic details.[52]

As the eighteenth century drew to a close, the victory of the Linnaean system seemed almost complete. In England, his followers founded the Linnean Society in 1788 and began publishing its *Transactions* three years later. Linnaean societies sprang up in France as well, and in 1790 the French revolutionaries put up a statue to Linnaeus. By the end of the century, Linnaean taxonomy was, in Stafleu's words, "almost sanctified."[53]

Linnaeus's sexual classification system has long since given way to more complex natural taxonomies, but his binomial nomenclature persists two hundred years later. The International Code of Botanical Nomenclature, started in 1905, regards *Species plantarum* (1753) and the fifth edition of *Genera plantarum* (1754) as the official starting point of botanical nomenclature. Even zoologists base their nomenclature on the tenth edition of Linnaeus's *Systema naturae* (1758).

Not only information but also the very language of science was transformed by Linnaeus. The Linnaean vocabulary was precise, terse, and organized. His method of using Greek and Latin roots, prefixes, and suffixes to create an entirely new vocabulary inspired the new chemistry and other sciences.[54]

The Paris School of Biology

In Paris, the Linnean system was challenged by two other ways of studying natural history: a narrative tradition exemplified by Buffon and a natural system of classification elaborated by Adanson, Jussieu, and Lamarck. The most celebrated naturalist of his time, after Linnaeus himself, was Georges-Louis Leclerc, comte de Buffon (1707–1788). Whereas Linnaeus aimed to clarify the plant kingdom for the benefit of an international community of scientists, Buffon's goal was to instruct a lay audience of educated French readers in the mysteries of the animal kingdom. The contrast between their intended audiences explains the differences in these men's approaches to both nature and language.

Buffon began his career by attacking Linnaeus in a manifesto entitled "De la manière d'étudier & de traiter l'Histoire Naturelle" (On the manner of studying and dealing with natural history), read to the Royal Academy of Sciences in 1744 and published in the first volume of his *Histoire naturelle* in 1749.[55] He condemned the Linnaean classification as completely artificial, "the least sensible and the most monstrous of all":

> As the characteristics of genera are taken from almost infinitely small parts, one must have a magnifying glass in hand in order to recognize a tree or a plant; the size, the shape, the exterior aspect, the leaves, all the obvious parts no longer serve any purpose; only the stamens, and if you cannot see the stamens, you know nothing, you have seen nothing.[56]

Linnaeus's method, Buffon maintained, "has lumped together into the same class the mulberry and the nettle, the tulip and the barberry, the elm and the carrot, the rose and the strawberry, the oak and the burnet." He concluded: "Would it not be simpler, more natural, and more true to say that a donkey is a donkey and a cat is a cat, than to demand, without knowing why, that a donkey be a horse and a cat be a lynx?"[57]

Buffon's attack was not directed at the artificiality of Linnaeus's system but at the very idea of classification. To classify implies the existence of a discontinuous series with clear delineations. Buffon denied that nature was discontinuous, for he believed that the number of species was infinite: "Everything that can be, is." If nature seemed discontinuous, it was only because of human ignorance, and the gaps between species would gradually be filled in as knowledge increased. Hence, every classification system, even the most "natural," was as arbitrary as the alphabetical order in a dictionary. In contrast to Linnaeus, for whom genera were natural groupings, Buffon believed that naming and classifying were only human constructs and methods of analysis: "This manner of thinking has made us imagine an infinity of false relationships between natural beings. . . . It is to impose on the reality of the Creator's works the abstractions of our mind."[58]

Buffon criticized not only Linnaeus's classification system but also his language and nomenclature: "This manner of knowing is not a science, it . . . is at most a convention, a medium of communication from which no real knowledge can come." As a result,

> by multiplying names and representations, the language of science has become more difficult than the science itself. . . . If all of this were not presented with the appearance of a mysterious order and wrapped in Greek and botanical erudition, would it have taken so long to notice how ridiculous such a method is?[59]

Buffon's answer was to write clearly: "Well-written works are the only ones which will pass on to posterity: the multitude of information, the singularity of facts, even the novelty of discoveries are no guarantees of immortality. . . . such things are outside of man, style is man himself." Writing must be "simple, neat, and measured. . . . the only ornament one should give it is nobility of expression and the proper choice of terms. . . . in a word, it must be done in such a way that it can be read without boredom or effort."[60] Science meant, above all, description: "Natural objects are only well defined if they are exactly described." "The only true way to advance science is to work at the description and the history of the different things which compose it."[61] For Buffon, the essence of science was narrative, not classification or analysis.

Buffon was not merely prolific, like so many of his contemporaries; he was encyclopedic. In 1749, while serving as intendant of the royal botanical garden, he began publishing his fifteen-volume *Histoire naturelle générale et particulière, avec la description du Cabinet du roy* on humans and animals (1749–1767), followed by a nine-volume natural history of birds (1770–1783), a seven-volume supplement on quadrupeds (1774–1789), and five volumes plus an atlas on minerals (1783–1788). He was one of the great literary figures of his time, a gifted science writer whose mastery of the French language is admired and imitated to this day. Although his knowledge of nature was awesome, much of his information was based on the research of others; he contributed less to science than his contemporaries believed.[62]

In spite of his opposition to artificial systems of classification, Buffon could not simply describe organisms at random. To make nature comprehensible to his readers, he had to organize its chaotic profusion in a logical manner; he was, after all, a child of the Enlightenment. Rather than imposing a classification that claimed to reflect the essence of nature, he arranged the animal kingdom in order of decreasing familiarity to humans (or, rather, to Frenchmen):

> One judges the objects of Natural History in terms of the relations they have with him. Those which are the most necessary and useful to him will take the first rank. For example, he will give preference in the order of animals to the horse, the dog and the cow. . . . then he will concern himself with those which, while not so familiar to him, [still] inhabit the same locales and the same climates, like the deer, rabbit and all the wild animals. . . . It will be the same for the fishes, the birds, the insects, the testaceans and all the other productions of Nature; [man] will study them in proportion to the use that he can make of them. . . . This most natural order of all, is the one we have decided should be followed . . . ; and we believe that this simple and natural means . . . is preferable to the most highly refined and elaborate taxonomic methods, because none of these is more arbitrary than our own.[63]

Hence, having rejected Linnaeus's sexual system of classification, Buffon came up with an alternative that was completely anthropocentric. At first, he asserted that only species were truly natural and that all the other categories Linnaeus used—classes, orders, genera—were imaginary constructs. Yet in the course of his career, he gradually came to recognize the existence of natural genera; thus, in his *Histoire naturelle des oiseaux* (1770–1783), he grouped birds by genus rather than by species or by their utility to humans.

Late-eighteenth-century Paris was the home of several other remarkable thinkers—Bernard and Antoine-Laurent de Jussieu, Michel Adanson, and Jean-Baptiste de Lamarck—whose approach to nature differed from both Linnaeus's static classification system and Buffon's literary descriptions. Their goal was to find a natural system of classification, one that took into account not just the stamens and pistils but also the seeds and fruits, the cotyledons, and the vegetative and other characteristics of plant life, thereby revealing the very laws of nature. In doing so, they transformed natural history into biology.

The pioneer of the natural system of classification was Bernard de Jussieu (1699–1777), chief botanist at the Jardin du Roi, the botanical garden of Paris. He knew the Linnaean system well, for he had translated the fourth edition of *Systema naturae* into French. Unlike Linnaeus, however, he preferred to use a microscope to study a small number of plants in detail, including their morphology, growth, nutrition, and other characteristics. He did not publish the results of his investigations but instead taught other botanists.[64]

One of the members of his circle was Michel Adanson (1727–1806). During his youth, Adanson spent six years in Senegal as an employee of the Compagnie des Indes, where he collected thousands of botanical and zoological specimens. Unable to adapt Linnaeus's classification system to the flora of Africa, he sought affinities on a broader scale:

> There is no doubt that there can only be one natural method in botany, that which considers the totality of all the parts of plants. One must consider root, stems, leaves, flowers, fructification, in fact, all the parts, qualities, properties and faculties of plants. . . . From this totality is born the conformity, the affinity, which unites plants and divides them into classes or families.[65]

His books *Histoire naturelle du Sénégal* (1757) and *Famille des plantes* (1763) proved that a natural system of classification was possible, though difficult. Unfortunately, Adanson rejected not only Linnaeus's classification system but also his nomenclature, by then the standard language of botany.[66] As a result, his works were largely forgotten.

The man most responsible for integrating Linnaeus's nomenclature with Adanson's natural classification was Bernard de Jussieu's nephew Antoine-Laurent (1748–1836), who moved to his uncle's house in Paris in 1765. There, he had access to his uncle's herbarium, to the royal gardens and herbarium, and to the thirty thousand specimens collected by Philibert Commerson, a naturalist who had accompanied Louis-Antoine de Bougainville on his voyage to the Pacific in 1766–1769. According to Stafleu:

> Jussieu's delimitation of families and genera was greatly helped by this superior material; it prevented him from repeating some of Adanson's errors due to insufficient information, and it strengthened him in his belief that such a diversity of forms was better dealt with by means of a natural classification than through the too rigid and simplistic Linnaean scheme.[67]

With all this material at hand, Antoine-Laurent de Jussieu was able to di-
vide the plant kingdom into fifteen classes and one hundred families
(equivalent to Linnaeus's orders), while retaining Linnaeus's genera and
species. In his book *Genera plantarum* (1789), he combined the sophistication of
a natural classification system with the simplicity of the Linnean nomenclature.[68]

The combination of Linnaean nomenclature and natural classification
was enshrined in the *Dictionnaire de botanique,* part of the publisher Charles-
Joseph Panckoucke's 199-volume *Encyclopédie méthodique* (1782–1832).[69] Panckoucke hired Jean-Baptiste de Lamarck (1744–1829) to write the four-volume
Dictionnaire de botanique, which covered two thousand genera of plants with
nine hundred illustrations. At Panckoucke's request, Lamarck organized it
according to the Linnean system, giving detailed descriptions of plants,
their morphology, their geographic distribution, and just about everything
known about them at the time.[70] The combination of the binomial
nomenclature and the natural classification system became the method of
choice for the leading botanists of the late eighteenth and early nineteenth
centuries.[71]

Nothing shows quite so clearly the distinction between systematics (a
method of organizing information) and science (a way of explaining nature) as the question of affinities. The term *affinities* refers to the resemblances between species that allowed them to be grouped into genera and,
more distantly, into orders and classes. Why did so many plant species re-
semble one another so closely?

Linnaeus did not question the affinities he found, believing that was
how plants had been since the Creation. Buffon, on the other hand, once
he had admitted that animal species formed genera, could not help won-
dering why. As an educated eighteenth-century Frenchman, he was too
much the skeptic to accept the Creation myth at face value. Instead, he
speculated that species could change over time, and that closely related
species might well have a common ancestor. In his "Discours sur la
dégénérescence des animaux" (Discourse on the degeneration of animals),
published in 1766, he considered the relations between Old World and New
World quadrupeds. Grouping them into thirty-eight "families" (his term
for genera), twenty-four in the Old World and fourteen in the New, he concluded that some species must have descended from "a more ancient state
of nature." Thus, American "tigers" differed from Old World tigers because
of "the long influence of their new situation."[72] The concept of affinity
thus led him, gradually, toward the notion of degeneration:

> One can also say that the monkey is of the same family as man, that it is
> a degenerate man, that man and monkey have a common origin, like

the horse and the donkey, that each family, among animals as among plants, had only one origin, and even that all animals have descended from a single animal that, over time, produced through perfection and degeneration, all the other races of animals.[73]

This proto-evolutionism was pure speculation, and dangerous speculation at that, for it challenged creationist dogma. Such was Buffon's authority, however, and such was the readiness of the French intelligentsia to question religious doctrines, that these speculations fell on fertile ground. Although Buffon began by offering to replace Linnaeus's information-management approach to nature with a literary one, in the end, the two approaches were more complementary than antagonistic. The question of affinities that Linnaeus presented without explanation and that Buffon speculated about provided, in fact, the key to the emergence of biology and the background for the Darwinian revolution.[74]

Lavoisier and the French Revolution in Chemistry

In the life sciences, classification and nomenclature preceded the emergence of an explanatory theory by over a century. In contrast, chemistry developed a new classification system, a new nomenclature, and an explanatory theory almost at the same time.

Before the eighteenth century there was no standard chemical nomenclature but instead a hodgepodge of terminologies derived from alchemy, pharmacy, metallurgy, glassmaking, cloth dyeing, and other sources. Alchemical tradition, for instance, equated metals, celestial bodies, and Roman gods: iron was Mars, bronze Jupiter, gold the Sun, silver the Moon, copper Venus (except when it was Mars), lead Saturn, and, of course, mercury was Mercury. Following this tradition, when Martin Klaproth discovered a new metal, he named it uranium after the planet discovered by William Herschel in 1781, who had called it Uranus after the sky god of the Greeks. Alchemists coined allegorical names and symbols in part to confuse the uninitiated but also, and more important, because they believed such names would endow them with the power to penetrate the mysteries of nature, the "hidden relations between the microcosm and the macrocosm."[75]

Compounds and other elements had less noble designations. Many were given culinary names because they looked like familiar foods (even when they were toxic): oil of vitriol, cream of tartar, sugar of Saturn, butter of antimony, saffron of Mars, liver of sulfur, and milk of magnesia are but a few examples. Others were named after a geographic location (vitriol of Cyprus, blue of Prussia, Epsom salt), their supposed medicinal properties, or the names of their inventors (febrifugal salt of Sylvius, Homburg's sedative salt, liquor of Libavius). Yet others had mysterious-sounding but meaningless names like powder of Algaroth or colcothar. Pharmacists who invented new compounds often deliberately misnamed them to hide their composition from rivals. Some compounds had multiple names; for example, potassium sulfate was called panacea duplicata, arcanum holsteiniense, tartarus vitriolatus, sal polychrestum Glaser, and half a dozen other expressions. The old vocabulary was not merely illogical; it also could be dangerous.[76]

Chemists attacked alchemy as a fraud perpetrated by charlatans. In 1749, Pierre Joseph Macquer (1718–1784) wrote:

> Chemistry had become an occult and mysterious science; its expressions were only figures, its phrases were metaphors, its axioms were enigmas; in a word, the salient characteristic of its language was to be obscure and unintelligible. These chemists, in wanting to hide their secrets, had made their art useless for humanity and thus contemptible.[77]

Criticizing the old terminology was one thing; devising a new one was another matter. Yet by the mid–eighteenth century, because of the proliferation of new compounds resulting from their own experiments, chemists faced a growing need for a systematic nomenclature. From 1700 to 1780, the number of known neutral salts increased from a dozen to several hundred, that of known metals rose from ten to seventeen, that of known acids from six to eighteen. Chemistry courses proliferated in European universities, as did communications among chemists.[78]

Many chemists, eager to avoid confusing alchemical terms, referred to compounds with long phrases that described their characteristics or their method of preparation. Thus the Swedish mineralogist Cronstedt used the expression "terra calcarea Acido Vitrioli saturata seu mixta" (chalk earth saturated or mixed with vitriolic acid) to refer to what we call calcium sulfate; and Antoine Lavoisier, before he coined the word *oxygen,* called this gas "the best and most respirable part of the air" or even "pure air . . . which is more air than ordinary air."[79] With the proliferation of new compounds, the situation in chemistry was reminiscent of that faced by botanists before Linnaeus, when plants had either idiosyncratic names or long, complicated descriptions. If Linnaeus's binomial nomenclature had brought order to the kingdom of plants, why couldn't the same be done for chemicals?

Not surprisingly, the first step in the direction of a new language of chemistry was an attempt to formulate a binomial nomenclature for salts, in imitation of Linnaeus. In his *Dictionnaire de chymie* (1766), a standard reference work, Macquer wrote:

> It would be proper to give the same denomination *vitriol* to all vitriolic salts with a metallic base, and to name, for example, *vitriol d'or,* the vitriolic salt composed of vitriolic [i.e., sulfuric] acid and gold; *vitriol d'argent, ou*

de lune, the salt resulting from the union of the same acid with silver, and so on. Perhaps it would be correct to include under the general name *vitriol,* all vitriolic salts whatsoever.[80]

For other compounds, however, such as the salts of still-undiscovered metals (sodium, potassium, calcium, aluminum), he retained the old names, for example, "sel vitriolique à base de terre argileuse" (vitriolic salt based on clay earth, i.e., ammonium sulfate), "sel ammoniaque secret de Glauber" (sodium tartrate), and "cristaux de Vénus" (copper acetate).[81]

Other chemists also helped create a new chemical nomenclature. One was the Swedish mineralogist Torbern Bergman (1735–1784), a pupil of Linnaeus who tried to apply his mentor's Latin binomial nomenclature to minerals.[82] He, too, began his career by criticizing the old vocabulary:

> As far as denominations are concerned, I think salts need a reform: The old names are absurd and intolerable and the most reasonable ones are based upon properties that are either wrong, uncertain or common to several substances. The number of salts is growing steadily, that is why it is necessary to establish a few constant rules.[83]

In his *Dissertatio de attractionibus electivis* (1775), Bergman used names like "magnesia aerata" and "calx nitrata" to identify the results of "elective attractions," that is, chemical reactions. When writing in Swedish, however, he used descriptive phrases like "järn uplöst i luftsyra" (iron saturated with aerial acid).[84]

A few years later, the Royal Academy of Sciences of Uppsala published Bergman's "Meditationes de systemate fossilium naturali," in which he described the principles of his chemical nomenclature.[85] Acids, alkalis, and metals should have one-word names; the names of metals should end in *-um* (thus *platina*—"little silver" in Spanish—became *platinum*); and neutral salts should have a two- or three-word name referring to their constituent elements.

Bergman's nomenclature did not have the impact he expected, for two reasons. He dealt with natural minerals rather than the gases that were then causing so much excitement among chemists, and he wrote in Latin, which by the 1780s was no longer the language of scholars.[86] Nonetheless, his efforts inspired and encouraged his French contemporary Louis-Bernard Guyton de Morveau (1737–1816).

Guyton de Morveau's first criticisms of the old chemical vocabulary appeared in an article in the supplement to Diderot's *Encyclopédie* in 1777: "It is much better if the technical terms of a science express nothing which is known and recall no . . . false resemblances which lead beginners astray and always astonish the most educated people."[87] Thus, he proposed replacing the word *foie* (liver), used to describe reddish substances, with the Latin word *hepar* (liver), which did not carry the connotation of food. In this, he was clearly influenced by Bergman, whose works he had translated into French.

In an article entitled "Mémoire sur les dénominations chymiques" (1782), he explained his philosophy of language:

> The state of perfection of the language is an indication of the state of perfection of the science itself; its progress can be certain and rapid only in so far as its ideas are represented by precisely determined signs, correct in their meaning, simple in their expression, convenient in use and easy to remember, in which are retained as far as possible, without error, the analogy which brings them together, the system by which they are defined and the etymology by which their meaning can be guessed.

He proposed to replace both the old alchemical nomenclature and the long descriptive phrases (e.g., "liqueur alkaline saturée de la matière colorante du bleu de Prusse") with a new vocabulary that would follow certain simple rules: every substance should have a name, not a descriptive phrase; elements should have one-word names, and compounds should have names indicating their composition; for poorly understood substances, one should prefer words having no intrinsic meaning to words with a false meaning; and new words should be derived from Greek roots.[88]

Guyton de Morveau was clearly following Bergman's example, but with a difference: whereas Bergman had used Latin, Guyton wrote in French, insisting that "names should be chosen with due regard to the genius of the language for which they were formed. . . . This rule is not the least important." His preference for Greek over Latin roots may have been motivated by anti-Jesuit feelings. Consequently, his proposals were well received in France, if not elsewhere.[89]

Guyton de Morveau's proposals brought him to the attention of Antoine-Laurent Lavoisier (1743–1794), a wealthy and influential member of the Academy of Sciences, at the very moment when Lavoisier was challenging the fundamental paradigm of chemistry, the phlogistic theory, to which all chemists, including Guyton, adhered. From the 1750s on, experiments with gases had led to dozens of new substances, chemical reactions, and hypotheses to explain them. The flurry of discoveries was making chemistry ever more complicated and confusing.

Lavoisier rejected the old explanation based on the mysterious "phlogiston" and proposed that one of the gases that composed the air was the "creator of acid" ("oxygen" in Greek) and a participant in burning and roasting ("oxidation") and many other chemical reactions. He also sought a way to quantify chemical reactions instead of describing them with occult expressions like "affinity" and "sympathy." He asserted that in chemical reactions, "nothing is lost and nothing is created," meaning that elements are only separated or combined in new ways. He presented his theory in numerous papers, in particular in "Réflexions sur la phlogistique," read to the Academy of Sciences in 1785.

When Lavoisier's paper failed to persuade his audience, he changed tactics and decided that his new chemistry needed an entirely new language. Meanwhile, Guyton de Morveau had arrived in Paris in late 1786, and by February 1787, had been persuaded by Lavoisier to abandon phlogiston and adapt his nomenclature to the oxygen theory. Along with two friends of Lavoisier and members of the Academy (Antoine François de Fourcroy and Claude Louis Berthollet) and two young laboratory assistants (Jean Henri Hassenfratz and Pierre Auguste Adet), they worked out a completely new system of chemistry.[90]

On April 18, 1787, Lavoisier read his "Mémoire sur la nécessité de réformer & de perfectionner la nomenclature de la Chimie" (Report on the need to reform and perfect chemical nomenclature) to the Academy of Sciences. Two weeks later, on May 2, Guyton de Morveau presented his "Mémoire sur le développement des principes de la nomenclature méthodique" (Report on the development of the principles of methodical nomenclature).[91] Their papers were published together as *Méthode de nomenclature chimique,* along with an essay on chemical symbols and two dictionaries to translate between the old and the new chemical vocabularies.[92] It was a classic case of what Thomas Kuhn called a "scientific revolution."[93]

Lavoisier's essay was a philosophical discourse on the relationship between facts, ideas, and words. In this, he was strongly influenced by the philosopher Condillac, who regarded algebra as the model language.[94] According to Lavoisier,

> Languages have as their purpose not only, as is commonly believed, to express ideas and images by signs: they are also true analytical methods with which we go from the known to the unknown, up to a point, in the manner of mathematicians. . . . thus an analytical method is a language; a language is an analytical method, and these two expressions are, in a certain sense, synonymous.
>
> We will have three things to distinguish in every physical science. The series of facts that constitute the science; the ideas that refer to the facts; and the words which express them. The word must give birth to the idea; the idea must depict the fact. . . . As it is words that conserve and transmit ideas, the result is that it would be impossible to perfect science without perfecting the language.
>
> It is time to rid chemistry of obstacles of all sorts which retard its progress; to introduce a true analytical spirit. We have clearly established that it is by perfecting the language that this reform must be achieved.[95]

For Lavoisier, words were the instruments of knowledge. A change in vocabulary both reflected and induced a change in science itself. What he proposed was not just a new set of names to apply to known chemicals but an analytical method of naming substances by their chemical composition, one that would lead to further discoveries.[96]

He left it to Guyton de Morveau to describe how the new method worked. Simple substances—earths, metals, alkalis, radicals of acids, and "principles" like oxygen, hydrogen, light, and caloric—were given simple names. Compounds were to be named after the elements that formed them, with suffixes indicating the degree of saturation with oxygen: *-ique* indicating complete saturation and *-eux* for partial saturation. Thus sulfur formed both *acide sulfurique*, or sulfuric acid (H_2SO_4), and *acide sulfureux*, or sulfurous acid (H_2SO_3). In turn, the salt formed by sulfuric acid was named *sulfate*, while that formed by sulfurous acid became *sulfite*, and a compound without oxygen was a *sulfure* (sulfide in English).[97] Thus, the new nomenclature ignored the appearance or utilitarian value of substances, and even their propensity to react with one another, concentrating instead on their composition. In other words, it mirrored the newly developed laboratory techniques of analyzing of substances into their constitutive elements.[98]

Given the state of chemical knowledge, the nomenclature was clearly just a beginning. To substances that were not yet understood, Lavoisier and Guyton gave temporary names such as *acide muriatique* (later renamed hydrochloric acid). Without the atomic theory, they could not assign quantitative prefixes to indicate the degree of oxygenation (as in the modern names carbon *mon*oxide and carbon *di*oxide).

The last third of the *Méthode de nomenclature chimique* was taken up by the "Synonymie ancienne et nouvelle" and the "Dictionnaire pour la nouvelle nomenclature chimique." The "Synonymie" translated the old terms into the new nomenclature; for example, "base de l'air vital" was translated as "oxygène," "esprit de Vénus" as "acide acétique," "foie d'antimoine" as "oxide d'antimoine sulfuré," and "sel d'Epsom" as "sulfate de magnésie." The "Dictionnaire" contained 1,055 new chemical terms but only 361 old ones; it was twice as long as the "Synonymie" because many chemicals were so new they had never received a traditional name. Indeed, half the new names referred to substances that were discovered later, as Lavoisier had predicted. His nomenclature was not just a list of new names, or even only a method of naming, but a guide to future research.[99]

Both the nomenclature and the oxygen theory spread rapidly. The *Méthode* was reprinted six times between 1787 and 1791. Its ideas were widely publicized in Lavoisier's journal *Annales de Chimie* and in chemistry textbooks such as Lavoisier's *Traité élémentaire de chimie* (1789), Chaptal's *Elémens de chimie* (1790), and Fourcroy's *Elémens d'histoire naturelle* (3d ed., 1789). The *Méthode* and the new texts were quickly translated into English, German, Italian, and Spanish. Translations into English and the Romance languages simply adopted the French vocabulary (e.g., oxygen, *oxígeno, ossigeno*). German translations, however, reconstituted the new nomenclature with Germanic roots in place of Greek ones, for example, *Sauerstoff* (sour substance) for oxygen and *Wasserstoff* (water substance) for hydrogen.[100]

As expected, the new system provoked strong reactions. Older members of the Academy and merchants who sold chemicals rejected the new nomenclature. French traditionalists criticized it for being offensive to "good usage," that is, to the genteel language of the salons. Jean-Claude de la Métherie, editor of the influential journal *Observations et Mémoires sur la Physique,* criticized it for using "harsh and barbaric words that shock the ear and are not at all in the spirit of the French language."[101]

British chemists either tried to save the phlogiston theory or rejected all theorizing, for fear that one sect would impose its views on everyone else, or that every sect would invent its own language. Joseph Black denounced the new nomenclature as an example of the French "rage for systems."[102] Henry Cavendish complained:

> If the giving of systematic names becomes the fashion it must be expected that the other chemists who differ from these in theory will give other names agreeing with their particular theories, so we shall have as many different sets of names as there are theories. . . . I do not imagine indeed that their nomenclature will ever come into use, but I am much afraid that it will do mischief by setting people's minds afloat and increasing the present rage of name-making.[103]

And Thomas Jefferson commented:

> One single experiment may destroy the whole filiation of his terms and his string of sulfates, sulfites and sulfures may have served no other end than to have retarded the progress of the science by a jargon, from the confusion of which time will be required to extricate us.[104]

The oxygen theory was not an instant success but took two or three generations of chemists to displace phlogiston.[105] However, students and younger chemists quickly adopted the new nomenclature because it expressed quantities of substances, it offered a guide to future research, and it swept away the old alchemical vocabulary.[106] It has been the basis for chemical vocabulary since the 1790s. As historian of chemistry William Brock explains, "A modern chemist, on looking at a chemical treatise published before Lavoisier's time, would find it largely incomprehensible; but everything written by Lavoisier himself, or composed a few years after his death, would cause a modern reader little difficulty."[107]

Chemical literature in the late eighteenth century was overwhelmingly narrative. Symbols were known but were associated with the esoteric illustrations of alchemical texts, in which a circle with a dot in the middle represented the Sun (i.e., gold), a crescent represented the Moon and silver, and so on. Some symbols dated back to the Egyptians, their original significance long since lost.[108]

Nonetheless, chemists recognized the usefulness of symbols as abbreviations for long verbal expressions. Lavoisier and Guyton's *Méthode de nomenclature chimique* included an essay by Lavoisier's laboratory assistants Hassenfratz and Adet, proposing a new system of chemical symbols. Simple substances were to be represented by short lines, metals by circles, acids by squares, and alkalis and earths by triangles containing initials (F for iron, M for muriatic, A for acetic, etc.). Compounds required combinations of shapes and ended up more confusing than enlightening.[109] Though Lavoisier praised the new symbols, all the authors neglected them in their later works, probably because they were too costly to set in print.[110] Guyton used them, but only in his courses at the Ecole polytechnique.[111]

After Lavoisier, the next advance in both chemistry and chemical notation system was the work of John Dalton (1766–1844), the man who originated the atomic theory. Dalton visualized atoms as tiny balls and symbolized them on paper "by a small circle, with some distinctive mark; and the combinations consist in the juxta-position of two or more of these."[112] Thus, he represented oxygen as a circle, hydrogen as a circle with a dot, and azote (nitrogen) as a circle with a vertical line. For metals, he placed initials inside circles: C for copper, I for iron, N for nickel, Ar for arsenic, and so on. Compounds were shown by combining circles. To represent water, he drew two circles, one empty, the other with a dot. More complex compounds required more circles; alum, for instance, needed twenty-five. This system allowed Dalton to show not only the proportion of atoms of each element in a compound but also their arrangement.[113]

While simpler than Hassenfratz and Adet's, Dalton's symbols were still a typographer's nightmare. In 1813/1814, Dalton's contemporary Jöns Jakob Berzelius (1779–1848) took the next logical step: he eliminated Dalton's little circles.[114] Instead, he represented each element by one or two letters of its Latin name, for example, S for sulfur, Si for silicium, Su for stannum (tin), C for carbon, Co for cobaltum (cobalt), and Cu for cuprum (copper). Multiple atoms of an element would be shown by a number, and compounds by the + sign; for instance, water became $2H + O$ and carbonic acid (i.e., carbon dioxide), $C + 2O$. Having come up with a very simple set of symbols, Berzelius then proceeded to complicate it. A bar through a letter meant two atoms; oxygen was shown by a dot above a compound instead of the letter O; likewise, he replaced S for sulfur with a superscript comma. He deleted the plus sign and moved the number of atoms in a compound from the left to the right; for example, $2H + O$ became H^2O.[115]

Even with all these variations, Berzelius's system remained the most logical, the fastest to memorize, and—most important—the easiest to typeset. Dalton was not pleased:

Berzelius' symbols are horrifying; a young student in chemistry might as well learn Hebrew as make himself acquainted with them. They appear like a chaos of atoms . . . to equally perplex the adept of science, to discourage the learner as well as to cloud the beauty of the Atomic Theory.[116]

Other chemists, however, gradually came around. In 1834, Edward Turner in England and Justus von Liebig in Germany adopted the Berzelius system.[117] Two years later, the Committee on Chemical Notation of the British Association for the Advancement of Science recommended the Berzelius notation system. It was well adapted to expressing chemical equations, such as $2H + O = H^2O$, and, even more important, it proved essential in the newly emerging organic chemistry, where compounds were too complex to explain in words.[118] The language of chemistry had become, as Lavoisier had hoped, "a true analytical methods with which we go from the known to the unknown, up to a point, in the manner of mathematicians."

The Metric System

Anyone who has learned the metric system cannot help but be impressed with how logical and practical it is and wonder why Anglo-Saxons, otherwise so proud of their efficiency and common sense, still cling to their medieval, illogical system of weights and measures. If that seems paradoxical, consider two other paradoxes in the history of weights and measures. The French people, who invented the metric system, resisted using it for two generations. Meanwhile, the first country to enjoy a legally enforced and popularly accepted system of weights and measures was not France but Great Britain.

Weights and measures serve very different purposes for the common people who use them, for the government officials who enforce them, and for the scientists who develop them. Social historian Witold Kula has seen in the contentious history of weights and measures a reflection of social struggles between lords and peasants, or between feudalism and capitalism. Here I will focus on the role of scientists in creating the metric system and how their needs affected the outcome of the social struggles their system provoked.

From an information-systems perspective, the metric system is a nomenclature: the names it gives to units of measurement are precisely defined and related to one another in a consistent, coherent manner. To scientists, it is as valuable as the botanical or chemical nomenclatures. In countries that have officially adopted it, the metric system, devised by and for scientists, is imposed by law on everyone else. Its advent in revolutionary France symbolized the defeat of the Old Regime by an intelligentsia imbued with the ideals of the Enlightenment.

Prerevolutionary weights and measures were amazingly diverse. According to Witold Kula, eighteenth-century Europe had 391 different measures called *pound* and 282 called *foot* (or their equivalents).[119] Ronald Zupko, a historian of metrology, counted 1,000 standard units of measurement in France, with 250,000 local variations.[120] Arthur Young, who traveled through France just before the Revolution, commented that "the infinite perplexity of the measures exceeds all comprehension. They differ not only in every province, but in every district, and almost every town."[121]

The situation was even worse than he thought: in a single town, the same word often represented different units, depending on what was being measured and who did the measuring. The Parisian unit of length, the *toise du Châtelet,* competed with the *toise de l'Académie* or *du Pérou* and with the *toise du Nord,* used by scientists who measured the arc of the meridian (see chapter 4).[122] The *arpent,* a measure of area, had forty-eight separate values in the different parishes of the Paris region.[123]

Units varied not only from place to place but also for measuring different substances in the same place. Paris had three measures for cloth alone.[124] Wheat, oats, salt, coal, and oil were measured with different units of volume.[125] The same unit of the same product could produce different measurements, depending on the transaction: when a landlord received payment in wheat from his tenants, for example, he used a wide, shallow container filled to heaping, but when he sold, it was with a tall, narrow container with the contents combed flat.[126]

Standards proliferated as time went on. Rights to weigh and to measure were privileges of lords and guilds, for which they extracted fees. After the mid–eighteenth century, landed aristocrats, threatened by new taxes, became increasingly rapacious in squeezing their tenants. The right to measure also provided merchants a profit from their customers, and inspectors a bribe from their victims. And it provided endless litigation for legions of lawyers.[127]

Such a state of affairs offended monarchs and their ministers, who thought weights and measures should be a royal privilege. Since Charlemagne, monarchs had issued hundreds of decrees and laws in an attempt to impose their own units on their entire kingdom, but all had failed; the profusion of weights and measures was simply too valuable to local power holders for them to give up.[128]

In the Age of Reason, this assertion of royal privilege was joined by a powerful new voice: that of scientists. As soon as it became possible, in theory, to measure the earth, scientists realized that to do so they needed a reliable unit of measurement. From the start, geodesy and scientific metrology went hand in hand.

The first proposal to reform weights and measures for scientific reasons dated from 1670, when the amateur scientist Gabriel Mouton suggested deriving a unit of measurement from the arc of the meridian, a fraction of the circumference of the earth passing through the poles that could be measured both on the ground and astronomically, by observing the latitude of its endpoints. Mouton's suggestion was echoed by Abbé Jean Picard, then engaged in measuring the arc between Paris and Amiens, and later by the astronomers Christiaan Huygens and Jean-Dominique Cassini.

These private suggestions entered the realm of public discussion when Charles-Marie de la Condamine (1701–1774) returned from his expedition to Peru (see chapter 4). In 1745, he presented a proposal to the Academy of Sciences for a "common and invariable" unit of measurement based on the length of a pendulum that beat once per second at the equator; this was to be the *toise du Pérou* or *de l'Académie*. Like Mouton's, his system was to be based on the measurement of a natural phenomenon, expressed in decimals to make calculations easier.[129] Long before the French Revolution, scientists advocated two characteristics of the metric system, the natural unit and decimal arithmetic.

By the late eighteenth century, royal administrators were becoming increasingly concerned with metrology, for it affected their ability to control grain supplies, and hence to prevent famines and maintain order in times of crisis.[130] Furthermore, the artillery corps was eager to simplify the calibers of cannon and the weights of cannonballs and was even thinking about using interchangeable parts for muskets; all of these required precise, accurate, and uniform measurements.[131]

The ideas of royal privilege and scientific reason came together in the reforms proposed by the physiocrat Robert Turgot (1727–1781). During his brief career as controller-general of finances from 1774 to 1776, he tried to introduce a reform of weights and measures, which he entrusted to the young mathematician Condorcet and the agronomist Mathieu Tillet (1720–1791).[132] The fall of the Turgot ministry is usually attributed to court intrigues and the opposition of vested interests, including the nobility that profited from its metrical privileges. As Witold Kula has argued, abolishing the old weights and measures could only happen along with the abolition of all other feudal privileges, in other words, in a revolution.[133]

Turgot's failure discouraged his successor, Jacques Necker (1732–1804). In his report to Louis XVI in 1778, Necker expressed his pessimistic assessment of the project:

> I considered the means necessary to make weights and measures uniform throughout the kingdom; but I doubt whether the value that would result would be proportional to the difficulties of every sort that this operation would entail, given the changes that would be necessary

in a multitude of sales contracts, feudal obligations and other acts of every kind.[134]

Diderot's *Encyclopédie* shared this ambivalence. Under "Mesure" it stated: "It is clear that people will never agree among themselves to use the same weights and measures. But it is very possible in a country subject to a single master." And the entry "Poids" (weight) said:

> The diversity of weights is one of the most embarrassing aspects of commerce, but it is an irremediable inconvenience. Not only is it impossible to reduce the units of weight in all nations to a single one, but even reducing the different units of weight in a single nation is not feasible.[135]

Under the circumstances, the best that could be done was to publish tables of conversion of weights and measures—which proliferated in that period.[136]

Metrology was a theme in the famous *cahiers de doléances,* or notebooks of grievances, which communes and corporations produced in the spring of 1789 in response to the calling of the Estates General. Kula exaggerated only a little when he wrote: "The voice of the people rose up in the whole country to demand the unification of measures and the abolition of the metrical privileges of the lords."[137] Hundreds of *cahiers* complained about the proliferation of standards and their abuse by lords and merchants, and demanded "one king, one law, one weight, one measure," or something along those lines.[138] Scientists and their revolutionary supporters took a simple popular demand and hijacked it for their own ends.

Proponents of metrical reform, thwarted for decades, found their opportunity with the creation of the National Assembly in 1789. Condorcet presented his ideas on the subject to Charles-Maurice de Talleyrand-Périgord (1754–1838), a rising star in the National Assembly. In early 1790, Talleyrand presented to the assembly his *Proposition . . . sur les poids et mesures,* advocating a new system of weights and measures to be devised by the Academy of Sciences in cooperation with the Royal Society of London. This system was to be "taken from nature," that is, based on the length of a seconds-beating pendulum.[139]

The assembly sent the proposal to the Academy of Sciences for review. The Academy set up a committee of scientists, including Condorcet, Lavoisier, Tillet, the astronomer Charles Borda, and the mathematician Joseph Louis Lagrange. In its report to the Academy in March 1791, this committee recommended the use of the decimal system and a unit of length based on the arc of the meridian, rather than the pendulum.

The Academy then created a commission to work out the details of the new system. The commission included Borda, Condorcet, Lagrange,

Lavoisier, and the mathematicians Pierre-Simon de Laplace and Gaspard Monge, the most brilliant mathematical and scientific minds in the world at that time. These were the men who devised the metric system, which the Assembly adopted in March 1791.[140] Lavoisier boasted: "Nothing so great and so simple, so coherent in all its parts, has ever come from the hand of man."[141]

Rather than simply pick an existing standard, such as the *toise* of Paris, the scientists insisted that the basic measurement of length should be both natural and precise. *Natural* meant that it should be based on the length of an object in nature that could be measured repeatedly, always with the same results. Three such objects were proposed: the length of the seconds-beating pendulum, the circumference of the earth at the equator, and the circumference of the earth through the poles. Although the length of a seconds-beating pendulum was simple and cheap to calculate, it could not be measured with the necessary degree of precision; furthermore, its calculation involved another unit, the second, that was arbitrary and not decimal. The length of the equator was a more elegant idea, but it was impossible to measure with the instruments available at the time. That left the circumference through the poles, or the meridian.

As will be described in chapter 4, scientists had measured the length of an arc of the meridian several times over the previous century, each time with a greater degree of accuracy. The commission proposed to measure it once more, this time between Dunkirk and Barcelona, cities that had the advantage of being on the same meridian, equidistant from the forty-five-degree parallel north, and at sea level. Coincidentally, only in France were the requisite conditions found to make a measurement that would be valid for the entire world (not the only such coincidence in the thinking of French revolutionaries at the time). Once that distance was known, it would be easy to determine the distance from the pole to the equator; dividing that distance by ten million gave a unit of length—the meter—that was both natural and exact.[142]

The eminent scientists on the commission were working, of course, for the greater good of mankind, but in the process they also helped their profession. To measure the arc of the meridian from Dunkirk to Barcelona would take years and would require the efforts of dozens of mathematicians, astronomers, cartographers, and others. Indeed, this project required more funds than the annual budget of the Academy of Sciences and was the main source of support for French scientific research after the Academy was closed during the Terror.[143]

In the spring of 1793 the Academy of Sciences presented its recommendations to the new parliament, the National Convention. Pending the completion of the meridian project, it recommended a provisional meter of 3 *pieds* and 11.44 *lignes*.[144] It proposed that decimal arithmetic be used not only for the weights and measures we now associate with the metric system but also for many other purposes: 10 days in a week, 10 hours in a day, 100 minutes in an hour, 100 seconds in a minute, and 100 degrees in a right angle. Merchants and accountants had used decimal arithmetic since Arabic numerals were introduced to Europe in the Renaissance, but applying it to other measures was such a novel idea that one of its advocates, Prieur de la Côte d'Or, had to explain it: "If you consider units of the same sort ranked in decreasing order, each one is ten times smaller than the one immediately preceding, and ten times bigger than the one that follows."[145]

To prevent confusion with the old measurements, the academicians introduced a new nomenclature based on logic rather than tradition. The basic units of measurement were to receive new names: *mètre, litre, gramme, are* (an area of 10 × 10 meters), and *stare* (a cubic meter). Multiples by 10, 100, 1,000, and 10,000 were to receive the Greek prefixes *déca, hecto, kilo,* and *myria,* respectively, while submultiples received the Latin prefixes *déci, centi,* and *milli.* The new nomenclature was not accepted without debate. One side used an argument inspired by Condillac and Lavoisier: "It is almost impossible to reason correctly without a language aptly made." Opponents argued: "These names, novel and unintelligible to the large majority of our citizens, are not necessary for the maintenance of the Republic."[146]

On August 1, the Committee of Public Instruction decreed that the new system would become obligatory in July 1794 and set up a Temporary Commission of Weights and Measures to implement it.[147] Meanwhile, the National Convention, led by Robespierre and the Committee of Public Safety, was becoming more and more radical. It abolished the Academy of Sciences and purged several members the Commission of Weights and Measures, including Borda, Laplace, and Lavoisier, tainted by association with the monarchy.[148] The membership of this and later commissions and agencies changed frequently but always included highly respected scientists.

The survey of the arc of the meridian from Dunkirk to Barcelona was completed and a definitive standard presented to the government in June 1799 and officially adopted on December 10.[149] That decree did not end the matter, however, for public resistance to the metric system was widespread. Farmers and artisans interpreted the strange names and the unfamiliar arithmetic as a new way of cheating them. The Agency of Weights and Measures complained that government officials, even artillery officers, continued to use the old units.[150]

Meanwhile, the politics that had brought about the metric system came full circle when the government was overthrown by the military adventurer Napoleon Bonaparte. Within less than a year, Napoleon replaced the Greco-Latin nomenclature with a system of his own devising, using old terms for the new units: *mille* for a kilometer, *doigt* (finger) for centimeter, *trait* (line) for millimeter, *pinte* for liter, *livre* (pound) for kilogram, and so on.[151] Six years later, he abolished the revolutionary calendar. In 1812, he backtracked some more on weights and measures, keeping the meter but abolishing the rest of the nomenclature and replacing the decimal divisions with fractions: a *livre* was half a kilo, divided into sixteen *onces* and each *once* into eight *gros.* This measure, designed to win conservative support on the eve of Napoleon's invasion of Russia, only sowed more confusion.[152]

For two generations, the metric system remained associated with Jacobinism, the most radical faction in the French Revolution. Not until 1837, after decades of confusion and waffling, did a French government (and a moderate one at that) bring back the metric system in its pure form, decimals, Greco-Roman names, and all. Since January 1, 1840, it has been the only legal system in France. Even so, it has taken a century of public education, economic development, and law enforcement to make it universally accepted.

In other countries, the metric system suffered from an additional handicap: it was foreign. In 1790, Talleyrand had hoped to interest the British in a joint reform of weights and measures, but the tension between the two countries soon defeated that attempt. Eight years later, with French troops occupying the Low Countries and northern Italy, he invited representatives of other European states (except Russia and Britain) to join France in adopting the metric system. As in France, coercion and backtracking caused chaos in weights and measures throughout Europe. Slowly and haltingly, however, the metric system gained ground, often in conjunction with major political turning points: in Italy and Germany at the moment of their unification; upon the creation of Poland and Yugoslavia in 1919; at the independence of India in 1947; and after the Communist revolutions in Russia (1918) and China (1959).[153]

Two countries have resisted the metric system to this day: Britain and the United States. In eighteenth-century Britain, the problem of weights and measures was not as acute as in France, for most people used the same arbitrary and unscientific units: the troy pound of twelve ounces, the London, or avoirdupois, pound of sixteen ounces, and the yard, made in 1758–1760 and deposited in the House of Commons.

Several reformers proposed a new system of weights and measures, including a unit of length based on the seconds-beating pendulum, coherence between the units, and decimal arithmetic. By 1793, however, such proposals not only were rejected as "French" but also encountered opposition from industry and trade.[154]

Not until 1814, with the end of the Napoleonic Wars, did Parliament turn its attention to weights and measures. Finally, in 1824, it enacted the imperial system of weights and measures, with three basic units: the yard, the troy pound, and the imperial gallon, the latter being defined as ten pounds of distilled water at sixty-two degrees Fahrenheit and thirty inches of mercury. All other units (quarts, pints, bushels, ounces, inches, etc.) were based on these three.[155] Unlike the metric system, the imperial system was not "natural," coherent, or decimal. However, it was widely accepted from the start and enforced by a corps of inspectors. In a country that was rapidly industrializing, in other words, mass-producing goods to standard dimensions, trustworthy measurements were essential to business and gave British goods an advantage throughout the empire and in overseas markets.

Americans were even more ambivalent about the metrical reform than the British. Thomas Jefferson, who introduced the decimal currency, caught the enthusiasm for metrical reform when he was ambassador to France. In 1790, at the request of President Washington, he proposed a decimal system similar to the French, but Congress took no action.[156] Many years later, in 1821, John Quincy Adams issued the *Report upon Weights and Measures,* in which he extolled the virtues of the metric system:

> The establishment of such a system so obviously tends to that great result, the improvement of the physical, moral, and intellectual condition of man upon earth; that there can be neither doubt nor hesitancy in the opinion that the ultimate adoption and universal, though modified, application of that system is a consummation devoutly to be wished.

To bring about that devoutly wished-for consummation, Adams trusted public opinion, not Congress:

> The final prevalence of this system beyond the boundaries of France's power must await the time when the example of its benefits, long and practically enjoyed, shall acquire that ascendancy over the opinions of other nations which gives motion to the springs and direction to the wheels of power.[157]

When Congress finally took an interest in the reform of weights and measures in 1828, it was to legalize ancient customary units: the yard and the troy and avoirdupois pounds, equal to those of Britain, and the Queen Anne gallon of 1707 and the Winchester bushel of 1702, abolished in Britain in 1824.[158]

To understand the significance of the metric system and why it took so long to find acceptance, we need to review its salient characteristics. First and foremost, the metric system was meant to be a universal and trustworthy set of standards, officially certified and enforced, to replace the myriad units of the Old Regime. This is what the writers of the *cahiers de doléances* had demanded, and this is why it succeeded in the end. But it had four other characteristics, introduced by scientists but irrelevant to the general public. The first of these was its "naturalness." People had always used natural units of time, the day and the year. But the fact that a meter was one ten-millionth the distance from the pole to the equator, rather than a bit more or a bit less, made little difference to farmers, merchants, landlords, or anyone but scientists.

The second characteristic upon which scientists insisted was that the system should be internally coherent. The unit of area had to be the square of the unit of length, the unit of volume had to be its cube, and the unit of weight had to be that of a given volume of distilled water at a specified temperature. In later years, scientists were able to define units of energy, mass, electricity, and so on, in terms of the original units, extending the integrated system. But how a volume was related to a unit of length or of weight was of little interest to the public, as long as a liter or a gram was the same at all times and in all places.

The third characteristic was decimal arithmetic. The academicians proclaimed base 10 as the most "natural" because humans sometimes counted on their fingers. But people also used other bases with other virtues. Base 12, the duodecimal system, was divisible by 6, 4, 3, and 2, whereas base 10 was divisible only by 5 and 2. Time (24 hours, 60 minutes, 60 seconds), angles (360 degrees), eggs, and oysters were, and still are, measured in base 12. For many everyday purposes, such as tailoring, carpentry, and market transactions, units that could be divided by 2 over and over, like inches, were easier to manipulate mentally than decimals. Only in written mathematics, and especially with such operations as long division or finding square roots, was the decimal system a real improvement. That is why scientists and philosophes wanted it so much, and why the French people began to appreciate it only after a public education system had spread the skills of written arithmetic.

The last characteristic of the metric system was its nomenclature. It may be impossible to reason scientifically without a language aptly made; yet a nomenclature that is coherent and logical to scientists clashes with the way people speak. The purpose of the metrical nomenclature was the same as that of the botanical and chemical nomenclatures: to associate precise terms with specific phenomena and to show the connections between such phenomena. But no government has dared order its citizens to say *Canis familiaris* or *Pisus sativum* or *Sodium chloride* instead of dog or pea or salt, the way the metric terminology has replaced the old weights and measures.[159]

The French Revolution is often associated with the "rise of the bourgeoisie" and, by extension, with a free market. To attribute the metric system to the desire to encourage a free market is to stretch a point too far, however.[160] To be sure, a free market requires uniform and reliable weights, measures, and other standards.[161] But it does not require anything like the metric system. The solution chosen by Britain and the United

States—the two nations most devoted to laissez-faire capitalism—met the needs of business. The metric system, by contrast, was the system of choice of scientists and, by extension, of philosophes and their revolutionary followers: it was the rationalist and scientific solution, not the capitalist one. That is why, in Anglo-Saxon countries, only scientists use the metric system.[162]

Science does not just accumulate data and find patterns in nature; it also seeks to explain these patterns. Yet finding patterns requires classifying and naming natural phenomena. Hence classification and nomenclature are the foundations upon which explanations can be built and influence those explanations.

Linnaeus classified plants into genera in order to bring some clarity and logic into their naming, but his classification avoided the issue of explanation. Or rather, he fell back on a theological explanation for genera, namely, that they were God-given and fixed since Creation. By rejecting his artificial system for a more subtle natural classification, his successors confronted the affinities they found among living things of different species not only within genera but also at higher levels: How to explain the fact that plants and animals form natural groups? By the late eighteenth century, neither randomness nor God's will seemed a satisfactory answer to this question. Biology was born of the need to find in nature itself an explanation for the affinities that the Linnaean classification systems had revealed.

The urge to classify and name was at the heart of the chemical revolution as well. In chemistry, however, classifying, naming, and explaining happened simultaneously, which is why we call it a revolution. Lavoisier and Guyton de Morveau invented not just a logical way of naming chemicals but a way of expressing the relationships among them, in other words, how they are formed; unlike the vernacular "rust," the name "ferric oxide" tells us this is a compound of iron (*ferrum* in Latin) and oxygen. In the Berzelius notation system, "Fe_2O_3," gives us even more information—the number of atoms in each molecule—in an even more succinct way.

At the end of the eighteenth century, three demands coincided to produce the metric system: a popular demand for a uniform, trustworthy system of weights and measures; a scientific demand for a system of measurement that was natural, mathematically simple, and internally coherent; and a political upheaval that valued innovation for its own sake. The system that emerged was no compromise but the triumph of science, backed by the force of law, over a recalcitrant popular culture.

Science has many legacies. Grand theories to explain the mysteries of nature capture the spotlight, followed, more recently, by the technological spin-offs of scientific research. But science also sets an example of information management. The classification systems and nomenclatures of the eighteenth and early nineteenth centuries not only were essential to further advances in the natural sciences but also provided models for other fields of knowledge.

Notes

1. On Linnaeus's sojourn in Holland, see Wilfrid Blunt, *The Compleat Naturalist: A Life of Linnaeus* (New York: Viking, 1971), 94–123; Norah Gourlie, *The Prince of Botanists: Carl Linnaeus* (London: Witherby, 1953), 120–47; and Heinz Goerke, *Linnaeus*, trans. Denver Lindley (New York: Scribner's, 1973), 27–29.

2. Gourlie, *Prince of Botanists*, 147.

3. Frans Antonie Stafleu, *Linnaeus and the Linnaeans: The Spreading of Their Ideas in Systematic Botany* (Utrecht: Oosthoek, 1971), 337.

4. *Oeuvres de Condorcet* (Paris: Fermin Didot, 1847), 2:153, quoted in Pascal Duris, *Linné et la France, 1780–1850* (Geneva: Droz, 1993), 125.

5. Goerke, *Linnaeus*, 33.

6. Stafleu, *Linnaeus and the Linnaeans*, 97.

7. Jean Le Rond d'Alembert, *Discours préliminaire de l'Encyclopédie*, (Picavet edition, Paris, 1894), 111, quoted in Max Fuchs, "La langue des sciences," in *Histoire de la langue française des origines à 1900*, ed. Ferdinand Brunot (Paris: Colin, 1930), 6:600.

8. Fuchs, "La langue des sciences," 6:526–75.

9. René Antoine Ferchault de Réaumur, *Memoire pour servir à l'histoire des insectes*, 6 vols. (Paris: Imprimerie Royale, 1734–1742); Charles Bonnet, *Traité d'insectologie*, 2 vols. (Paris: Durand, 1745); Guillaume Antoine Olivier, *Entomologie ou histoire naturelle des insectes avec leurs caractères génériques et spécifiques, leur description, leur synonymie et leur figure enluminée*, 6 vols. (Paris: Baudoin, 1789–1808).

10. John Ray, *Historia plantarum*, 3 vols. (London: H. Faithorne, 1686–1704), cited in Ernst Mayr, *The Growth of Biological Thought: Diversity, Evolution, and Inheritance* (Cambridge, Mass.: Belknap Press, 1982), 162.

11. W. T. Stearn, "The Background of Linnaeus's Contributions to the Nomenclature and Methods of Systematic Biology," *Systematic Zoology* 8 (1959): 8; Gunnar Broberg, "The Broken Circle," in *The Quantifying Spirit in the Eighteenth Century*, ed. Tore Frängsmyr, John L. Heilbron, and Robin E. Rider (Berkeley: University of California Press, 1990), 67; and Mayr, *Growth of Biological Thought*, 157–62.

12. On botanical classification and systematics, see V. H. Heywood, *Plant Taxonomy*, 2d ed. (London: Edward Arnold, 1976); and Charles Jeffrey, *Introduction to Plant Taxonomy*, 2d ed. (Cambridge: Cambridge University Press, 1982).

13. Mayr, *Growth of Biological Thought*, 156–58.

14. Alan G. Morton, *History of Botanical Science: An Account of the Development of Botany from Ancient Times to the Present Day* (London: Academic Press, 1981), 256–57; Henri Daudin, *De Linné à Jussieu, méthodes de la classification et l'idée de série en botanique et en zoologie, 1740–1790* (Paris: Alcan, 1926), 25–33; Julius von Sachs, *History of Botany (1530–1860)*, trans. E. F. Garnsey (Oxford: Clarendon, 1890), 68–77.

15. Maurice P. Crosland, *Historical Studies in the Language of Chemistry* (Cambridge, Mass.: Harvard University Press, 1962), 139–40; Fuchs, "La langue des sciences," 6:614.

16. Mayr, *Growth of Biological Thought*, 187.

17. An example for book lovers might be the difference between organizing one's books by topic, as in the Library of Congress system, and arranging them by height or alphabetically by authors' names. Another example, fraught with more serious consequences, is how we judge people: sometimes by their capacities (the natural classification), more often by race and gender (the artificial one).

18. Carl von Linné, *Critica botanica* (Leiden, 1737), aphorism 256.

19. von Sachs, *History of Botany*, 90. More recently, John Lesch designated Linnaeus as the founder of eighteenth-century systematics; see "Systematics and the Geometrical Spirit," in *The Quantifying Spirit in the Eighteenth Century*, ed. Tore Frängsmyr, J. L. Heilbron, and Robin E. Rider (Berkeley: University of California Press, 1990), 74–79. See also Mayr, *Growth of Biological Thought*, 172.

20. See James L. Larson, *Reason and Experience: The Representation of Natural Order in the Work of Carl von Linné* (Berkeley: University of California Press, 1971); William Thomas Stearn, "Introduction," in Carl von Linné, *Species plantarum: A Facsimile of the First Edition*, 2 vols. (London: The Ray Society, 1957), 22–26; and John Lewis Heller, *Studies in Linnaean Method and Nomenclature* (New York: P. Lang, 1983).

21. Today, with millions of species to classify, biologists need a far more complex set of categories: species, family, suborder, order, class, subphylum, phylum, and kingdom.

22. Quoted in Stafleu, *Linnaeus and the Linnaeans*, 61–62.

23. Quoted in ibid., 28.

24. Mayr, *Growth of Biological Thought*, 173–77.

25. The very idea that plants could have sex horrified the prudes of the day. In 1737, the clergyman-botanist Johann Siegesbeck protested that God never would have allowed such "loathsome harlotry": "Who would have thought that bluebells, lilies and onions could be up to such immorality?" See Blunt, *Compleat Naturalist*, 120–21; and James L. Larson, "Linnaeus and the Natural Method," *Isis* 58 (1967): 309–10. The sexual system has recently come under attack for a different reason, namely, that Linnaeus determined the class (a higher taxon) by the number of male stamens and the order (a lower taxon) by the number of female pistils; see Londa Schiebinger, "The Loves of Plants," *Scientific American*, February 1966, 110–15.

26. Stafleu, *Linnaeus and the Linnaeans*, 64, 115–22; Larson, *Reason and Experience*, 58, 97.

27. Linnaeus, *Philosophia botanica*, aphorism 159, quoted in Morton, *History of Botanical Science*, 266–67.

28. Stafleu, *Linnaeus and the Linnaeans*, 28.

29. Linnaeus, *Philosophia botanica*, aphorism 151, quoted in Stafleu, *Linnaeus and the Linnaeans*, 57–58.

30. Stafleu, *Linnaeus and the Linnaeans*, 79–80, 93–97; Crosland, *Historical Studies in the Language of Chemistry*, 140.

31. Larson, *Reason and Experience*, 123–27.

32. Stafleu, *Linnaeus and the Linnaeans*, 100–102.

33. Duris, *Linné et la France*, 123–24.

34. Larson, *Reason and Experience*, 122.

35. Stafleu, *Linnaeus and the Linnaeans*, 86−87; Heller, *Studies in Linnean Method and Nomenclature*, 43, 55−58.

36. Heller, 43−49, 55−58.

37. Stafleu, *Linnaeus and the Linnaeans*, 103−8; Larson, *Reason and Experience*, 135−37; Heller, *Studies in Linnaean Method and Nomenclature*, 41, 60; Stearn, "Background of Linnaeus's Contributions," 7−13.

38. Linnaeus, *Critica Botanica* (1737), aphorism 322, quoted in Stearn, "Background of Linnaeus's Contributions," 5. *Dill.* and *Dillen.* refer to J. J. Dillenius; *elth.* to *Hortus Elthamensis* (1732); *gissens.* to *Catalogus Plantarum sponte circa Gissam nascentium* (1719); and *gener.* to *Nova Plantarum Genera* (1719).

39. Heller, 62−75, 125. Eighteenth-century librarians faced the same problem with books that botanists faced with flowers; see Broberg, "Broken Circle," 52.

40. Mayr, *Growth of Biological Thought*, 178.

41. On Jean-Jacques Rousseau, see "Lettres élémentaires sur la botanique" and "Fragmens pour un Dictionnaire de termes d'usage en botanique," in *Oeuvres complètes*, 4 vols. (Paris: Gallimard, 1959−1969), 4:1174, 1207−8, cited in Duris, *Linné et la France*, 103−5. On Goethe, see *Goethe Schriften zur Naturwissenschaft* (Frankfurt: Insel, 1981), 36−63, 230−72; and James L. Larson, "Goethe and Linnaeus," *Journal of the History of Ideas* 28 (1967): 590−96.

42. Cf. Antoine Gouan, *Flora Monspeliaca* (1765), cited in Stafleu, *Linnaeus and the Linnaeans*, 267−71.

43. James L. Larson, *Interpreting Nature: The Science of Living Form from Linnaeus to Kant* (Baltimore: Johns Hopkins University Press, 1994), 17.

44. Miguel Angel Puig-Samper, "Difusión e institucionalización del sistema linneano en España y América," in *Mundialización de la ciencia y cultura nacional: Actas del Congreso Internacional "Ciencia, descubrimiento y mundo colonial,"* ed. Antonio Lafuente, Alberto Elena, and María Luisa Ortega (Madrid: Doce Calles, 1993), 350−52.

45. Ibid., 358.

46. Eduardo Estrella, "Introducción del sistema linneano en el virreinato del Perú," in Lafuente, Elena, and Ortega, *Mundialización de la ciencia y cultura nacional*, 344−48.

47. Per Kalm, *En Resa till Norra America*, 3 vols. (Stockholm: L. Salvii, 1753−1761), translated as *Travels into North America* by John R. Foster (Barre, Mass.: Imprint Society, 1972).

48. Stafleu, *Linnaeus and the Linnaeans*, 151−53, 199−202, 228−38.

49. See Harold B. Carter, *Sir Joseph Banks, 1763−1820* (London: British Museum, 1988); Patrick O'Brian, *Joseph Banks: A Life* (Boston: Godine, 1993); and John Mac-Kenzie, ed., *Imperialism and the Natural World* (Manchester: Manchester University Press, 1989).

50. Stafleu, *Linnaeus and the Linnaeans*, 111−14, 211−38. The influence of Banks's herbarium on botanical practices is similar to that of the Library of Congress classification system on academic libraries throughout the United States.

51. Ibid., 205.

52. Ibid., 238.

53. Ibid., 239.

54. Fuchs, "La langue des sciences," 6:613−14.

55. Georges-Louis Leclerc, comte de Buffon, "Premier discours de la manière

d'étudier & de traiter l'Histoire Naturelle," in *Histoire naturelle, générale et particulière, avec la description du Cabinet du roi* 13 vols. (Paris: Imprimerie royale, 1749–1767).

56. Quoted in Daudin, *De Linné à Jussieu*, 26–27.

57. Duris, *Linné et la France*, 33–34.

58. Ibid.

59. Fuchs, "La langue des sciences," 6:589; Duris, *Linné et la France*, 34–35.

60. Duris, *Linné et la France*, 35.

61. Philip R. Sloan, "The Buffon-Linnaeus Controversy," *Isis* 67 (September 1976): 356–75; Duris, *Linné et la France*, 32–36; Fuchs, "La langue des sciences," 6:590.

62. Charles C. Gillispie, *Science and Polity in France at the End of the Old Regime* (Princeton, N.J.: Princeton University Press, 1980), 143–51.

63. Buffon, "Premier discours," 14b, quoted in Sloan, "Buffon-Linnaeus Controversy," 359–60.

64. Daudin, *De Linné à Jussieu*, 118–19; Morton, *History of Botanical Science*, 296–300; Stafleu, *Linnaeus and the Linnaeans*, 267–78; von Sachs, *History of Botany*, 109–15.

65. Michel Adanson, *Histoire naturelle du Sénégal: Coquillages. Avec la relation abrégée d'un voyage fait en ce pays, pendant les années 1749, 50, 51, 52 et 53* (Paris: Bauche, 1757), quoted in Morton, *History of Botanical Science*, 304. See also Daudin, *De Linné à Jussieu*, 121–22; Stafleu, *Linnaeus and the Linnaeans*, 311–17.

66. Fuchs, "La langue des sciences," 6:592, 643; Morton, *History of Botanical Science*, 308; Stafleu, *Linnaeus and the Linnaeans*, 320; Lesch, "Systematics and the Geometrical Spirit," 79–82.

67. Stafleu, *Linnaeus and the Linnaeans*, 227.

68. Gillispie, *Science and Polity*, 151–55; Duris, *Linné et la France*, 143–45; Stafleu, *Linnaeus and the Linnaeans*, 320–32.

69. *Encyclopédie méthodique, ou par ordre de matières . . .*, 199 vols. (Paris: Panckoucke, 1782–1832).

70. Daudin, *De Linné à Jussieu*, 190–200; Morton, *History of Botanical Science*, 314, 347, 355; Gillispie, *Science and Polity*, 161–62; Duris, *Linné et la France*, 146–47; Stafleu, *Linnaeus and the Linnaeans*, 332–39.

71. Larson, *Interpreting Nature*, 36–40; von Sachs, *History of Botany*, 122–41.

72. Daudin, *De Linné à Jussieu*, 129–41.

73. Buffon, *Histoire naturelle*, 4:382, quoted in Stafleu, *Linnaeus and the Linnaeans*, 307–8. The notion of degeneration was widespread in the eighteenth century; many believed that vernacular languages had degenerated from an original perfect language.

74. Mayr, *Growth of Biological Thought*, 209.

75. Marco Beretta, "The Grammar of Matter: Chemical Nomenclature during the 18th Century," in *Sciences et langues en Europe*, ed. Roger Chartier and Pietro Corsi (Paris: Ecole des hautes études en sciences sociales, 1966), 110–11.

76. On alchemical and early chemical terminologies, see Bernadette Bensaude-Vincent, "Une charte fondatrice," in *Méthode de nomenclature chimique, proposée par MM. Morveau, Lavoisier, Berthollet & de Fourcroy. On y a joint un nouveau système de caractères chimiques, adaptés à cette nomenclature, par MM. Hassenfratz & Adet*, new ed. (Paris: Seuil, 1994), 11–20; Crosland, *Historical Studies in the Language of Chemistry*, 5–88; Fuchs, "La langue des sciences," 6:641–52.

77. Pierre Joseph Macquer, *Elémens de chymie théorique* (Paris: Hérissant, 1749), ix, quoted in Fuchs, "La langue des sciences," 6:642 n. 2.

78. François Dagognet, *Tableaux et langages de la chimie* (Paris: Seuil, 1969), 16–17, 165; Bensaude-Vincent, "Charte fondatrice," 17–20; Crosland, *Historical Studies in the Language of Chemistry,* 130; Fuchs, "La langue des sciences," 6:652.

79. Crosland, *Historical Studies in the Language of Chemistry,* 124–30.

80. Pierre-Joseph Macquer, *Dictionnaire de chymie* (Paris, 1766), 2:673, quoted in W. A. Smeaton, "The Contributions of P. J. Macquer, T. O. Bergman and L. B. Guyton de Morveau to the Reform of Chemical Nomenclature," *Annals of Science* 10 (1954): 88.

81. Marco Beretta, *The Enlightenment of Matter: The Definition of Chemistry from Agricola to Lavoisier* (Canton, Mass.: Watson, 1993), 136–37; Crosland, *Historical Studies in the Language of Chemistry,* 136–37; Smeaton, "Contributions," 88–89.

82. On the connections between Linnaeus, Bergman, Guyton de Morveau, and Lavoisier, see Smeaton, "Contributions," 86–88; and Lesch, "Systematics and the Geometrical Spirit," 93–96.

83. Quoted in Beretta, "Grammar of Matter," 115.

84. Robert M. Caven and J. A. Cranston, *Symbols and Formulae in Chemistry: An Historical Study* (London: Blackie, 1928), 12–17; Crosland, *Historical Studies in the Language of Chemistry,* 135–51; Beretta, *Enlightenment of Matter,* 138.

85. Torbern Bergman, "Meditationes de systemate fossilium naturali," *Nova Acta Regiae Societatis Scientiarum Upsalensis* 4 (1784): 63–128, cited in Smeaton, "Contributions," 97.

86. Bensaude-Vincent, "Charte fondatrice," 22–23; Beretta, *Enlightenment of Matter,* 147–48; Crosland, *Historical Studies in the Language of Chemistry,* 148–49; Fuchs, "La langue des sciences," 6:648.

87. Louis-Bernard Guyton de Morveau, "Hépar," in *Supplément à l'Encyclopédie,* vol. 3 (1777), 347, quoted in Crosland, *Historical Studies in the Language of Chemistry,* 153–54.

88. Louis-Bernard Guyton de Morveau, "Memoire sur les dénominations chymiques, la nécessité d'en perfectionner le système, & les règles pour y parvenir," *Observations sur la Physique, sur l'Histoire Naturelle et sur les Arts* 19, no. 1 (1782): 370–82. See Wilda Anderson, *Between the Library and the Laboratory: The Language of Chemistry in Eighteenth-Century France* (Baltimore: Johns Hopkins University Press, 1984), 128; Smeaton, "Contributions," 92.

89. Bensaude-Vincent, "Charte fondatrice," 24–28; Dagognet, *Tableaux et langages de la chimie,* 18–19, 53–55; Duris, *Linné et la France,* 127; Fuchs, "La langue des sciences," 6:649–57; Beretta, *Enlightenment of Matter,* 153–57; Crosland, *Historical Studies of the Language of Chemistry,* 154–66.

90. Bensaude-Vincent, "Charte fondatrice," 30–39.

91. Arthur Donovan, *Antoine Lavoisier: Science, Administration and Revolution* (Oxford: Blackwell, 1993), 157–69; Beretta, *Enlightenment of Matter,* 181–84; Smeaton, "Contributions," 102–5.

92. Antoine Laurent Lavoisier and Louis-Bernard Guyton de Morveau, *Méthode de nomenclature chimique* (Paris: Cuchet, 1787).

93. Thomas S. Kuhn, *The Structure of Scientific Revolutions* (Chicago: University of Chicago Press, 1962).

94. Etienne Bonnot de Condillac, *La logique, ou les premiers développemens de l'art de penser* (Paris: L'Esprit, 1780).

95. Antoine Laurent Lavoisier, "Memoire sur la nécessité de réformer & de perfectionner la nomenclature en Chimie," in *Méthode de nomenclature chimique* (1787), 5–7, 13–14, 17.

96. For a discussion of the new method of nomenclature, see Aaron Ihde, *The Development of Modern Chemistry* (New York: Harper and Row, 1964), 77–79; Bensaude-Vincent, "Charte fondatrice," 40–41; Beretta, *Enlightenment of Matter,* 203–11; Crosland, *Historical Studies in the Language of Chemistry,* 180–82; and Fuchs, "La langue des sciences," 6:663–73.

97. Louis-Bernard Guyton de Morveau, "Memoire sur le développement des principes de la nomenclature méthodique," in *Méthode de nomenclature chimique* (1787), 27–74.

98. Bensaude-Vincent, "Charte fondatrice," 41–42.

99. Beretta, "Grammar of Matter," 118–22.

100. Jean-Antoine Claude Chaptal de Chanteloup, *Elémens de chimie,* 3 vols. (Montpellier, 1790); Antoine François de Fourcroy, *Elémens d'histoire naturelle et de chimie,* 3d ed., 4 vols. (Paris: Cuchet, 1789); Antoine Laurent Lavoisier, *Traité élémentaire de chimie, présenté dans un ordre nouveau et d'après les découvertes modernes* (Paris: Cuchet, 1789). See Donovan, *Antoine Lavoisier,* 176–77.

On the diffusion of the new nomenclature, see Bernadette Bensaude-Vincent and Ferdinando Abbri, eds., *Lavoisier in European Context: Negotiating a New Language for Chemistry* (Canton, Mass.: Science History Publications, 1995); and Bensaude-Vincent, "Charte Fondatrice," 55.

101. Jean-Claude de la Métherie, "Essai sur la nomenclature chimique," *Observations et mémoires sur la physique* 31 (1787): 274, quoted in Jan Golinski, "The Chemical Revolution and the Politics of Language," *Eighteenth Century* 33 (1992): 244–45.

102. Beretta, "Grammar of Matter," 124.

103. Quoted in Beretta, *Enlightenment of Matter,* 224.

104. Quoted in Crosland, *Historical Studies in the Language of Chemistry,* 212–14.

105. Bensaude-Vincent, "Charte fondatrice," 55–56.

106. Beretta, "Grammar of Matter," 124–25.

107. William H. Brock, *The Norton History of Chemistry* (New York: Norton, 1993), 88. Needless to say, the Guyton-Lavoisier nomenclature has been revised and elaborated many times since 1787, notably to handle the proliferation of complex organic substances; see Bensaude-Vincent, "Charte fondatrice," 59–60.

108. Caven and Cranston, *Symbols and Formulae in Chemistry,* 6–12; Crosland, *Historical Studies in the Language of Chemistry,* 227–34.

109. Crosland, *Historical Studies in the Language of Chemistry,* 237–55; Caven and Cranston, *Symbols and Formulae in Chemistry,* 18–25.

110. Lavoisier, *Traité élémentaire;* Pierre Auguste Adet, *Leçons élémentaires de chimie* (Paris, 1804).

111. Bensaude-Vincent, "Charte fondatrice," 50–51.

112. John Dalton, *A New System of Chemical Philosophy* (Manchester, 1808), 216.

113. Crosland, *Historical Studies in the Language of Chemistry,* 217–19, 256–63; Caven and Cranston, *Symbols and Formulae in Chemistry,* 25–27; Brock, *Norton History of Chemistry,* 138–39.

114. J. J. Berzelius, "Experiments on the Nature of Azote, of Hydrogen and of Ammonia and upon the Degrees of Oxidation of which Azote is Susceptible," *Annals of Philosophy* 2 (1813); Berzelius, "On the Chemical Signs and the Method of employing them to express Chemical Proportions," *Annals of Philosophy* 3 (1814).

115. Brock, *Norton History of Chemistry,* 154–55; Caven and Cranston, *Symbols and Formulae in Chemistry,* 30–38; Crosland, *Historical Studies in the Language of Chemistry,* 270–74; Ihde, *Development of Modern Chemistry,* 112–14.

116. Quoted in Ihde, *Development of Modern Chemistry,* 115.

117. Edward Turner, *Elements of Chemistry,* 4th ed. (London, 1834); Justus von Liebig, "Ueber die Constitution des Aethers und seiner Verbindungen," *Annalen der Pharmacie* 9 (1834).

118. Crosland, *Historical Studies in the Language of Chemistry,* 276–80; Brock, *Norton History of Chemistry,* 155–57; Ihde, *Development of Modern Chemistry,* 115–18.

119. Witold Kula, *Les mesures et les hommes,* trans. Joanna Ritt (Paris: Maison des sciences de l'homme, 1984), 254 n. 3.

120. Britain, in contrast, had only sixty-four legal units, and fewer than sixty-four thousand unofficial local units. See Ronald E. Zupko, *Revolution in Measurement: Western European Weights and Measures since the Age of Science* (Philadelphia: American Philosophical Society, 1990), 113, 176–77.

121. Quoted in Ken Alder, "A Revolution to Measure: The Political Economy of the Metric System in France," in *The Values of Precision,* ed. M. Norton Wise (Princeton, N.J.: Princeton University Press, 1995), 43.

122. Zupko, *Revolution in Measurement,* 114.

123. Jean-Claude Hoquet, *La métrologie historique* (Paris: Presses universitaires de France, 1995), 23.

124. J. L. Heilbron, "The Measure of Enlightenment," in *The Quantifying Spirit in the Eighteenth Century,* ed. Tore Frängsmyr, J. L. Heilbron, and Robin E. Rider (Berkeley: University of California Press, 1990), 207.

125. Zupko, *Revolution in Measurement,* 116–17; Alder, "Revolution to Measure," 43.

126. Kula, *Les mesures et les hommes,* 149–53; Hoquet, *La métrologie historique,* 26, 108–9.

127. Kula, *Les mesures et les hommes,* 149–53.

128. Ibid., 114–16; Alder, "Revolution to Measure," 46; Hoquet, *La métrologie historique,* 24.

129. Zupko, *Revolution in Measurement,* 123–35; Kula, *Les mesures et les hommes,* 163; Heilbron, "Measure of Enlightenment," 208–10; Gillispie, *Science and Polity,* 113.

130. Kula, *Les mesures et les hommes,* 159–60.

131. Ken Alder, *Engineering the Revolution: Arms and Enlightenment in France, 1763–1815* (Princeton, N.J.: Princeton University Press, 1997).

132. Gillispie, *Science and Polity,* 22.

133. Kula, *Les mesures et les hommes,* 210, 254.

134. Quoted in ibid., 162; see also Zupko, *Revolution in Measurement,* 136.

135. Quoted in Kula, *Les mesures et les hommes,* 163.

136. Heilbron, "Measure of Enlightenment," 210–11.

137. Kula, *Les mesures et les hommes,* 169.

138. Ibid., 169–79.

139. Ibid., 211, 226; Heilbron, "Measure of Enlightenment," 218–19; Zupko, *Revolution in Measurement,* 137–38.

140. William Hallock and Herbert T. Wade, *Outlines of the Evolution of Weights and Measures and the Metric System* (New York: Macmillan, 1906), 47; Zupko, *Revolution in Measurement,* 142–47; Kula, *Les mesures et les hommes,* 212.

141. Quoted in Kula, *Les mesures et les hommes,* 250 n. 116.

142. Heilbron, "Measure of Enlightenment," 220–24; Kula, *Les mesures et les hommes,* 212, 226; Zupko, *Revolution in Measurement,* 146–47. Ironically, scientists have long since given up this definition of the meter as much too gross and have gone back to measuring distance by time: in the late twentieth century, a meter is defined as the distance light travels in a vacuum in 1/299,792,458 second. Hoquet, *La métrologie historique,* 120.

143. Alder, "Revolution to Measure," 51–52; Heilbron, "Measure of Enlightenment," 224–27.

144. Today that would be 1,000.3262 millimeters.

145. Quoted in Hoquet, *La métrologie historique,* 110.

146. Quoted in Heilbron, "Measure of Enlightenment," 214–15.

147. Zupko, *Revolution in Measurement,* 157–61; Hoquet, *La métrologie historique,* 1110–11; Heilbron, "Measure of Enlightenment," 213–14.

148. Kula, *Les mesures et les hommes,* 227–38; Zupko, *Revolution in Measurement,* 148–55. For a time Lavoisier, under arrest, was accompanied by guards to meetings of the commission; he was executed on May 8, 1794.

149. Hollock and Wade, *Evolution of Weights and Measures,* 63; Heilbron, "Measure of Enlightenment," 235.

150. Kula, *Les mesures et les hommes,* 235–37; Alder, "Revolution to Measure," 56–60; Heilbron, "Measure of Enlightenment," 236–37.

151. Zupko, *Revolution in Measurement,* 162–71.

152. Kula, *Les mesures et les hommes,* 241–43; Zupko, *Revolution in Measurement,* 171–72.

153. Witold Kula (*Les mesures et les hommes,* 254–67) devotes considerable attention to the spread of metrification and its connections with revolutions. See also Hoquet, *La métrologie historique,* 114–16.

154. Zupko, *Revolution in Measurement,* 79–104.

155. F. G. Skinner, *Weights and Measures: Their Ancient Origins and Their Development in Great Britain up to AD 1855* (London: HMSO, 1967), 108–9; Hoquet, 38–39, 119; Zupko, *Revolution in Measurement,* 105–12, 177–81.

156. Zupko, *Revolution in Measurement,* 139–42; Hallock and Wade, *Evolution of Weights and Measures,* 110–15.

157. John Quincy Adams, *Report upon Weights and Measures* (Washington, D.C., 1821), 90–91, 135, quoted in Hallock and Wade, *Evolution of Weights and Measures,* 117–18.

158. Skinner, *Weights and Measures,* 107.

159. Neither the old vocabulary nor the old arithmetic has disappeared, however: to this day, the French refer to a 125-gram package of butter as "un quart de livre" (a quarter of a pound).

160. See, for example, Alder, "Revolution to Measure," 41.

161. Lawrence Busch and Keiko Tanaka, "Rites of Passage: Constructing Quality in a Commodity Subsector," *Science, Technology, and Human Values* 21 (1996): 3–27.

162. Ironically, under the pressure of science, the metric system has infiltrated the British fortress: in 1897, Parliament made metric units optional in science, medicine, and pharmacology, and in 1951 the British Empire Scientific Conference redefined the imperial units by reference to metric units: a yard is now 0.9143 meters, and a pound is 0.453592 kilograms! See Kula, *Les mesures et les hommes*, 268–70.

3

TRANSFORMING INFORMATION

The Origin of Statistics

> How do I love thee? Let me count the ways.
> ELIZABETH BARRETT BROWNING,
> *Sonnets from the Portuguese*

WE LIVE IN A SEA OF NUMBERS. SURROUNDED BY A CULTURE OF STATISTICS—IQs, grade point averages, gross domestic products, batting averages, Dow-Jones Industrial Averages, probabilities of precipitation—it is not easy to imagine a world just awakening to the meaning of numbers.

Statistics, in the sense of numbers representing data, first appeared in the eighteenth century and became a regular feature of the cultural landscape in the early nineteenth century. Nothing illustrates better the transformative power of numbers than the changing views of one of the era's most influential thinkers, Thomas Robert Malthus.[1]

Malthus (1766–1834) will always be remembered for his lapidary statements such as: "Population, when unchecked, increases in a geometrical ratio. Subsistence only increases in an arithmetical ratio." This statement sounds mathematical, as if it were a law of nature, yet ominous: "if unchecked," disaster will surely strike.[2] That is how Malthusians, then and now, have always read it. Malthus wrote these words in 1798 to refute giddy optimists like the Marquis de Condorcet and William Godwin, who believed in the inevitability of progress. Though sincere, he wrote his *Essay on Population* without benefit of data. It aroused a passionate debate and encouraged the government to undertake the first census in British history in 1801.

Armed with census data, Malthus revisited his ideas. He published a second edition in 1803 and, in later years, four more revised editions; they bore the same title but a different subtitle, for they were really a different work: many times longer, full of information, and much more refined. In the course of his life, Malthus changed his thinking about population and subsistence. He no longer predicted an inevitable demographic disaster but instead realized that "in no state that we have yet known, has the power of population been left to exert itself with perfect freedom."[3] Unlike North Americans and "uncivilized" peoples, Europeans kept their numbers under control by preventive checks, rather than waiting for famines to bring populations in line with the food supply: "An infrequency of the marriage union from the fear of a family . . . may be considered . . . as the most powerful of the checks, which in modern Europe, keep down the population to the level of the means of subsistence."[4] Even England could be saved through education: if the poor were educated, they would stop breeding like animals and learn to behave with moral restraint like their betters. Thus did statistics turn a Cassandra into a liberal.

There have always been numerate people, for merchants and bureaucrats had been keeping accounts since ancient times. What was new in the Age of Reason and Revolution was the idea that numbers could be used to analyze something other than money, such as population, health and illness, nature, or even divine Providence.[5]

One source of interest in statistics was a concern for public health. The epidemics that struck Europe and North America in the seventeenth and early eighteenth centuries, in particular the plague and smallpox, aroused not only fear but also a desire to be informed, to understand, to predict, and to prevent. From this urge came "political arithmetic," the first attempt to apply numerical methods to the study of population and public health.

Another source of demand was political and economic, for quantification was closely tied to mercantilism, that is, the attempt to apply commercial and accounting methods—balance sheets, profit-and-loss statements—to entire states and their peoples. Critics of government saw in statistics a useful weapon with which to point out deficiencies in the political system and to suggest improvements.

Numerical data required amounts of information so large that only institutions like the state or the church had the resources to gather it. With few exceptions, such information was hard to come by, and the institutions that gathered it did not often make it public. Until the end of the eighteenth century, individuals had very little reliable information on which to exercise their numerical skills. Elaborate controversies and ill-informed speculations were as common in the Age of Reason as theological disputes in the Middle Ages.

In the course of the eighteenth century, as the governments of Europe grew more elaborate and better organized, the quantifying spirit affected officials as well as the educated public. The officials' demand for information accelerated the collection of numerical data. This trend, slow and sporadic during most of the eighteenth century, grew frenetic during the period of revolutions and wars at the end of the century. Eventually, the interaction of public demand and growing government ushered in the statistical movement of the mid–nineteenth century, with its censuses, statistical bureaus, and statistical societies. Our world was shaped by that movement.

Political Arithmetic and the Divine Order

What we call statistics was known in the seventeenth and eighteenth centuries as *political arithmetic*. Its beginnings date back to 1662, the year a London tradesman named John Graunt (1620–1674) published *Natural and Political Observations Made upon the Bills of Mortality*. The bills of mortality were reports published by the Company of Parish Clerks of London, giving the number of christenings and burials, along with the cause of death, in each Anglican parish in London. First issued sporadically in the fifteenth century, they had become a regular weekly feature of London life after 1603, warning townspeople of the approach of epidemics and the relative healthiness of the different parishes.[6]

What John Graunt did was to apply familiar accounting methods to these weekly bills. By making certain assumptions (e.g., the proportion of women of childbearing age in the population and the number of people per household) and arranging the data from the bills into tables, he was able to make a number of interesting deductions: the number of inhabitants of London, the number of men and of women in each age-group, and the male:female ratio at birth and at different ages. He discovered that the death rate in London was higher than the birth rate, yet the population was growing thanks to migration from the countryside. He also showed that deaths from chronic or endemic diseases outnumbered those from the epidemics that terrified people.[7]

Graunt's book was a great success, especially after the plague struck London in 1665, and led to his election to the Royal Society. His work inspired several other political arithmeticians, beginning with his friend the physician William Petty (1623–1687). A prolific author, Petty wrote *Observations upon the Dublin-Bills of Mortality* in 1683 and *Further Observations upon the Dublin-Bills* in 1686. He also coined a term for his and Graunt's method of analysis in his *Political Arithmetick*, completed in 1679 and published in 1690. In it he dealt not only with population but also with land values, manufacturing, navigation, agriculture, and every other aspect of the economy and public life he could describe with numbers.[8] His enthusiasm for numbers came from his belief—still prevalent today—that numbers are more factual than words:

The Method I take . . . is not very usual; for instead of using only comparative and superlative Words, and intellectual Arguments, I have taken
the course . . . to express myself in Terms of *Number, Weight* or *Measure;* to
use only Arguments of Sense, and to consider only such Causes, as have
visible Foundations in Nature; leaving those that depend upon the mu-
table Minds, Opinions, Appetites, and Passions of particular Men.[9]

Also in that first generation was Gregory King (1648–1712), who used the
hearth tax records, along with some assumptions about the number of persons per "hearth," or household, to estimate the population of England
both at the time and well into the future. The tract he wrote in 1690, "Natural
and Political Observations and Conclusions upon the State and Condition of
England," was not published until 1802, but its conclusions appeared in a
work by Charles Davenant (1656–1714) entitled *Essay upon the Probable Methods of
Making a People Gainers in the Balance of Trade* (1699); his title reveals the mercan-
tilist motivations behind his brand of political arithmetic.[10]

The early political arithmeticians used incomplete and unreliable
sources, their methods were crude, and their conclusions often were biased. Political arithmetic was of more than academic interest, however, for
in quantifying life and death, it touched upon a very contentious issue: the
respective roles of humans and of divine Providence in causing diseases,
births, and deaths. As the first attempt to quantify society, the arithmeticians' contribution to the culture of information must rank with those of
more famous philosophers.

The relationship between political arithmetic and health was complex and
reciprocal. The movement had arisen from an interest in the impact of the
plague and from the availability of bills of mortality listing the causes of
death. Many of these "causes" were neither precise nor scientific, however.
Among the reported causes we find "act of God," "decay of nature," "water in the head," or "weakness." But two diseases produced obvious and un-
deniable symptoms: the plague, which caused dark, painful swellings in
the armpits and groin, and smallpox, which covered the body with sores.
The plague could be neither prevented nor cured, and people fled upon
hearing of its arrival. Smallpox, however, could be prevented, and its pre-
vention caused a controversy in which political arithmetic played a major
role.

Before the eighteenth century, inoculation—the deliberate injection
into a healthy person of pus from someone suffering from smallpox—was
practiced in Turkey, China, and parts of Africa. In the 1720s, Lady Mary
Wortley Montagu, wife of the ambassador to Constantinople, publicized it
in England by having her own children inoculated. The practice caught on
among the aristocracy and the royal family when the Princess of Wales had
her daughters inoculated in 1722.

Despite its fashionable appeal, inoculation had two drawbacks: it was a risky procedure—some healthy people died after being inoculated—and theological conservatives thought it thwarted the will of God. The pamphlet literature of the 1720s brought out interesting epistemological issues; those who favored inoculation presented quantitative evidence—the proportion of infected persons who died of smallpox versus the proportion of those inoculated—whereas those who opposed it preferred case studies or moral arguments. In the end, fashion combined with the evidence of numbers to win the argument, and inoculation spread widely in the English population.[11]

Much the same happened in British North America. Beginning in 1704, the *Boston News-Letter* published a monthly bill of mortality, but without listing the causes of death. Ministers preached sermons in which the deaths of persons of every age, including children, were offered as evidence of God's will. Yet the smallpox epidemic of 1721 caused a split in the ranks of those concerned with public health. Cotton Mather and other ministers advocated inoculation, while opponents like Samuel Grainger denounced it as interference with predestination. Although both sides used numbers in a sloppy way, the evidence of the inoculationists must have been the more persuasive, for when smallpox returned in 1730 and 1752, inoculation had become popular, and the argument that disease was a "visitation for sins" lost its appeal.[12]

Inoculation was late in coming to France, not for lack of numerate people but because of the rigid nature of its medical institutions. The medical profession was controlled by the faculties of medicine, especially that of Paris. This official guild maintained that disease was the result of an imbalance between the four humors in an individual's body; from this perspective, quantifying the diseases of a large group of people made little sense. Physicians had no interest in mathematics, nor did they care for mathematicians meddling in medical affairs. When celebrated mathematicians such as Charles-Marie de la Condamine, Daniel Bernoulli, and Jean d'Alembert used the calculus of probability to defend inoculation, doctors dismissed their arguments. Despite the doctors' opposition, inoculation spread in France, as it had in England, as an aristocratic fashion later imitated by the bourgeoisie. It also appealed to the rationalist administrators of the last decades of the Old Regime. In 1775, Finance Minister Robert Turgot established the Commission for Epidemics, which his successor, Jacques Necker, turned into the Royal Society of Medicine to gather information about public health and epidemics.[13]

In every era, those who believe in God prove his existence in their own fashion. Is it surprising that in an age that worshiped reason, some should have attempted to offer a proof of God based on logic and observation?

Among the first such "natural" theologians to see the hand of God in population statistics was John Arbuthnot (1667–1735), physician to the queen of England. In 1710 the journal *Philosophical Transactions* published his "Argument for Divine Providence, taken from the constant Regularity observ'd in the Births of both Sexes," based on the London bills of mortality for the years 1629–1710. Arbuthnot noted that more male babies were christened than females, but that males had a higher death rate than females because, as he put it, "the external Accidents to which are Males subject (who must seek their Food with danger) do make a great havock of them." Because these two phenomena canceled each other out, he concluded that "among innumerable Footsteps of Divine Providence to be found in the Works of Nature, there is a very remarkable one to be observed in the exact Ballance that is maintained between the Numbers of Men and Women."[14] The discovery of such demographic regularities was hailed by Protestant ministers. In British North America, as historian Patricia Cohen has noted, "The faithful were exhorted in church to study the numerical patterns of death and to use demographic facts to reflect on their own mortality, ever a fit subject for a Christian to contemplate."[15]

The most thorough and detailed attempt to prove the existence of God through demography was the work of Johann Peter Süssmilch (1707–1767), a Prussian pastor and military chaplain. In 1742 he published the first edition of *Die göttliche Ordnung in den Veränderungen des menschlichen Geschlechts, aus der Geburt, Tode und Fortpflanzung desselben erwiesen* (The divine order in the changes in the human race, proved by the birth rate, death rate and propagation of the species); a second edition, in two volumes, followed twenty years later. Süssmilch incorporated figures from Hannover, Sweden, Prussia, and Württemberg, the cities of London, Rome, Stockholm, and Berlin, and 1,056 villages; in those numbers, he found regularities governing the ratios of births to deaths, of male to female births, and of deaths in cities and in the country.

Süssmilch believed in large numbers: "If I have a hundred cases in support of my conclusion, then nothing to the contrary can be drawn from one case."[16] His quantification was straightforward, almost literary. For example, after giving numerous statistics on villages, towns, and cities, he drew some generalizations:

> It follows from all the evidence which has just been presented that the death rate:
>
> 1) is, in the countryside, between 1/42 and 1/43 in good years, or 1/38 for a combination of years.
>
> 2) Taking the average of the two ratios, we can establish the death rate at 1/40 in the villages. To use the rule, we must know what sort of year we are dealing with.
>
> 3) In small towns, the death rate is 1/32.

4) In larger cities, like Berlin, it is 1/28.

5) In even larger cities, like Rome, London, etc., it reaches 1/24 and 1/25.[17]

Having thus noted the contrast between rural and urban death rates, he drew ethical, religious, and political conclusions, which fit nicely with his antiurban and anti-Catholic preconceptions. Thus, he ascribed the high death rates in cities to "too soft an upbringing" and "frequent and gross sensual excesses":

> By impure pleasures, they will have caught diseases that corrupt the blood and which are very difficult to cure; that is when the flower of youth fades, strength becomes exhausted, and this leads to a premature death. In the lists for Rome . . . , we note the existence of 600 prostitutes who are publicly tolerated because of the taxes they pay, and perhaps because of the large number of unmarried men, or because of a bad police or powerful protection which do not allow them to be suppressed. . . . What poison, spread in the bodies of the inhabitants and which kills, surreptitiously, like a plague! . . . How many youths are not dragged into sin by public incitements, and how many of them see their strength prematurely exhausted?

Süssmilch contrasted this decadence to the healthfulness of rural life:

> The contagious poison is seldom found in villages. People are more modest. There is more decency, at least natural decency, among the country folk. The supervision of the clergy and the teachings of the Church are a dike against impudence. Hard work also protects against the disorder of passions.[18]

Süssmilch's goal was to prove the existence of God by showing that the law of large numbers reconciled predestination at the level of populations with free will for individuals. In the process of serving religion, however, he also gave wide publicity to the importance of demographic statistics for human affairs, and in particular for the state, for his figures showed that the size of a country's population was closely related to its power and security—a matter of considerable interest to the rulers of Prussia. The implication was that rulers had a duty to ensure the growth of the population under their care.[19]

The Depopulation Controversy

Political arithmetic, the inoculation controversy, and the arguments over narrative versus numerical statistics were all expressions of the quantifying spirit of the eighteenth century. But the quantifiers had little to go on, for governments were slow to develop the necessary administrative tools to obtain information, and, when they had some, they revealed very little of it to the public: bills of mortality from certain cities, the returns of the hearth and other taxes, and, late in the century, the first population figures for Sweden, Spain, and the United States. Filling the gulf between demand and supply was speculation, the product of deductive reason unfettered by empirical evidence. Interestingly, the two most notorious examples, the depopulation theory and the Malthusian hypothesis, were at opposite ends of the spectrum.

The depopulation controversy began in 1721 with the publication of *Lettres persanes* by the Baron de Montesquieu (1689–1755), who wrote:

> After a calculation as exact as possible in these sorts of matters, I found that there are on earth barely one fiftieth as many people as there were in ancient times. What is astonishing is that the world is losing people every day, and if this continues, in ten centuries it will be but a desert.[20]

Montesquieu's information (what there was of it) came from the vastly inflated estimates of the population of Rome in the works of the classicists Justus Lipsius and Gerardus Vossius.[21] In his most influential work, *L'esprit des lois* (1748), he went a step further, arguing that despotic governments caused a decline in the number of their subjects.

Montesquieu's claims were widely repeated, notably in Louis de Jancourt's articles "France" and "Mariage" in Diderot's *Encyclopédie*.[22] What made the depopulationist idea so popular, despite the lack of supporting evidence, was its political implications. Many philosophes believed that a growing population was a sure sign of prosperity, and prosperity was the result of good government. Hence, if the population declined, that was proof that the government was bad. As Jean-Jacques Rousseau (1712–1778) explained:

> What is the object of any political association? It is the protection and the prosperity of its members. And what is the surest evidence that they are so protected and prosperous? The numbers of their population. . . . the government under which . . . the citizens do most increase and multiply is infallibly the best. Similarly, the government under which a people diminishes in number and wastes away, is the worst. Experts in calculation, I leave it to you to count, to measure, to compare.[23]

Depopulationists simply reversed the logic of this argument. Starting with the premise that the government of France was not doing its job, they concluded that the population *must* be shrinking. Thus the Marquis de Mirabeau (1715–1789) argued, in his influential work *L'ami des hommes, ou traité de la population* (1756), that France was losing population because of bad agricultural practices and overconsumption by the rich, but he provided no numerical data to support his assertions.[24] Similarly, the physiocrat François Quesnay claimed that the population of France had dropped from twenty-four million in 1650 to sixteen million in 1750, but he gave no source for his figures.[25]

English political arithmeticians had exercised their minds on the published bills of mortality since the late seventeenth century; in France, political arithmetic began only in the 1740s because far less information was available to the public. By calling attention to the importance of population, it led first to more careful evaluations by political arithmeticians, then to official surveys, and finally to full-fledged censuses.

Among the first who tried to determine the population of France in a more inductive way was the comte de Buffon (1707–1788), author of the forty-four-volume *Natural History*. His volume on mankind, published in 1749, included figures on baptisms, marriages, and burials in Paris to calculate the growth of population; but his figures were inflated, for he had no information about the deaths of infants who did not get a church burial.[26]

In 1762, the geographer Jean-Joseph Expilly (1719–1793) published the *Dictionnaire géographique, historique et politique des Gaules et de la France*, in which he attempted to calculate the population on the basis of the hearth tax returns and scattered birth records. Taking various coefficients from scattered samples and some Swedish statistics, he estimated that cities contained six inhabitants per hearth and the countryside four, for a national average of five.[27] He was followed by Louis Messance (1733–1799), secretary to the intendant La Michodière, and Jean-Baptiste Moheau, secretary to the intendant Anget de Montoyon; these two men had access to some secret government figures but by no means enough to give accurate results.[28] Finally, Pierre-Simon de Laplace (1749–1827), one of the founders of the mathematics of probability, applied his concepts to population; in *Sur les naissances, les mariages et les morts* (1783), he demonstrated that reducing the margin of error in the calculation of the population required a sampling of at least one million inhabitants.[29]

What all these political arithmeticians did was to calculate a "universal multiplier" from a sample of parish baptismal records and population surveys of a few localities, then multiply that constant by the number of baptisms in all of France. The value of the multiplier depended, of course, on the sample selected and on how much it was "corrected" by comparing the resulting figures with hearth, poll, and other taxes, wheat consumption figures, and whatever other information was at hand. Expilly's multiplier was 28, Messance used 25, Moheau 25.5, and Laplace 26. The result was a population estimate that varied from 20.9 million (Expilly 1762) to 24 million (Laplace 1793).[30]

Whatever their differences, the French political arithmeticians proved that the population of France was the largest of any country in Europe, and that it was rising. By the 1780s, they had laid the depopulationist thesis to rest. In the process, they showed that the patient accumulation of data and plodding accounting techniques could invalidate the brilliant insights of famous philosophers.

The depopulationist theory also appeared in England, albeit later and in a less ideological form than in France. The issue that interested most writers was not whether the world had fewer people than in Roman times but whether the population of England was currently declining, or had done so since the Glorious Revolution of 1688. In 1755–1757, *Philosophical Transactions* published articles for and against the depopulation theory. In two books, *Observations on Reversionary Payments* (1771) and *Essay on the Population of England and Wales* (1780), Richard Price (1723–1791) synthesized the literature on political arithmetic and used tax returns to prove that the population had declined by 25 percent since the late seventeenth century. The problem was not with his arithmetic but with his sources, for he had no clear way to relate the hearth, window, or liquor taxes with the number of inhabitants. The political arithmetician William Wales (1734?–1798) attempted to remedy this defect by sending questionnaires to correspondents throughout the country, asking them about the number of houses, and to parish clergy, requesting information from their parish registers for the years 1688–1697, 1741–1750, and 1771–1780. In *An Inquiry into the Present State of Population in England and Wales* (1781), he concluded that the population was growing, not shrinking.[31]

Although Wales preceded him, the idea of a growing population is irrevocably associated with Thomas Malthus. What is astonishing about Malthus is not his method nor his contribution to historical demography; it is the fame that has surrounded his name for the past two centuries, while other, more careful demographers have long since been forgotten. No doubt, once the world's population begins to decline, Malthus will be forgotten and the memory of the depopulationists will be resurrected from oblivion.

Statistics in the Old Regime

The word *statistics* was first used by Gottfried Achenwall (1719–1772) to describe "the study of the state." It appeared in English in 1770 in a translation of J. F. von Bielfeld's *Elements of Universal Erudition* and was popularized by Sir John Sinclair in his twenty-one-volume *Statistical Account of Scotland* (1791–1799). In 1797, the *Encyclopaedia Britannica* described statistics as "a word lately introduced to express a view or survey of any kingdom, country or parish."[32] Not until the first decade of the nineteenth century did it acquire its current meaning of information presented in numerical form, and only in the 1830s was it used in its second meaning as the calculus of probabilities, a branch of mathematics.

The obvious answer to the controversies over population would have been to take a census. Yet the French government, though not terribly solicitous of the liberties of its citizens, hesitated to do so, for it believed that a census would arouse popular resistance. Furthermore, the basic assumption of a census—that individuals are equal and therefore can be added up—conflicted with the aristocratic view that humans are not only unequal but incommensurate. Only in the colonies, where European settlers clearly understood the connections between the demands of the state and their own security, were censuses successful.[33]

Yet the ministers and intendants of an absolutist monarchy with enlightened pretensions needed information in order to conduct the affairs of state in a rational manner. The last century of the Old Regime abounds in their demands and in the haphazard responses they elicited.[34]

In 1664, Prime Minister Jean-Baptiste Colbert (1619–1683) ordered intendants to furnish good maps, information on bishoprics and abbeys, the military and the nobility, magistrates and the quality of justice, finances and tax collection, the estates of the crown, natural resources, navigable rivers, commerce, industry, horse-breeding farms, and counterfeit coinage. Three years later, in the "Code Louis," he ordered parish priests to present their registers of baptisms, marriages, and burials to a royal judge every year. By these acts, he revealed just how little the government knew about the activities of its own administration, let alone the nation's resources and people.[35]

Throughout the eighteenth century, Colbert's successors repeated his initiative. The controllers-general of finance and other officials regularly bombarded their indendants with requests for information about houses, families, beggars, professions, resources, industries, soils, and even "the greater or lesser kindness and intelligence of the local culture." Almost all their initiatives fizzled out for lack of administrative support.[36]

The questions the controllers-general of finances asked show how concerned they were with economic and demographic problems. But their main motive was to increase tax revenues, and that connection with taxation is precisely why enumerations aroused popular resistance. The inadequacy of the data collected by the French monarchy also stemmed from provincial and local administrations that were far too rudimentary and decentralized to satisfy its needs. Although the government's demands for information were peremptory, the vague questions produced responses that could be neither compared nor added up.

In any event, the information contained in the responses was considered a state secret. When Expilly asked for information for his geographic dictionary, the controller-general responded:

> I do not think it is appropriate to give M. l'abbé d'Expilly a copy of this
> report; the information it contains on the different branches of industry
> and commerce and on the finances and talents of the inhabitants is re-

served for the administration and must not be divulged: it will suffice to give him some general notion on the population and on some historical facts that can be published without inconvenience.[37]

As we shall see, not even a revolution could close the gap between the central government's insistence on knowing everything immediately and some very lethargic and inadequate responses from the provinces.

Unlike the French, the British government had few pretensions of absolute power and operated more openly under the scrutiny of Parliament. It neither demanded nor expected to know everything at once, but made more modest demands.

Ever since the Glorious Revolution of 1688, there had been a vast increase in the number of official documents, such as treasury minutes, account books of the excise tax, and navy muster books. Some of these records were statistical, beginning in 1696 with those of the inspector-general of imports and exports. During the eighteenth century, government bureaus developed complex record-keeping systems to ensure the implementation of official policies. Although the bureaucrats tended to be secretive, they were under pressure from their ministers, from members of Parliament, and from special interest groups to reveal the information they gathered.[38]

The nation that originated bills of mortality and political arithmetic hesitated to take the next step. In 1753, a bill was introduced into the House of Commons "for Taking and Registering an Annual Account of the Total Number of People, and the Total Number of Marriages, Births, and Deaths." It was defeated after members of the House of Lords denounced it as "totally subversive of the last remains of English liberty . . . the most effectual engine of rapacity and oppression that was ever used against an injured people. . . . Moreover, an annual register of our people will acquaint our enemies abroad with our weakness." Another member of Parliament claimed that his constituents "looked upon the proposal as ominous, and feared lest some great public misfortune or an epidemic distemper should follow the numbering."[39] These words reveal the true grounds for opposition to the census: fear of the government, of foreigners, and of God.

With the exception of Süssmilch, eighteenth-century German intellectuals preferred what was then called *descriptive,* or *nonquantitative, statistics* to political arithmetic. Descriptive statistics were especially popular at the University of Göttingen, whose professors tried to put some order into the massive accumulation of available information about the countries of Europe. In this, they were following in the footsteps of the Cameralists, seventeenth-century writers who sought to maximize the welfare of the myriad German principalities through detailed regulations.[40]

Achenwall, a professor at Göttingen and the author of *Abriss der Staatswissenschaft der europäischen Reiche* (Outline of state knowledge of the European kingdoms; 1749), was in the tradition of the naturalists and encyclopedists of his day, for his approach was taxonomic rather than quantitative. He emphasized the economic resources of states, such as climate, land, population, manufacturing, transportation, and money.[41] According to historian Susan Mahoney, for Achenwall a statistician's duty was "to trace these connections among moral, material, economic, political, and religious causes and to measure their net effects, producing a total and integrated picture of the constitution."[42] Although his descriptions were narrative, whenever possible he used quantitative data, which permitted comparisons, a matter of great interest in a Germany still divided into hundreds of microstates.

In a similar vein, Anton Friedrich Büsching (1724–1793) proposed to write a geographic description of the world; his six-volume *Neue Erdbeschreibung* (New description of the earth; Hamburg, 1754–1771), only got as far as the states and cities along the Baltic Sea, with a special emphasis on Copenhagen.

After Achenwall and Büsching, German statisticians split into two factions, according to their attitude toward quantification. August F. W. Crome, a professor at the University of Giessen, incorporated numerical tables in his economic atlas, *Producten-Karte von Europa* (Product map of Europe; 1782), and in *Über die Grösse und Bevölkerung der sämtlichen europäischen Staaten* (The size and population of the various European states; 1785).[43] For A. L. von Schlözer, Achenwall's disciple and successor at Göttingen, however, statistics was "history frozen for a moment," while history was "statistics in motion."[44] He and the Göttingen school denounced quantitative data as "lower statistics," as opposed to the "higher" descriptive statistics that alone could account for such important qualities as national character and the love of liberty. Despite this rearguard effort, descriptive statistics had become passé by 1812, when the Prussian state began collecting quantitative data in a serious way.[45]

Sweden was the first sizable country to have reliable population figures. There, Lutheran ministers had been required to keep parish registers since 1686, and because Sweden had few inhabitants of other faiths, these registers reflected the population fairly accurately. In 1749, the Royal Academy of Sciences campaigned for a Commission of Tables to which pastors would report their parishes' births, marriages, deaths, and total population. From these figures, the secretary of the Academy, Pehr Wargentin, calculated the population of Sweden by region, age, sex, marital status, and profession, along with births and deaths. These figures were reserved for the Riksdag and the king until the 1760s, after which they were made public. Though this was not a real census but an official exercise in political arithmetic, the figures published by Wargentin and his successor, Henrik Nicander, probably were the most accurate known before the 1830s.[46]

Statistics in France, 1789-1815

From the very start of the Revolution, the revolutionary leaders sought information about the nation they had inherited. The traditional curiosity of government officials was greatly magnified by the growing emergency, the hostility of France's neighbors, and the wars that followed. Besides the number of potential recruits and taxable resources, the new leaders also wanted information on eligible voters, on suspects and subversives, on beggars and vagabonds, and on harvests, food stocks, and prices. Furthermore, they believed that information was a public good and wished to disseminate it in order to educate and enlighten the citizenry.

Different branches of government made different demands, sometimes overlapping, sometimes conflicting. In December 1789, the Constituent Assembly decreed that all municipalities list their active citizens for electoral purposes. In June 1790, the Committee of Division, which had replaced the old provinces and generalities with departments, ordered local administrators to furnish information on the population and resources of the new departments. A month later, the Committee on Mendicancy called for a census of inhabitants by canton and township, including taxpayers, children under fourteen, the old, the infirm, the ill, vagabonds, and beggars.

In January 1791, the Legislative Assembly demanded lists of all inhabitants, their profession and marital state, as well as the number of children, servants, houses, and resources. In July, municipalities were ordered to keep accurate lists of all their inhabitants, including all political suspects. They were also asked for information on plows, mills, cattle, horses, pigs, and other food stocks, as well as manufactures of metal, glass, textiles, soap, leather, and other necessities. Only 123 of the 36,000 communes in France obeyed this command.[47]

In September 1792, the Legislative Assembly was replaced by the National Convention, a legislature with a radical agenda and a voracious appetite for information. At first, it tried enlisting the enthusiasm of local administrators. Its Committee of Public Works, charged with organizing a census, sent a circular to its agents:

> The Commission sends you instructions and three forms to fill out in order to obtain an exact knowledge of the population of the French territory. All citizens are expected to combine their zeal and their enlight-

enment to ensure the success of such an important operation, for it can have no other goal but the happiness of the People. . . . Today, all means of public prosperity are on the agenda and we can no longer neglect to know one of its most essential elements, the population. An enumeration of free men! Can one conceive of the idea without carrying it out? Entrusting it to patriotic administrators is to promise in advance speed and success![48]

When enthusiasm did not yield the expected results, the National Convention made peremptory demands and harassed local administrators with circulars and reminders. The dreaded Committee of Public Safety, for instance, ordered local administrators to provide information on 123 different subjects, all within three days, or else their communities would be denounced as "suspect and evil intentioned."[49]

The enthusiasm of the revolutionary leaders in Paris was not matched by the ability of local administrators to furnish the required data, nor that of a bureaucracy to process it. The result was a flood of miscellaneous, disorganized, and often unreliable information. Of the reports that flooded in from the provinces, some may have been accurate and others based on guesswork. We will never know, for France was at war, and tons of reports were either turned into cartridges for the army or burned to heat public buildings.[50]

In October 1795, as the revolutionary fervor abated, the radical National Convention was replaced with the more conservative Directory. In November 1795, Pierre Bénézech, the Directory's first minister of the interior, wrote to departmental administrators:

> It is essential that you let me know as soon as possible the state of your department as it comes under the constitutional government. This way and by comparison . . . with the situation in which France will find itself in a few years, we will know the advantage of a free government and the good we will have done.[51]

His successor, François de Neufchâteau, regularly sent out circulars demanding information "on the population and animals of every species" and on "anything that may be useful, interesting, or remarkable in your department, from every point of view," even Roman ruins.[52]

In December 1799, Napoleon Bonaparte overthrew the Directory and put his brother Lucien in charge of the Interior Ministry. Lucien wrote to his prefects:

> I am interested in all information that can let me know the state of the Republic from every point of view: agriculture, commerce, industry, arts, etc. I assemble all the information that comes to me and I intend to form a general picture. You will be sure to write at the top of the letters that accompany your tables the words: Statistics of the Republic.[53]

In November 1800, Jean Antoine Chaptal, who succeeded Lucien Bonaparte, formed the Statistical Bureau, charged with collecting all possible economic or demographic information. Chaptal was even more energetic than his predecessors in requesting reports from the departmental prefects; he demanded to know everything immediately. He asked for data on hospitals, topography, beggars, grain prices, roads, taxes, education, and "the public mood." He expected monthly reports on "the moral and physical situation of the department." He announced: "I think we must create a complete corpus of all information and give the nation an exact knowledge of its riches and resources." A ministry employee provided a more practical motive: "Quite precise details are needed about the habits, prejudices, opinions, customs, and energy of the inhabitants, so that the government can decide the forms of surveillance, repression, encouragement and protection most suited to obtain the best results in each different locality."[54]

These many demands got little response. The purges of the National Convention had denuded departmental offices of competent employees and relevant documents; local administrators who were left were paralyzed by fear or inertia. The prefects, though educated men, did not have competent staffs, nor were they trained in collecting and summarizing information. Two-thirds of the mayors, on whom the prefects relied for local data, were illiterate. The resulting "prefects' statistics" were compilations of miscellaneous and incomparable data, some descriptive, some numerical, and many that were imprecise or misleading. Likewise, the "census" of 1801, which Lucien Bonaparte had ordered, took two years to complete and was so flawed by errors and undercounting that it was practically useless.[55]

Yet much of the information the Statistical Bureau gathered was made available to the public. The consul Cambacérès, one of Napoleon's associates, helped found the Société statistique de Paris in 1803, which defined statistics as "the art of presenting an exact inventory of the remarkable and truly existing things in a State." True to this German conception of statistics, it arranged for translations of works by Schlözer and Achenwall. The years 1795–1803 saw the appearance of numerous works of descriptive statistics, beginning with the government's *Descriptions abrégées des départements* in 1797, followed by Sébastien Bottin's *Annuaire politique et économique* in 1799 and Victor Herbin's *Statistique générale et particulière de la France et de ses colonies* in 1803.[56]

After Napoleon crowned himself emperor on December 2, 1804, he ordered the Société statistique de Paris dissolved and a veil of secrecy drawn over all official reports.[57] The information demanded by the central government became more specific. Minister of the Interior Nompère de Champagny ordered the prefects to provide monthly reports on grain stocks and food prices, manufactures, and trade. He demanded special reports on cotton, chestnuts, honeybees, and orange trees.[58] The prefects were also to report on crimes and police measures, on "the attitude of the people," and on the conduct of local administrators.[59] At the same time, the local administrations were now better able to respond to these more specific requests. Graduates of the prestigious *grandes écoles,* well trained in mathematics, helped the prefects gather the data requested by the ministries.[60]

Nevertheless, the improved efficiency of official data gathering did not occur without epistemological and political struggles. The first directors of the Statistical Bureau under Napoleon were of a literary bent and much attracted to the German idea of statistics. Alexandre Deferrière dismissed quantitative statistics with a bon mot: "The most exact determination of the number of vegetables that France produces will not bring forth one additional cabbage in her gardens."[61] His successor, Jacques Peuchet, addressed his book *Statistique élémentaire de la France* (1805)

> to French spirits . . . who cannot stand the aridity of tables, no matter how exact they may be. . . . We must reject [the method] which by enigmatic formulas, algebraic calculations, or geometrical figures, pretends to present or analyze that which is much simpler to say naturally and without obscurity.[62]

However, one of Peuchet's subordinates, Emmanuel Duvillard, was a mathematician with a different outlook. In his *Mémoire sur le travail du Bureau de statistique* (1806), he criticized "men who shine by the seductive varnish of their elegant style." He went on to suggest that facts "which can be presented en masse, with details, and on the exactness of which one can rely, must be presented in tables. This form . . . facilitates connections, the understanding of relationships and the work of the mind."[63]

Napoleon was not interested in the epistemological disputes between descriptive statisticians and political arithmeticians. He put a bureaucrat, Charles Etienne Coquebert de Montbret, in charge of the bureau, with instructions to produce data on the economy. The reports it produced between 1806 and 1812, especially those on harvests and food prices, were among the most reliable to be found anywhere at that time.[64]

After 1810, Napoleon's endless campaigns and the continental blockade sapped the French economy. As the government grew ever more authoritarian, its interests shifted from the poor, who needed assistance, to the classes with taxable resources. It began inquiring into the fortunes of wealthy families, even their daughters' dowries, beauty, and chances of marriage.[65] In November 1811, Napoleon asked for "a complete statistic of manufactures, divided by industry, to include all establishments, each with the number of workers, quantity and value of production—all to be submitted to him within eight days." When the bureau could not provide the in-

formation he needed fast enough, he closed it.[66] Interior Minister Monta-
livet explained: "A Statistical Bureau was created twelve years ago, but has
not obtained any important or complete results. . . . Its work . . . was too
theoretical, it was conceived with too broad a view and embraced too many
details."[67]

The First Censuses

Much confusion surrounds the word *census*. Some writers argue that the
first census was taken in the late eighteenth century in the United States,
Sweden, or Spain, while others mention "censuses" in biblical or classical
times. For the sake of clarity, then, let us use *census* to refer to an attempt to
count all the people in a country at a given point in time, and *enumeration* to
refer to all other estimates based on counting hearths or households or religious events like baptisms, marriages, and burials.

All enumerations before the eighteenth century had direct administrative purposes. When King David instructed his commander, Joab,
to "go, number Israel," Joab counted "valiant men that drew the sword"
(2 Sam. 24:1–3). Besides counting potential recruits for the army, enumerations were also carried out to determine how many men could be drafted
for corvée labor and how many households, or "hearths," could be taxed.
The purpose of the Domesday Book of 1086 was to improve the collection
of taxes. Enumerators seldom counted women and children, nor did they
count clergy and nobles.

For these reasons, such enumerations as existed before the late eighteenth century generally encountered stiff resistance. Popular opposition
was sometimes given a religious explanation, referring to the pestilence
that is said to have struck Israel after King David's enumeration (1 Chron.
27:14–17). But there were also practical reasons for commoners to flee at the
approach of the enumerators, for these were often tax collectors, army re-
cruiters, or other agents of repression. Given the resistance they encountered, it was not unusual for enumerators to present their superiors with
numbers that were often erroneous, if not fictitious.[68]

The first true census of a large country was the Spanish census of 1787.[69]
In the course of the eighteenth century, the Bourbon monarchy of Spain
conducted several surveys of the kingdom's population. The first, the
"Vezindario general" of Campoflorido (1717), was a traditional counting of
hearths, done for tax purposes and therefore inaccurate. The count of
Aranda's census of 1768–1769 was the first to count individuals, not hearths,
but most scholars consider it unreliable. In 1787, the reforming minister José
Floridablanca ordered a new census, in part to prove to foreigners "that the
kingdom is not as empty as they and their writers believe." Unlike previ-

ous enumerations, this census was conducted in a few months by civil, not ecclesiastical, authorities. It showed an increase of 1.5 million inhabitants since Aranda's enumeration of twenty years earlier. Although modern demographers believe it undercounted the population by 10 percent, it is still the most accurate European census before 1800, and the only reliable Spanish census before 1857.[70]

The United States, the first revolutionary nation-state, was the second to conduct a census. The authors of the Constitution of 1787 agreed, in Article 1, Section 2, to take a census every ten years in order to apportion both the expenses of the national government and the seats in the House of Representatives on the basis of state populations; thus they ensured that the urge to reduce taxes was counterbalanced by the desire to increase representation.

The act of March 1, 1790, directed the census takers, supervised by U.S. Marshals, to ask a few simple questions: the name of the head of the household, the number of free white males age sixteen and over, the number under sixteen, the number of females, the number of other free persons, and the number of slaves. The official number of inhabitants of each state was calculated by adding the number of free persons and three-fifths of the number of slaves; nontaxpaying Indians were not counted. To James Madison's disappointment, the first census did not inquire into occupations, "the kind of information extraordinarily requisite to the Legislator, and much wanted for the science of Political Economy."[71]

Because the population of the United States was scattered throughout a large area with poor transportation, the census takers took eighteen months to gather, collate, transmit, and publish their data. The report, signed by Secretary of State Thomas Jefferson in October 1791, was fifty-six pages long and showed a population of 3,929,214 inhabitants, fewer than Jefferson had hoped.[72]

Ascertaining the number of inhabitants in the British Isles, the subject of so much controversy over the previous century, became an urgent necessity during the wars of the French Revolution. The manpower demands of the armed forces and the bad harvest of 1800 convinced Parliament of the need for an accurate count. By the Population Act of December 1800, it authorized a census, to be supervised by John Rickman, the clerk of the House of Commons. The actual enumeration was undertaken in England and Wales by the Overseers of the Poor, aided by constables, church officials, and "substantial householders"; in Scotland, it was done by schoolmasters. In each parish or township, the census takers noted the number of houses and the number of males and females in each house (but not their ages), along with their occupation in one of three categories: agriculture; trade, manufacturing, or handicrafts; and others. In addition, Anglican pastors were asked to furnish lists of baptisms and burials for every tenth year from 1700 through 1780 and for every year from 1781 on, and the number of marriages for each year between 1754 and 1800. Unlike the census, these figures were incomplete, for they excluded all non-Anglicans.[73]

The results were published in December 1801. To the surprise of many, the census did not provoke public discontent, and the results were deemed satisfactory at the time. It was repeated following much the same pattern under Rickman's direction in 1811, 1821, and 1831. Not until the census of 1841 were any major improvements forthcoming.[74]

Americans: A Calculating People

The American people, delighted with their new nation, wanted it to compare favorably with the old countries of Europe. Eager to learn as much as they could about their country and their home states, they wrote and read memoirs, almanacs, gazetteers, travel accounts, and descriptive works of all sorts. These works combined the narrative approach of German academic geography with a fondness for numbers, wherever they could be found. The exemplar, in this as in so much else in American culture, was Jefferson. He took notes wherever he went, especially in his beloved home state, which he described in profuse detail in *Notes on the State of Virginia*.

After the American Revolution, a whole literature sprang up to describe and glorify every state and territory in the Union, as well as cities like New Haven and Philadelphia. Jefferson's work was still mostly verbal, but works written after 1790 were filled with statistics of every sort, which they presented as "authentic facts." As the author of a book on Philadelphia explained, "In composing a work like the present, the author is of the opinion that the chief object ought to be the multiplication of facts, and that the reflections arising out of them, should be left to the reader."[75]

To foreigners, Americans seemed obsessed with numbers. In a review of Adam Seybert's *Statistical Annals*, an eight-hundred-page description of the United States published in 1818, the *Edinburgh Review* commented that Americans were "vulgar and arithmetical," for they valued things that could be counted, like population and trade, over culture, science, and art.[76] And the English traveler Thomas Hamilton wrote of the inhabitants of New England: "Arithmetic, I presume comes by instinct among this guessing, reckoning, expecting, and calculating people."[77] But the reverence for numbers served a political purpose, for opinions seemed to threaten the still precarious unity of the nation, whereas "facts" would bring them together: "Did all men know alike, though imperfectly, their opinions must be the same," wrote the *Literary Magazine and American Register* in 1804.[78]

Vital statistics were kept, if at all, in a haphazard manner until the mid–nineteenth century. As in England, they began as parish registrations of christenings, marriages, and burials. In 1791, the American Academy of Arts and Sciences collected sixty-two parish registers in order to produce a table of life expectancies. In 1804, New York established an Office of City Inspector, which gathered reports of births from physicians and midwives, of marriages from the clergy, and of burials from sextons and cemetery caretakers. In New Orleans, Dr. Bennet Dowler gathered data on the number and age of deaths from tombstone inscriptions; from these data, the "graveyard arithmetician" drew too rosy a picture of life expectancy, for it did not include the poor. Mortality statistics remained insufficient and unreliable until Massachusetts passed its Registration Act in 1842, followed by other states in the 1840s and 1850s.[79]

Statistics served not only to satisfy people's curiosity and inflate their pride but also to bring about changes in society. American physicians, by and large, took a deductive approach, preferring to think of medicine as an art rather than a science. Beginning in the 1830s, however, a few young physicians who had returned from studying in Paris showed a concern for note taking and record keeping. The American Medical Association, founded in the mid-1840s, bombarded its members with questionnaires and filled its annual transactions with quantitative reports. By the midcentury, the profession increasingly turned to "rational medicine," based on accurate records, statistical analysis, and an empirical approach to medicine.[80]

The United States may have lagged behind Europe in the analysis and reform of medicine and public health, but in the use of statistics for moral reform, Americans were at the forefront of progress. In 1816, the Massachusetts Society for the Suppression of Intemperance reported on the incidence of drunkenness and vice. The following year the Philadelphia Society for Alleviating the Miseries of Public Prisons issued statistics on crimes, criminals, and jails, while the Boston Society for the Moral and Religious Instruction of the Poor reported that pauper children had memorized 54,029 verses, 1,899 hymns, and 17,779 answers to catechisms. In 1830, the New York Moral Reform Society collected statistics on prostitution and licentiousness.

What historians have called the Second Great Awakening was more than a philanthropic and proselytizing movement. The attempts to quantify behavior revealed a craving for knowledge and a faith in the power of statistics. In order to do something about vagrants or licentious persons or children without schooling, reformers first had to know how many there were and then count how many were saved or cured. Even in matters of piety and morality, Americans had become a "guessing, reckoning, expecting, and calculating people."[81]

The development of the U.S. Census parallels the development of the nation, but with a considerable lag. Like the census of 1790, those of 1800 and

1810 asked only the most basic demographic questions, namely, the numbers of free white males and females in five age categories, of other free persons, and of slaves. As in 1790, there was a tug-of-war between those, like Madison, who wanted data on people's occupations and those who saw this as an intrusion on their privacy and a way to squeeze more taxes from citizens. As a compromise, the secretary of the Treasury published "A Statement of the Arts and Manufactures," an inaccurate document.[82]

Gradually, censuses grew more elaborate. The 1820 census asked about occupations and, for the first time, divided the black population by age and sex. The 1830 census introduced printed schedules mailed out to the U.S. Marshals; in addition to the earlier questions, it enumerated the deaf, dumb, and blind, and produced a 163-page report.[83]

The census of 1840 was far more elaborate than its predecessors, with eighty-two inquiries rather than the four included in 1790 and 1800 or the twenty in 1820. At the urging of President Martin Van Buren and the American Statistical Association, founded the year before, the census takers asked questions about Revolutionary War pensioners, schools and colleges, mining and manufactures, illiterates, idiots, the insane, and much else. As Patricia Cohen has demonstrated, the sheer volume of raw data and the incompetence of the head of the Census Bureau, William Weaver, and his staff of amateur statisticians led to one of the most embarrassing fiascos in the history of statistics. By an odd combination of errors in enumeration and analysis, the census report showed that the percentage of insane individuals in the black population increased as one went farther north. Defenders of slavery seized upon this finding as evidence of black insanity and of the harmful effects of freedom for blacks; opponents, led by former president John Quincy Adams, saw in the census a conspiracy of Southern slavers concocting phony statistics for vile political purposes.[84] The census of 1840 shattered the naive faith that "facts" would bring the nation together. As Cohen explains:

> The story of the census of 1840 is a story of innocence lost. Out of it arose a more general recognition that statistics could sometimes lie. Practitioners of the science of statistics had to adopt a defensive posture and a measure of caution about numbers, for they now knew that their numbers could be challenged by other sets of numbers.[85]

"Social Physics" in France and Belgium after 1815

The French Restoration governments of Louis XVIII (1815–1824) and Charles X (1824–1830) fired many of Napoleon's officials and canceled their reports. Yet they could not turn back the clock to prerevolutionary times, for a new attitude toward social statistics had entered the culture; as the mathematician

Laplace put it: "Let us apply to the political and moral sciences the method based on observation that has served us so well in the natural sciences."[86]

A combination of necessity and administrative competence led the Ministries of War, Commerce, and Justice to issue their own statistical series on recruitment, foreign trade, and justice, respectively. The Ministry of Justice was the first to collect complete statistics on a regular basis, because it had a long tradition of careful paperwork, and because crimes and sentences were rigorously defined.[87] In its *Compte général de l'administration de la justice criminelle,* first issued in 1827, it announced its credo: "Exact knowledge of facts is one of the first necessities of our form of government: it illuminates discussions, it simplifies them, it gives them a clear basis by substituting the positive and certain lights of experience to the vagueness of theories."[88] "Issued" does not mean "published," nor does it mean "kept secret." Instead, these reports were printed in very limited editions reserved for high dignitaries. Yet they soon leaked out, for they aroused a special interest among bourgeois readers worried about crime.[89] André-Michel Guerry (1802–1866), director of criminal statistics in the Ministry of Justice, was the first to systematically examine the raw figures of the *Compte général* in his *Essai sur la statistique morale de la France,* published in 1833. In this book, complete with tables, maps, and graphs, he showed how crime rates are related to location, wealth, education, economic activities, and other factors, but he did not draw inferences from his analysis.[90]

The July Monarchy (1830–1848) transformed a reluctant dribble of statistics into a flood. In 1834, Commerce Minister Adolphe Thiers established the Bureau de statistique générale (renamed Statistique générale de France, or SGF, in 1840). This bureau, headed by Alexandre Moreau de Jonnès (1778–1870), published data collected from other branches of government on such matters as public works, agriculture, commerce, mining, penitentiaries, savings banks, and much else. Beginning in 1831 and every five years thereafter, it also published the census data gathered by the Ministry of the Interior; these were the first true censuses in France, as opposed to the glorified estimates that previously had passed for censuses.[91]

Unlike the British, the SGF showed more interest in economic matters than in public health. Yet France, too, had physicians who were concerned with public health, vital statistics, and epidemiology, many of them army surgeons discharged at the end of the Napoleonic Wars. The *Annales d'Hygiène Publique et de Médecine Légale,* founded in 1829, published the results of their inquiries, as well as articles on poverty, alcoholism, crime, prostitution, and delinquency, all of which constituted what was called "moral statistics."[92]

By the 1830s, western Europe and the United States were experiencing what Ian Hacking has called an "avalanche of printed numbers."[93] Governments

gathered and published great amounts of statistics for quantification en-
thusiasts to digest and ponder. Their concerns were partly scientific (to understand and explain social phenomena) and partly political (to reform society through state action).

Before it became a nation in 1830, Belgium had been part of Napoleonic
France and then of the Kingdom of the Netherlands, neither of which inspired much trust in officialdom among the Belgian people. The census of
1830, taken just before Belgium broke away from the Netherlands, proved
unreliable, for municipalities underestimated their populations in order to
furnish as few recruits as possible. After independence, the new kingdom
reorganized its administration and began publishing national statistics. To
do so, Interior Minister Liedts turned to his friend Adolphe Quetelet (1796–
1874).[94]

Quetelet was a man of numerous talents and enormous energy.
Trained as a mathematician, he became a teacher of mathematics, physics,
and astronomy. From 1823 to 1825 he lived in Paris, where he was influenced
by the mathematicians Laplace and Jean-Baptiste Fourier. His modus
operandi was to assemble as many numerical observations as he could and
then look for regularities. He was also an enthusiastic organizer; in 1833,
while on a visit to England, he persuaded the British Association for the
Advancement of Science to start a statistical branch. Back in Belgium, he
organized the Commission centrale de statistique in 1841, the census of
Brussels in 1842, and the national census in 1846. In 1853, he organized and
presided over the first International Statistical Congress, at which he called
for cooperation in developing uniform methods and terminologies in statistical publications.[95]

Quetelet's approach was to apply mathematics to social phenomena,
something he called "social physics" or "the science of man." Thus, when
he noticed that the birth and death rates changed with the seasons, rising
when the temperature fell and falling when it rose, he was inspired to
write: "If you want to represent geometrically the law of births as well as
that of deaths, you will find a transcendent curve which greatly resembles
a sine-curve. One could give it the equation: $y = a + b \sin x$."[96] He discovered a striking regularity in the distribution of heights of French army recruits, which he called the "binomial curve" (now known as the normal,
or "bell," curve). He noted that the average growth rate of children resembled a hyperbola.[97]

He also investigated "moral" statistics, such as marriages, suicides, and
crimes. In the official French statistics on criminal justice, he discovered
"the *frightening exactness* (constancy) with which crimes occur." In an article
entitled "Recherches sur le penchant au crime aux différens âges" (Research on the propensity to crime at different ages), he wrote: "I do not fear
to see the table of degrees of propensity to crime at the different ages as de-

serving as much confidence as the one I gave for heights or that I could give for the weight and strength of men, or those we have on mortality." He discovered that the propensity to crime correlated not only with age but also with sex, education, ethnicity, climate, the seasons, and much else. He showed, for example, that men's propensity to commit crimes rose sharply from age ten to age twenty-three, then declined gradually. He published these and other correlations in an influential book entitled *On Man and the Development of His Faculties, or an Essay in Social Physics.*[98]

Statistics were the most valuable precisely where causal mechanisms—of crime, illness, or height—were least understood.[99] By jumping from correlations to curves and equations, Quetelet hoped to formulate the laws of society comparable to the laws of physics. In this he was not alone, of course, for one finds similar views in the works of Arbuthnot, Süssmilch, Malthus, and Auguste Comte, among others. Quetelet became famous, however, for his glorification of the "average man."

As an astronomer, he noticed that the distribution of many measurements of a single item—the position of a star, for instance—resembled the distribution of single measurements of many items, such as the height of conscripts. Just as astronomers considered the average of many measurements to represent the closest approximation to a theoretically exact measurement, so Quetelet concluded that the average of many measurements of humans represented not only the "average man" but also an ideal type free from both excess and defect:

> The man whom I considered is the analog in society of the center of gravity in bodies; he is a fictional being for whom everything happens according to the average results obtained for society. If the *average* man were determined for a nation, he would represent the type of that nation; if he could be determined for all men, he would represent the type for the entire human race.[100]

He believed that idealizing the "average man" would make the arts and literature more representative of society and would improve politics by drawing politicians' attention to public opinion.

The combination of social physics and the average man created some troublesome philosophical problems. If individual differences were deviations from an ideal "average" and if society was ruled by "laws," then free will was reduced to "a capricious element acting within a narrow circle of possibilities."[101] Thus, he said: "The crimes which are annually committed seem to be a necessary result of our social organization.... Society prepares the crime and the guilty is only the instrument by which it is accomplished."[102] And, more generally:

> Man, as an individual, seems to act with the greatest freedom; his will seems to know no limits, and yet ... the more individuals one observes,

the more the individual will shrinks to make room for the series of general facts that result from causes that allow society to exist and conserve itself.[103]

Quetelet had lived through the revolution of 1830, which had changed the monarchy in France and detached Belgium from the Netherlands. Yet he interpreted revolution as a physical phenomenon: "not a rupture, not progress, but the reestablishment of an equilibrium." He believed that social statistics, by revealing the strains in society, would allow wise governments to institute reforms in time to avoid revolutions. Statistics, having failed to satisfy reactionary monarchists and radical revolutionaries, finally found a home as the tool of moderate bourgeois reformers. As a statistician, Quetelet not only founded empirical sociology but also was a precursor of liberal reform movements.[104]

The British Statistical Movement

After the Napoleonic Wars, statistics penetrated British life and culture, until by the 1830s it had become a mania in intellectual circles. Government officials involved in finance, taxation, and recruitment found statistics of immediate practical interest. Actuaries, who had to determine the premiums on annuities and life insurance policies, devised life tables, or tables of life expectancies. But statistics interested many others as well, for they appealed to the same spirit of rationality that led the educated to believe in science, progress, and the perfectibility of man. Census statistics, like political arithmetic before them, were based on the premise that society consisted of individuals of equal value. Seeking patterns in numbers seemed a scientific way to understand society, at least in the inductive, Baconian approach to science. This notion appealed to businessmen and economists concerned with wealth, production, and income, as well as to physicians interested in health and the incidence of diseases. Together, these constituencies formed what Michael Cullen has called "the statistical movement."[105]

The first organization, or club, devoted to the subject was the Statistical Society of Manchester, founded in 1833 by thirteen physicians and industrialists "who felt a strong desire to assist in promoting the progress of social improvement."[106] That same year, the British Association for the Advancement of Science invited Adolphe Quetelet to speak at its annual meeting in Cambridge. Inspired by Quetelet, several members, among them Thomas Malthus, the mathematician Charles Babbage, and the economists Nassau Senior and Richard Jones, founded the Statistical Society of London.[107] In the prospectus of the society they proclaimed their credo:

The Statistical Society of London has been established for the purposes
of procuring, arranging and publishing "Facts calculated to illustrate the
Condition and Prospects of Society." The Statistical Society will consider
it to be the first and most essential rule of its conduct to exclude carefully all *opinions* from its transactions and publications—to confine its attention rigorously to facts—and, as far as it may be found possible, to
facts which can be stated numerically and arranged in tables.[108]

Behind this facade of unsullied objectivity, the founders of the society and
others that sprang up in its wake in other British cities were members of
the Whig political and intellectual elite. Deeply disturbed by the unprecedented social stresses caused by industrialization and urbanization, they
were convinced that Britain risked a political revolution like the one that
had swept parts of Europe in 1830. These were the men whose sense of social responsibility and fear of revolution led to the Reform Act of 1832, the
Factory Act of 1833, and the new Poor Law of 1834. As the Statistical Society
of Bristol explained in 1839:

In a simple state of society, a man may know tolerably well what his
duties to the poor are . . . but what shall be said of that artificial and complicated state of things when a nation manufactures for half the world—
and when the consequence unavoidably is the enormous distance between the labourer and his virtual and subdivided employer?[109]

The founders of the Statistical Society believed that disagreement with
their point of view was the result of ignorance and that this ignorance
would surely vanish as soon as they could marshal the "facts" in support
of their position. For them, statistics were a mode of discourse designed to
legitimize their perspective, rather than a retreat into mathematics—
hence, the close connections between fear of revolution, concern with social problems, and a craving for "facts" about society.

But where to find these "facts"? Among the first research projects of the
Statistical Society of London was a questionnaire distributed to police, hospitals, poor-law administrators, landlords, magistrates, and others who dealt
with the poor. (Not until the end of the century did anyone survey the poor
directly.) The responses were disappointing, however. It also soon became
clear that survey research required not only concern about social problems
and confidence in the relevance of statistics but also a great deal of money.

Besides being costly, research also was less effective than the founders
had originally hoped, for there were no direct links between information,
consensus, and reform. After the initial enthusiasm, attendance at Statistical Society meetings dropped sharply, and most of the groups folded, except for Manchester and London. By the 1840s, meetings of the Statistical
Society of London were attended mainly by civil servants and actuaries who
used numbers professionally.[110]

To find the data they needed, reformers and professional quantifiers turned to the government. The reforms of the 1830s coincided with data supplied by government agencies to parliamentary commissions. Statistics were part of the process of implementing reforms.

Until the 1830s, the data needed by members of Parliament were very hard to come by and full of errors. As William Jacob, controller of corn returns, said in 1832:

> Little statistical information has been collected, and that chiefly by the industry of the two Houses of Parliament, but that little has been so mingled with a vast mass of irrelevant, or unimportant, or tiresome details, and is scattered through such a number of ponderous folio volumes, that it has presented an appalling labour to all but the most indefatigable inquirers.[111]

Soon after the Reform Bill of 1832, several branches of government set up statistical bureaus. The Home Office, which had gathered data on crimes since 1810, began publishing regular reports in the 1830s. The Board of Trade provided Parliament with information on industrial and trade questions; it also printed any other information that came to hand, down to the amount of money taken from drunks by the Manchester police and returned to them after they sobered up. The army and navy also began collecting statistics, the most valuable of which were the reports prepared by Major Alexander Tulloch on sickness and mortality among British troops serving in the West Indies and other colonial outposts of the empire.[112]

The most important of the official statistical bureaus was the General Register Office (GRO). For a long time, dissenters and Catholics had protested that their births, marriages, and deaths were not registered by the Anglican pastors, and hence they did not have legal status; actuaries complained that vital statistics culled from parish registers were too incomplete to use in compiling accurate life tables; and physicians demanded better information on the causes of death. Finally, Parliament passed the Registration Act of 1836, bringing the registration of vital statistics for England and Wales under the GRO (Scotland set up its own office in 1855, and Ireland did so in 1863).[113]

The first registrar general, Thomas Lister, took great pains to establish the procedures for registration. England and Wales were divided into 626 registration districts in which local poor-law commissioners were appointed registrars and superintendent registrars. Although the registration of births and marriages was voluntary, the registration of deaths and their causes was considered extremely important because of the fear of epidemics. The registrars entered the data in register books and delivered copies for the preceding quarter to be verified by the superintendent registrars. The data were then sent on to the GRO to be verified again, sorted, indexed, bound, and deposited in locked fireproof iron boxes. By the end of the first year, the GRO had already accumulated 958,630 entries in twelve volumes.[114]

Once the GRO was established, it was the logical organization to conduct the census of 1841. The office hired 35,000 enumerators supervised by the local registrars of vital statistics. It printed schedules to be filled out by every household on the same day, asking the name, sex, age, occupation, and place of birth of each individual. All the schedules (and not just summaries, as in previous censuses) were then forwarded to the GRO to be compiled and analyzed by its statisticians. The result was a far more accurate count of the population than had ever been done before, in Britain or any other country, and a model for all future censuses.[115]

The most important employee of the GRO was William Farr (1807–1883), the compiler of abstracts under Thomas Lister and later the statistical superintendent under Lister's successor, George Graham. Farr had trained as a physician and soon began publishing articles on vital statistics, epidemiology, and medical reform in the *British Annals of Medicine*. From 1839 to 1880, he prepared most of the GRO's publications and testified before parliamentary committees. He was also a lifelong member of the Statistical Society of London, where he read many papers on socioeconomic conditions and vital statistics.[116]

Like other reformers, Farr believed that "the misery of the urban poor was due to remediable physical defects in the environment of modern cities."[117] By using statistics to reveal the incidence of disease and death, reformers believed they could improve the lives of the poor and put medicine on a more scientific basis—two radical ideas at the time. As Farr wrote in the first annual report of the registrar general:

> The deaths and causes of deaths are scientific facts which admit to numerical analysis; and science has nothing to offer more inviting in speculation than the laws of vitality, the variations of those laws in the two sexes at different ages, and the influence of civilisation, occupation, locality, seasons and other physical agencies, either in generating diseases and inducing death or in improving the public health.[118]

The outpouring of numerical data that issued from the GRO under Farr's direction had a significant impact on the cause of reform. It provided the ammunition for the most influential of all reformist tracts, Edwin Chadwick's *Sanitary Report on the Condition of the Labouring Population of Great Britain* (1842). Farr's *Weekly Returns* to the City Commission on the cholera epidemic of 1848 inspired Dr. John Snow to investigate the relation between cholera and the water supply, which led to his pathbreaking book, *On the Mode of Communication of Cholera* in 1854.[119]

The publications of the GRO were soon recognized as the most complete in the world. Three aspects were particularly important. The first of these was the data on mortality and life expectancy that allowed Farr to construct accurate life tables, important assets for the life and health insurance plans that proliferated in the mid–nineteenth century.[120]

The second use of statistics was not to predict but to influence mortality. For this, Farr published the mortality rates of different towns, rural areas, and urban neighborhoods. This was, of course, a refined version of the bills of mortality, now applied to all of Britain and revealing enormous disparities in the healthiness of rural and urban areas, and between different neighborhoods in the same city. Farr did not attribute the disparities to sin, as had Süssmilch, but to the environment. His data showed, for instance, that in Liverpool, previously thought to be healthy because it had such a fast-growing population, half the children died before reaching age six. Farr listed the sixty-three healthiest districts, those with death rates of ten per thousand or less. The average death rate of seventeen per thousand was declared a goal, and the public health law of 1848 required municipalities with death rates higher than twenty-three per thousand to institute sanitary reforms.[121]

Farr's third contribution was to give a more scientific basis to the classification of diseases. While some diseases, such as smallpox, plague, and cholera, were easy to identify, most other causes of death were lumped together under such fuzzy rubrics as "visitation by God" or "natural causes." Farr complained: "Each disease has in many instances been denoted by three or four terms, and each term has been applied to as many different diseases: vague, inconvenient names have been employed, or complications have been registered instead of primary diseases."[122] With the help of the British Medical Association, Farr insisted that physicians and coroners use more accurate terms on death certificates. This required establishing an acceptable system of classifying the causes of death, called a *nosology*. Farr's nosology, which he revised several times over his forty-year career, was used in Britain until the end of the century and is considered the foundation of today's International Classification of Diseases.[123]

This overview of the origin of statistics reveals national differences: the British interest in health, the French concern with economic data, and the American political and moral uses of numbers, not to mention Quetelet's search for the "average man" and Süssmilch's search for God. But behind the differences lies a common cultural phenomenon: the quantifying spirit, or the desire to reveal truths that could not be found in verbal descriptions. In all these cases, statistics were the expression of the need to master large quantities of information, to find patterns in those large quantities, to understand those patterns, and to use that understanding to control the world.

Social statistics had a long, complicated birth because it required the simultaneous development of two phenomena. One was an interest in explaining epidemics, crimes, demographic and economic changes, and other social phenomena in purely human terms, without falling back on supernatural explanations like "fate" or "God's will." The other was obtaining data that, by its very nature, could only come from organizations: parish records, tax rolls, administrative enumerations, and the like.

Quantification began during the Old Regime with a handful of political arithmeticians, professors, and government officials. In the Age of Revolution, it was seen as a means of connecting citizens with their nation and, in turn, of allowing governments to know and control their people. But in the rush of events, revolutionaries who demanded statistical information lacked the patience and administrative competence to gather and analyze it.

Not until after the Napoleonic Wars did the public demand for statistical information and for its supply by governments finally merge into the "avalanche of printed numbers" under which we are still buried. From that point on, statistics became the mode of discourse of moderates, people who eschewed both reactionary absolutism and violent revolution, but instead advocated progress through reform in matters of health, crimes, or morality. Americans were not the only "calculating people." So were all people who wanted to achieve progress in an orderly, rational manner: the bourgeoisie and bureaucrats of Europe and America, from that time to the present.

Notes

1. See William Petersen, *Malthus* (Cambridge, Mass.: Harvard University Press, 1979); and J. Dupâquier, A. Fauve-Chamoux, and E. Grebnik, eds., *Malthus Past and Present* (London: Academic Press, 1983), especially the essays by Nathan Keyfitz and Y. Charbit.

2. Thomas Robert Malthus, *An Essay on the Principle of Population, as it Affects the Future Improvement of Society. With Remarks on the Speculations of Mr. Godwin, M. Condorcet, and Other Writers* (London: J. Johnson, 1798), 7.

3. Thomas Robert Malthus, *An Essay on the Principle of Population; or, A View of its Past and Present Effects on Human Happiness; with an Inquiry into our Prospects Respecting the Future Removal or Mitigation of the Evils which it Occasions*, 2d ed., (London: J. Johnson, 1803), 4.

4. Thomas Robert Malthus, *An Essay on the Principle of Population; or, A View of its Past and Present Effects on Human Happiness; with an Inquiry into our Prospects Respecting the Future Removal or Mitigation of the Evils which it Occasions*, 4th ed., 2 vols. (London: T. Bensley, 1807), 1:579–80.

5. The culture of numbers has only recently begun to be investigated. Among the sources I have consulted, see in particular Michael J. Cullen, *The Statistical Movement in Early Victorian Britain: The Foundations of Empirical Social Research* (New York: Barnes and Noble, 1975); Alain Desrosières, *La politique des grands nombres: Histoire de la raison statistique* (Paris: La Découverte, 1993); Ian Hacking, "Biopower and the Avalanche of Printed Numbers," *Humanities in Society* 5 (1982): 279–95; Theodore M. Porter, *The Rise of Statistical Thinking, 1820–1900* (Princeton, N.J.: Princeton University Press, 1986); Tore Frängsmyr, J. L. Heilbron, and Robin E. Rider, eds., *The Quantifying Spirit in the Eighteenth Century* (Berkeley: University of California Press, 1990); James H. Cassedy, *Demography in Early America: Beginnings of the Statistical Mind, 1600–1800* (Cambridge, Mass.: Harvard University Press, 1969); and Patricia Cline Cohen, *A Calculating People: The Spread of Numeracy in Early America* (Chicago: University of Chicago Press, 1982).

6. John M. Eyler, *Victorian Social Medicine: The Ideas and Methods of William Farr* (Baltimore: Johns Hopkins University Press, 1979), 38; David V. Glass, *Numbering the People: The Eighteenth-Century Population Controversy and the Development of the Census and Vital Statistics in Britain* (New York: Heath, 1973), 15–16; Muriel Nissel, *People Count: A History of the General Register Office* (London: HMSO, 1987), 99; Andrea Alice Rusnock, "The Quantification of Things Human: Medicine and Political Arithmetic in Enlightenment England and France" (Ph.D. dissertation, Princeton University, 1990), 27–35.

7. Jacques Dupâquier and Michel Dupâquier, *Histoire de la démographie: La statistique de la population des origines à 1914* (Paris: Perrin, 1985), 130–37; Rusnock, "Quantification of Things Human," 42–52, 183–86.

8. Dupâquier and Dupâquier, *Histoire de la démographie,* 137–43; Rusnock, "Quantification of Things Human," 53–56.

9. Karin Johannison, "Society in Numbers: The Debate over Quantification in the Eighteenth-Century Political Economy," in Frängsmyr, Heilbron, and Rider, *Quantifying Spirit,* 348. Trust in numbers—the belief that numbers are more objective than words—was later in coming: Theodore Porter traces it to the late nineteenth and early twentieth centuries; see his *Trust in Numbers: The Pursuit of Objectivity in Science and Public Life* (Princeton, N.J.: Princeton University Press, 1995).

10. Dupâquier and Dupâquier, *Histoire de la démographie,* 144–52; Desrosières, *La politique des grands nombres,* 34–37; Rusnock, "Quantification of Things Human," 169–70, 194–97.

11. Rusnock, "Quantification of Things Human," 26–108.

12. Cohen, *Calculating People,* 87–106.

13. Rusnock, "Quantification of Things Human," 110–58.

14. Ibid., 211–13.

15. Cohen, *Calculating People,* 83.

16. Johann Peter Süssmilch, *Die göttliche Ordnung in den Veränderungen des menschlichen Geschlechts, aus der Geburt, Tode und Fortpflanzung desselben erwiesen* (Berlin: Grohls, 1742), 38–39.

17. Jacqueline Hecht, *J. P. Süssmilch (1707). "L'Ordre divin," aux origines de la démographie* (Paris: INED, 1979), 2:333.

18. Ibid., 339.

19. Ibid., 3—7; Desrosières, *La politique des grands nombres*, 95—96, 219—20; Dupâquier and Dupâquier, *Histoire de la démographie*, 166—72.

20. Montesquieu, *Lettres persanes*, ed. Paul Vernière (Paris: Garnier, 1960), letter CXII, p. 235.

21. Justus Lipsius, *Opera historica, politica, philosophica et epistolica*, 8 vols. (Antwerp, 1596—1625); Gerardus Johannes Vossius, *Gerardii Joannis Vosii Ars historica: De historicis graecis libri quatuor, De historicis latinis libri tres, Historiae universalis epitome: Opuscula et Epistolae* (Amsterdam, 1699).

22. Jacqueline Hecht, "L'idée du dénombrement jusqu'à la révolution," in *Pour une histoire de la statistique*, proceedings of "Journées d'étude sur l'histoire de la statistique," Vaucresson, June 23—25, 1976 (Paris: Institut national de la statistique et des études économiques, 1977), 53—54.

23. Jean-Jacques Rousseau, "Social Contract," in *Essays by Locke, Hume, and Rousseau*, ed. Ernest Barker, (New York: Oxford University Press, 1960), 280.

24. Victor de Riquetti, Marquis de Mirabeau, *L'ami des hommes, ou traité de la population*, 6 vols. (Avignon, 1756—1758).

25. Andrea Rusnock, "Quantification, Precision, and Accuracy: Determinations of Population in the Ancien Régime," in *The Values of Precision*, ed. M. Norton Wise (Princeton, N.J.: Princeton University Press, 1995), 24—25.

26. Dupâquier and Dupâquier, *Histoire de la démographie*, 174—75.

27. Bertrand Gille, *Les sources statistiques de l'histoire de France: Des enquêtes du XVIIe siècle à 1870*, 2d ed. (Geneva: Droz, 1980), 53—55; Rusnock, "Quantification, Precision, and Accuracy," 26.

28. Louis Messance, *Nouvelles recherches sur la population de la France, avec des remarques importantes sur divers objets d'administration* (Lyon: Frères Périsse, 1788); Jean-Baptiste Moheau, *Recherches et considérations sur la population de la France*, 2 vols. (Paris: Moutard, 1778).

29. Pierre-Simon de Laplace, *Sur les naissances, les mariages et les morts à Paris, depuis 1771 jusqu'en 1784; et dans toute l'étendue de la France, pendant les années 1781 et 1782* (Paris, 1783); see also Rusnock, "Quantification, Precision, and Accuracy," 30.

30. Hecht, "L'idée du dénombrement," 59—60; Dupâquier and Dupâquier, *Histoire de la démographie*, 174—98; Rusnock, "Quantification of Things Human," 162—63; Rusnock, "Quantification, Precision, and Accuracy," 25—28.

31. Glass, *Numbering the People*, 11—15; Nissel, *People Count*, 48—49; Rusnock, "Quantification of Things Human," 221—31.

32. Stuart J. Woolf, "Toward the History of the Origins of Statistics: France 1789—1815," in *State and Statistics in France, 1789—1815*, ed. Jean-Claude Perrot and Stuart Woolf (New York: Harwood, 1984), 82—83; Cullen, *Statistical Movement in Early Victorian Britain*, 10—11; Porter, *Rise of Statistical Thinking*, 24.

33. Jacques Dupâquier and Eric Vilquin, "Le pouvoir royal et la statistique démographique," in *Pour une histoire de la statistique*, proceedings of "Journées d'étude sur l'histoire de la statistique," Vaucresson, June 23—25, 1976 (Paris: Institut national de la statistique et des études économiques, 1977), 92—101.

34. Gille, *Les sources statistique de l'histoire de France*, 24—25.

35. Desrosières, *La politique des grands nombres*, 38—39; Rusnock, "Quantification of Things Human," 243—49.

36. Hyman Alterman, *Counting People: The Census in History* (New York: Harcourt, Brace, 1969), 46–47; Gille, *Les sources statistique de l'histoire de France,* 28–42, 60; Dupâquier and Vilquin, "La pouvoir royal et la statistique démographique," 85–90; Desrosières, *La politique des grands nombres,* 40; Hecht, "L'idée du dénombrement," 61–62; Rusnock, "Quantification, Precision, and Accuracy," 17–21; Rusnock, "Quantification of Things Human," 245–49.

37. Gille, *Les sources statistique de l'histoire de France,* 53.

38. John Brewer, *The Sinews of Power: War, Money, and the English State, 1688–1783* (New York: Knopf, 1989), 221–24.

39. Nissel, *People Count,* 48. See also Peter Buck, "People Who Counted: Political Arithmetic in the Eighteenth Century," *Isis* 73 (1982): 32.

40. Dorinda Outram, *The Enlightenment* (Cambridge: Cambridge University Press, 1996), 103–6.

41. Hecht, "L'idée du dénombrement," 1:43–44; Dupâquier and Dupâquier, *Histoire de la démographie,* 116; Desrosières, *La politique des grands nombres,* 29–30.

42. Susan Kadlec Mahoney, "A Good Constitution: Social Science in Eighteenth-Century Göttingen" (Ph.D. dissertation, University of Chicago, 1982), 120.

43. Dupâquier and Dupâquier, *Histoire de la démographie,* 112.

44. August Ludwig von Schlözer, *Theorie der Statistik. Nebst Ideen über das Studium der Politik überhaupt* (Göttingen: Vandenhoek and Ruprecht, 1804), 93, quoted in Mahoney, "Good Constitution," 116.

45. Dupâquier and Dupâquier, *Histoire de la démographie,* 126, 261–63; Desrosières, *La politique des grands nombres,* 220–21.

46. Edvard Arosenius, "The History and Organization of Swedish Official Statistics," in *The History of Statistics, Their Development and Progress in Many Countries,* ed. John Koren (New York: Macmillan, 1918), 537–47; Johannison, "Society in Numbers," 350–60; Dupâquier and Dupâquier, *Histoire de la démographie,* 71–72, 195, 289–90; Hecht, "L'idée du dénombrement," 66–68.

47. Jean-Noël Biraben, "La statistique de population sous le Consulat et sous l'Empire," *Revue d'Histoire Moderne et Contemporaine* 17 (July–August 1970): 359. Michel Lévy, "La statistique démographique sous la Révolution," in *Pour une histoire de la statistique,* 1:106; Dupâquier and Dupâquier, *Histoire de la démographie,* 292–93; Gille, *Les sources statistique de l'histoire de France,* 102–9.

48. Dupâquier and Dupâquier, *Histoire de la démographie,* 256–57.

49. Jean-Claude Perrot, "The Golden Age of Regional Statistics (Year IV–1804)," in Perrot and Woolf, *State and Statistics in France,* 14–15; Lévy, "La statistique démographique," 107.

50. Dupâquier and Dupâquier, *Histoire de la démographie,* 292–93; Woolf, "Toward the History of the Origins of Statistics," 99–103.

51. Gille, *Les sources statistiques de l'histoire de France,* 117–18.

52. Jean-Claude Perrot, "Golden Age of Regional Statistics," 18–19; Gille, *Les sources statistiques de l'histoire de France,* 116–20.

53. Biraben, "La statistique de population," 360.

54. Marie-Noëlle Bourguet, "Décrire, compter, calculer: The Debate over Statistics during the Napoleonic Period," in *The Probabilistic Revolution,* ed. Lorenz Krüger, Lorraine Daston, and Michael Heidelberger (Cambridge, Mass.: MIT Press,

1987), 306—7; Gille, *Les sources statistiques de l'histoire de France*, 125—28; Desrosières, *La politique des grands nombres*, 54—59.

55. Jean-Claude Perrot, "Golden Age of Regional Statistics," 20—21; Gille, *Les sources statistiques de l'histoire de France*, 116—21; Dupâquier and Dupâquier, *Histoire de la démographie*, 293; Bourguet, "Décrire, compter, calculer," 306—7.

56. Desrosières, *La politique des grands nombres*, 47; Dupâquier and Dupâquier, *Histoire de la démographie*, 126—27, 258.

57. Dupâquier and Dupâquier, *Histoire de la démographie*, 127.

58. Bourguet, "Décrire, compter, calculer," 313; Gille, *Les sources statistiques de l'histoire de France*, 131—35.

59. Woolf, "Toward the History of the Origins of Statistics," 126—29.

60. Jean-Claude Perrot, "Golden Age of Regional Statistics," 35.

61. Gille, *Les sources statistiques de l'histoire de France*, 123.

62. Desrosières, *La politique des grands nombres*, 49—50.

63. Ibid., 48—53.

64. Woolf, "Toward the History of the Origins of Statistics," 165.

65. Bourguet, "Décrire, compter, calculer," 312—14.

66. Woolf, "Toward the History of the Origins of Statistics," 118—20; Desrosières, *La politique des grands nombres*, 54; Gille, *Les sources statistiques de l'histoire de France*, 123—24; Dupâquier and Dupâquier, 260—61.

67. Biraben, "La statistique de population," 363.

68. Alterman, *Counting People*, 25—26, 49; Cassedy, *Demography in Early America*, 61—69; Dupâquier and Dupâquier, *Histoire de la démographie*, 76—102, 288—89; Hecht, "L'idée du dénombrement," 23—32.

69. Québec had a census in 1665, but it counted only 3,215 persons of European origin. See Hacking, "Biopower and the Avalance of Printed Numbers," 289; and Alterman, *Counting People*, 58.

70. Massimo Livi-Bacci, "Il censimento di Floridablanca nel contesto dei censimenti europei," *Genus* 43 (1987): 137—51; Jorge Nadal, *La población española: Siglos XVI a XX* (Barcelona: Ariel, 1984), 23—26.

71. Quoted in Cassedy, *Demography in Early America*, 215.

72. Margo J. Anderson, *The American Census: A Social History* (New Haven, Conn.: Yale University Press, 1988), 9—14; Carroll Wright and William C. Hunt, *History and Growth of the United States Census, Prepared for the Senate Committee on the Census* (Washington, D.C.: GPO, 1900), 12—17; Cassedy, *Demography in Early America*, 212—16; Alterman, *Counting People*, 170—95.

73. Livi-Bacci, "Il censimento di Floridablanca," 143.

74. Dupâquier and Dupâquier, *Histoire de la démographie*, 281—82, 296—97; Cullen, *Statistical Movement in Early Victorian Britain*, 12—13; Eyler, *Victorian Social Medicine*, 39—40; Nissel, *People Count*, 50—55; Glass, *Numbering the People*, 91—94; Porter, *Rise of Statistical Thinking*, 30—31.

75. Cohen, *Calculating People*, 150—55, 254 n. 3; Cassedy, *Demography in Early America*, 225—31. James Mease, *The Picture of Philadelphia* (1811), quoted in Cohen, *Calculating People*, 154.

76. Cohen, *Calculating People*, 169.

77. Thomas Hamilton, *Men and Manners in America* (1833), quoted in ibid., 175.

78. Quoted in Cohen, *Calculating People,* 155.

79. James Cassedy, *American Medicine and Statistical Thinking, 1800–1860* (Cambridge, Mass.: Harvard University Press, 1984), 16–20, 179–203.

80. Cassedy, *American Medicine,* 52–83.

81. Cohen, *Calculating People,* 170–73; Cassedy, *American Medicine,* 25–30.

82. Wright and Hunt, *History and Growth of the American Census,* 217–23; Cohen, *Calculating People,* 158–62; Anderson, *American Census,* 18–19.

83. John Cummings, "Statistical Work of the Federal Government of the United States," in Koren, *History of Statistics,* 671; Cohen, *Calculating People,* 164–65; Wright and Hunt, *History and Growth of the American Census,* 26–27, 85–87; Anderson, *American Census,* 23–25.

84. Cohen, *Calculating People,* chap. 6.

85. Ibid., 204.

86. Michelle Perrot, "Premières mesures des faits sociaux: Les débuts de la statistique criminelle en France (1780–1830)," in *Pour une histoire de la statistique,* 1:129–30.

87. Ibid., 126–27.

88. Ibid., 127.

89. Desrosières, *La politique des grands nombres,* 113, 302; Dupâquier and Dupâquier, *Histoire de la démographie,* 268; Jean-Claude Perrot, "Golden Age of Regional Statistics," 125–27; Gille, *Les sources statistiques de l'histoire de France,* 149, 170–71.

90. Michelle Perrot, "Premières mesures des faits sociaux," 130.

91. Desrosières, *La politique des grands nombres,* 185–88; Gille, *Les sources statistiques de l'histoire de France,* 150–211; Livi-Bacci, "Il censimento di Floridablanca," 140–41.

92. Porter, *Rise of Statistical Thinking,* 28–29; Desrosières, *La politique des grands nombres,* 104–8.

93. Hacking, "Biopower and the Avalanche of Printed Numbers."

94. Joseph Lottin, *Quetelet, statisticien et sociologue* (Paris: Alcan, 1912), 73–74.

95. Frank H. Hankins, *Adolphe Quetelet as Statistician,* Columbia Studies in History, Economics and Public Law 31, no. 4 (New York: Columbia University Press, 1908), 28–30; Lottin, *Quetelet,* 75–108; Dupâquier and Dupâquier, *Histoire de la demographie,* 394–96; Michelle Perrot, "Premières mesures des faits sociaux," 129–32.

96. Quoted in Lottin, *Quetelet,* 109–10.

97. Lambert Adolphe Jacques Quetelet, "Recherches sur la loi de la croissance de l'homme" (1831) and "Recherches sur le poids de l'homme aux différens âges" (1832), *Nouveaux mémoires de l'Académie royale des sciences et belles-lettres de Bruxelles* 7 (1832): 1–87.

98. Quetelet, "Recherches sur le penchant au crime aux différens âges" (1831), *Nouveaux mémoires de l'Académie royale des sciences et belles-lettres de Bruxelles* 7 (1832): 71; and *Sur l'homme et le développement de ses facultés, ou Essai de physique sociale,* 2 vols. (Brussels, 1835); see Hankins, *Adolphe Quetelet as Statistician,* 53–85; and Lottin, *Quetelet,* 120–27.

99. I am indebted to Joel Mokyr for this insight.

100. Quetelet, "Penchant au crime," 1.

101. Hankins, *Adolphe Quetelet as Statistician,* 89.

102. Quoted in ibid., 88.

103. Quoted in Michelle Perrot, "Premières mesures des faits sociaux," 133.

104. Lottin, *Quetelet*, 435ff.; Hankins, *Adolphe Quetelet as Statistician*, 86–102; Michelle Perrot, "Premières mesures des faits sociaux," 133.

105. Cullen, *Statistical Movement in Early Victorian Britain*.

106. Philip Abrams, *The Origins of British Sociology, 1834–1914* (Chicago: University of Chicago Press, 1968), 33.

107. Ibid., 11–15; Cullen, *Statistical Movement in Early Victorian Britain*, 77–82; Porter, *Rise of Statistical Thinking*, 31–32; Eyler, *Victorian Social Medicine*, 16–20.

108. Quoted in Eyler, *Victorian Social Medicine*, 13–15.

109. Abrams, *Origins of British Sociology*, 36.

110. Ibid., 18–19, 38–40; Eyler, *Victorian Social Medicine*, 15.

111. Quoted in Cullen, *Statistical Movement in Early Victorian Britain*, 19.

112. Ibid., 13, 24–25; Eyler, *Victorian Social Medicine*, 21–22. Philip D. Curtin, *Death by Migration: Europe's Encounter with the Tropical World in the Nineteenth Century* (New York: Cambridge University Press, 1989), 3, 43–47.

113. Eyler, *Victorian Social Medicine*, 37–43; Cullen, *Statistical Movement in Early Victorian Britain*, 29; Nissel, *People Count*, 10–11.

114. Eyler, *Victorian Social Medicine*, 43–46; Nissel, *People Count*, 19.

115. Nissel, *People Count*, 47–61; Eyler, *Victorian Social Medicine*, 40–41.

116. Nissel, *People Count*, 99–100; Eyler, *Victorian Social Medicine*, 8–15, 47–49.

117. Eyler, *Victorian Social Medicine*, 23.

118. Quoted in Nissel, *People Count*, 101.

119. Simon Szreter, "The GRO and the Public Health Movement in Britain, 1837–1914," *Social History of Medicine* 4 (December 1991): 435–63; Nissel, *People Count*, 98–106; Cullen, *Statistical Movement in Early Victorian Britain*, 35–43; Eyler, *Victorian Social Medicine*, 22–31.

120. Eyler, *Victorian Social Medicine*, 76–86.

121. Desrosières, *La politique des grands nombres*, 205–8; Eyler, *Victorian Social Medicine*, 80–82.

122. Quoted in Nissel, *People Count*, 102.

123. Nissel, *People Count*, 99–102; Eyler, *Victorian Social Medicine*, 45–60.

4

DISPLAYING INFORMATION

Maps and Graphs

So geographers in Afric maps
With savage pictures fill their gaps;
And o'er unhabitable downs
Place elephants for want of towns.
JONATHAN SWIFT, "On Poetry"

NOT ALL THOSE WHO CONTRIBUTED TO THE CULTURE OF INFORMATION WERE members of the bourgeoisie. In the area of visual representation, two names—Cassini and Harrison—illustrate how widely the culture of information had spread to all classes of society.

For over a century, four generations of Cassinis dominated French astronomy and cartography. The founder of this illustrious lineage, Giovanni Domenico Cassini (1625–1712), was a professor of astronomy at the University of Bologna when he was recruited to head the Paris Observatory in 1669. He became a French citizen, changed his name to Jean-Dominique Cassini, and entered into the privileged elite of the Old Regime. At the observatory, Jean Cassini discovered the rotation of the planets and developed a method of determining longitude by sighting the moons of Jupiter. He also launched the most elaborate cartographic project of his time, the map of France known as "la carte de Cassini."[1]

His son Jacques Cassini (1677–1756), known as Cassini II, succeeded him at the observatory and as a member of the French Academy of Sciences. Jacques carried on his father's work of measuring the arc of the meridian—a necessary but preliminary step in constructing an accurate map of France. In this effort, which was to take fifty years, Jacques Cassini was seconded by his son César-François Cassini de Thury (1714–1784), known (of course) as Cassini III, who was also a member of the Academy and director of the observatory. When César-François died in 1784, his son Jacques-Dominique (1748–1845), count of Cassini (Cassini IV), carried on as head of the observatory, member of the academy, and director of the map project. The Cassinis' *Carte de France,* completed in 1793, was a masterpiece of Old Regime cartography. Jacques-

Dominique's son Gabriel (1784–1832) broke with the family tradition and became a botanist.

In contrast to this story of distinction and privilege, John Harrison's life was one of struggle and hardship, rewarded by success only at the very end.[2] Harrison (1693–1776) was the son of a carpenter who taught himself how to build clocks. In 1714, Parliament had offered a prize of £10,000 for a clock accurate enough to be used to draw reliable maps of the oceans and determine a ship's position at sea and had established a Board of Longitude to award the prize. Learning of the prize, Harrison devoted the years 1728 to 1735 to building the most complex clock ever seen. Harrison's Number 1 was far more accurate than any previous clock, for it was unaffected by temperature changes, it operated without friction, and it needed no oil. It also weighed seventy-two pounds and stood three feet high, and was not meant to go to sea or to compete for the prize. Its accuracy was so astonishing, however, that the Board of Longitude awarded Harrison small subsidies to refine his methods. Harrison spent the next four years building his next clock, Number 2, and seventeen more years building Number 3. Both were experimental devices—large, complex, ungainly, and superbly accurate.

In 1757, Harrison announced that his next work would be much smaller. Two years later he presented his Number 4, a beautiful five-inch pocket watch that was easy to carry. It was, in the words of clock historian Rupert Gould, "the most famous timekeeper which has ever been or ever will be made."[3] The parliamentary board put Number 4 to the test on a voyage to Jamaica and back in 1761–1762; after several months at sea, the clock was off by only five seconds. Not satisfied, the board ordered another test, to Barbados and back. This time, the watch was one-tenth of a second fast per day, giving a longitude error of less than half a degree, better than Parliament had required. Still the board would not award the prize to Harrison, who was required to hand over all his clocks and allow other watchmakers to make copies. Even after he complied, the board awarded him just £7,500—only half the prize, even with his previous grants.

Harrison accused the board of bias, since one of its most prominent members was Nevil Maskelyne, inventor of a rival method. When Harrison appealed to George III, who was an amateur clockmaker himself, the king exclaimed, "By God, Harrison, I'll see you righted!" Finally, in 1773, fourteen years after he had completed Number 4 and just two years before his death, Harrison received the balance of his prize.

Visual Representation

As a means of conveying information, pictures have a distinct advantage over both writing and numbers. They come more "naturally"—humans have been making drawings, paintings, and sculptures for thirty thousand years or more, and small children understand pictures long before they can grasp letters or numbers. To express certain kinds of information (e.g., facial features), a picture is incomparably better than words.[4]

Even when a picture is meant to be informative, however, it does not necessarily convey information efficiently and correctly. To achieve a high degree of efficiency and accuracy, the graphical representation of information had to undergo a long process of evolution. The eighteenth and early nineteenth centuries made great contributions to the forms of visual representation designed to convey information. Though not high points in Western art, the number and diversity of these contributions is remarkable: illustrations of plants, animals, and parts of the human anatomy; engineering drawings and technical illustrations; maps, hydrographic charts, and geological sections; and statistical graphs.

In this chapter, I will consider two of these means of representing information visually: maps and graphs. Though the content of the information that maps and graphs carry is very different, they are quite similar in the ways they contain and convey that information. Whereas statistics and narratives are both one-dimensional, maps and graphs are two-dimensional and therefore can be grasped by *seeing* rather than *reading;* and, for many purposes, seeing is more efficient than reading.

Maps are a very old means of representing information, one that has evolved sporadically since ancient times. Advances in cartography in the eighteenth and early nineteenth centuries reflected not so much an increased knowledge of the world—although there was a great deal of that—as improvements in precision and accuracy; in other words, cartography became scientific.

Statistical graphs, in contrast, first appeared in the eighteenth century as the output of certain scientific instruments and as a means of presenting numerical data; in today's jargon, they were an analog version of data, whereas numbers were digital. Not surprisingly, their evolution tended to follow (with some delay) that of statistics as described in chapter 3, and they came into common use only in the nineteenth century. The same was true of a new form of visual expression that emerged in the 1820s, a hybrid of maps and graphs called *thematic maps.*

Mapping the Land

Improvements in maps can be measured in three ways. First are changes that reflect an increased knowledge of the world. In this respect, no period can compare with the fifteenth and sixteenth centuries, when mapmakers first produced, in cartographer Arthur Robinson's words, "a reduced image of the real world," rather than "symbolizing spiritually based meta-physical concepts."[5] Nonetheless, the eighteenth century added much to Europeans' knowledge of the world: the Pacific islands, Australia, and New Zealand. By the mid–nineteenth century, the interior of the two American continents and much of Asia had been filled in as well.

The second criterion of cartographic progress is precision. This means filling in small blanks with local knowledge—villages, the height of mountains—in other words, completing maps by increasing their information density. This is progress of a pedestrian sort, the result of patient work by surveyors and careful cartographers.

The third criterion of progress is accuracy: making maps represent more closely the true location of their elements, which required advances in geodesy, astronomy, surveying, and their associated instruments. This is the scientific aspect of cartography, and it is here that our period made its greatest contribution to knowledge of the earth.[6]

The positions of geographic features are represented on maps by reference to a grid of meridians of longitude and parallels of latitude. Travelers and navigators had long known how to determine their latitude by measuring the angle between the horizon and the North Star or, in the Southern Hemisphere and with somewhat more difficulty, by the Southern Cross. Yet determining latitude by the stars, while easy, would be accurate only if the earth were a perfect sphere. By the late seventeenth century, astronomers had reason to believe it was not.

In 1666, Jean-Baptiste Colbert (1619–1683), chief minister to Louis XIV of France, founded the Academy of Sciences and the Paris Observatory specifically to advance cartography and produce the maps needed for commerce, road building, navigation, and the military. The first result was the "map of France corrected by order of the King, based on the observations of the gentlemen of the Academy of Sciences," finished in 1682. It showed the west coast of France 1.5 degrees farther east and the Mediterranean coast half a degree farther north than had previously been thought; in other words, France had shrunk by several hundred square miles (see fig. 1).[7]

To staff the Academy, Colbert recruited two of the most famous scientists of his time. Christiaan Huygens (1629–1695), a mathematician, astronomer, inventor of the pendulum clock, and discoverer of the rings of Saturn, came for a few years, then returned to his native Holland. Jean-Dominique Cassini remained to launch the most elaborate cartographic project of his time, the map of France.

In the process of surveying France for the corrected map, the members of the Academy realized they needed to know the length of a degree of latitude along the arc of a meridian, an imaginary line from pole to pole. In 1669/70, the Abbé Jean Picard measured the arc of the meridian between

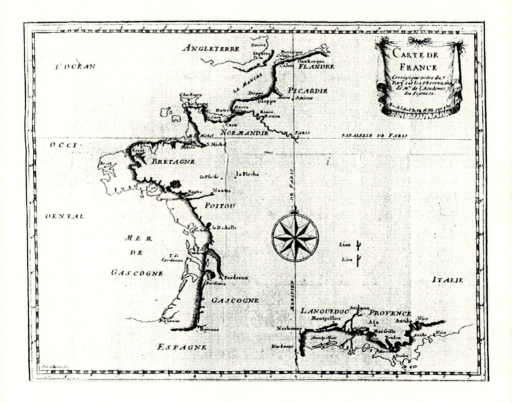

Figure 1.
Academy of
Sciences, map
of France, 1682.

Paris and Amiens. To measure long distances accurately, he adopted a system called *triangulation*, invented by the Dutch mathematician Willebrord Snell in 1615. Triangulation involved measuring a short distance—five miles or so—as accurately as possible on a flat surface; this was called the *baseline*. Then, using an instrument called a *theodolite*, Picard measured the angles between the baseline and a third point visible from both ends. Knowing one side and two angles of a triangle, he used a trigonometric table to calculate the length of the other two sides. This process was then repeated across the country, forming a chain of triangles of known dimensions.

In 1672/73, the astronomer Jean Richer, sent to French Guiana to measure the length of a seconds-beating pendulum, found that such a pendulum ran slower than in Paris, a sign that gravity was weaker in the Tropics. Huygens believed that this confirmed Isaac Newton's hypothesis that the earth bulged at the equator.[8] If that were true, then a degree of latitude would be longer at the pole than at the equator, thereby throwing off all maps.

The issue could be resolved only by further measurements. However, Colbert's death in 1683 temporarily halted all such research. In 1700, Cassini's son Jacques undertook to prolong the measurement of the arc of the meridian southward from Paris to Collioure at the southern tip of France. The results led him to conclude that the earth bulged at the poles, not the equator.

With Cassini II and the Academy on one side of the debate and Newton and Huygens on the other, the issue became politicized as one of France against England and Holland.[9] Political or not, the question could be answered only by scientific means. This meant taking two accurate measurements of a degree of latitude, one as close to the pole as possible, the other near the equator. Pierre-Louis de Maupertuis (1698–1759), the man who introduced Newton's theory of gravity to France, proposed to do just that. After many delays, Louis XV authorized two expeditions. The first, led by Pierre Bouguer and Charles-Marie de la Condamine, went to Peru to measure a degree of latitude at the equator; because of political difficulties and the rugged terrain, it took the expedition from 1735 to 1745 to complete its work. Meanwhile, a second expedition, led by Maupertuis, traveled to the northern end of the Gulf of Bothnia, on the Arctic Circle, in 1736/37. When the results of the two expeditions were compared, the Academy admitted that Newton was right: the earth is flattened at the poles by 1:178; or, expressed using modern measurements, a degree of latitude measured 109.92 kilometers (68.30 miles) in Peru, compared with 111.094 (69.03 miles) in Lapland.[10]

As these expeditions were heading out to determine the shape of the earth, the French government regained its interest in cartography. In 1733, Controller-General Philibert Orry (1703–1751) asked Cassini II to resume the survey of France, which had lain dormant since 1700 but was urgently needed by road and canal builders. Cassini realized it was futile to try to fit haphazard surveys to the Dunkirk-Paris-Collioure meridian measured earlier. What was needed was a new and exact set of triangles, which involved first taking a chain of triangles along a line through Paris at a right angle to the meridian, then covering all of France with triangles. Such a project was the basis for scientific—as opposed to descriptive—cartography and was the first trigonometric survey of a large area of the world. Under the direction of Jacques Cassini and his son César-François Cassini de Thury, the Paris Observatory published a map of France showing the exact location of the main towns and other prominent features, printed in 1744 on eighteen sheets. This was *La carte générale des triangles de Cassini,* begun by Cassini I over seventy years earlier (see fig. 2).[11]

Soon after, in 1747, Louis XV asked the Cassinis to undertake a much more ambitious project: a map of France at a scale of 1:86,400 (1 inch = 1.36 miles), the same scale as the first result of triangulation, a map of the environs of Paris printed in 1678. For this sort of map, a trigonometric survey was only the beginning. Surveyors had to fill in the first-order triangles with

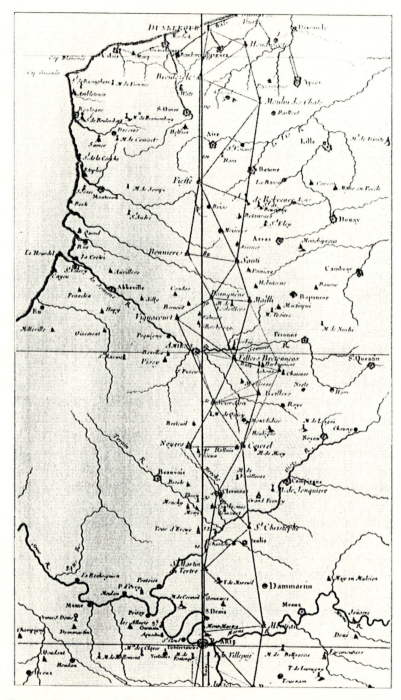

Figure 2. César-François Cassini de Thury, map of France (detail), from trigonometric survey, 1744.

second- and third-order ones and then add paths, rivers, buildings, hills, and myriad other details. Such a project required a large staff and many years of work. It was expected to produce 180 sheets, each 1,985 by 1,252 *lignes* (88 × 55.5 centimeters, or 35 × 22 inches) in size, to be issued at a rate of ten per year. They would be detailed enough to show forest paths, windmills, and the châteaux of the nobility, along with their owners' names. They would serve many purposes, such as building roads and fortifications and surveying the boundaries of the royal forests, Catholic dioceses, and large estates.[12]

Work began in 1748, with the Cassinis sending out ten teams with two surveyors in each to complete ten sheets at a time. The surveyors took angles and named the places they encountered with the help of local priests and nobles.

In 1756, just as the first sheets were being printed, the king abandoned the project as too costly. To carry on the work, Cassini III founded a private company, sold shares to important nobles and officials, and convinced various provinces and *généralités* to subsidize maps of their own areas. The work proceeded slowly. Fifty sheets had been printed by 1760, forty-five more by 1770, and another forty-five by 1780. When Cassini III died in 1784, all but Britanny had been mapped. (For a detail of Cassini's *Carte de France,* see fig. 3.) Only three to five hundred copies of each sheet were printed for shareholders and subscribers; few were sold piecemeal.[13]

The French Revolution revived interest in cartography, and the first revolutionary governments willingly subsidized the completion of the map of France, now directed by the son of Cassini de Thury, Jacques-Dominique Cassini, or Cassini IV. Completed in 1793, the Cassinis' *Carte de France* was the most accurate and detailed map of any country produced up to its time. Yet by the time it was finished, it was already obsolete, and it lacked consistency in details of woods and villages. In contrast to the precision with which it showed horizontal distances, its depiction of elevations, especially in mountainous areas, was very approximate and unreliable.[14]

Cartography, like everything else, was swept up in the Revolution. When the old provinces were replaced by *départements,* the Cassini map was redrawn to show the new boundaries. The Cassini enterprise was nationalized as a precious natural resource in 1793, and its maps were transferred to the Dépôt de la guerre, the army's cartographic service. From then until the end of the Napoleonic Wars in 1815, this organization produced maps of France and other European countries for the government and the army.[15]

In mapping their country, the English lagged behind the French by fifty years or more. Having a less centralized government than France, they left cartography to local notables and commercial publishers. Besides, their sci-

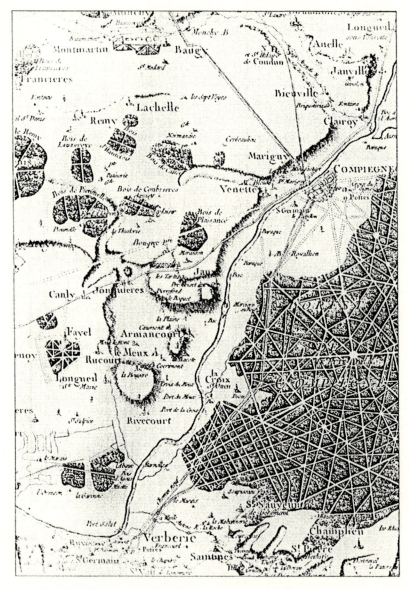

Figure 3. César-François Cassini de Thury, map of Compiègne, 1756.

entists and cartographers were more concerned with mapping the oceans than the land, as we shall see.

From the sixteenth century on, private surveyors had drawn numerous county maps, generally on a scale of one inch to the mile. These were basically road traverses, with distances paced off along the main roads, directions taken by magnetic compass, and the rest filled in by sketching. As cartographer Sir Charles Arden-Close pointed out: "Picturesque and interesting as the old county maps were, they leave a great deal to be desired on the score of accuracy. Errors of 10 per cent. or more may be found on Elizabethan maps; but similar errors exist even on the eighteenth-century maps."[16] The first map of Scotland, drawn by army surveyor William Roy after the Battle of Culloden of 1746, was, in his own words, "rather to be considered as a magnificent military sketch, than a very accurate map of the country."[17] The maps of Bihar and Bengal in India drawn by Major James Rennell in the 1770s and 1780s were more accurate than any produced in England.[18]

As the French had shown, only a trigonometric survey could produce an accurate map. The inspiration for such a survey came, not surprisingly, from France. In 1783, Cassini III proposed to connect the observatories of Paris and Greenwich by a chain of triangles that was already completed, on the French side, as far as Calais. The following year King George III and the Royal Society approved the project and appointed Roy, now a major-general and the inspector general of coasts, to direct it. To carry it out, the Royal Society ordered a three-foot theodolite from Jesse Ramsden, the best instrument maker in England. This large, complicated device (it weighed two hundred pounds) could read angles to within a tenth of a second of arc—a previously unheard-of precision—and took Ramsden thirty-five months to build.[19]

Roy, not content with determining the exact distance between Paris and Greenwich, insisted that the purpose of the triangulation "has always been considered of a still more important nature, namely, laying the foundation of a general survey of the British Islands."[20] Finally, in 1788, the chain of triangles linked Greenwich to Paris. Two years later, while correcting the proofs of *An Account of the Trigonometrical Operations by which the Distance between the Meridians of the Royal Observatories of Greenwich and Paris has been Determined*, Roy died.[21]

If France of the Old Regime gave the example, it was the French Revolution that provided the stimulus for a survey of England. In 1791, in response to fears of war, the duke of Richmond founded the Corps of Royal Military Surveyors and Draughtsmen to begin the trigonometric survey of England and Wales. The duke was master-general of the Ordnance; hence the name Ordnance Survey. The immediate need was to survey the southern coasts of England in anticipation of a French invasion. With a second three-foot theodolite from Ramsden, the surveyors finished a double chain of triangles from London to Land's End in 1795, then went on to survey Sussex and Kent. The first four sheets of the Ordnance Map, as it was thereafter called, were published in 1801. They showed Kent and parts of Essex and London at a scale of one inch to the mile.[22]

Once the southern counties were mapped, the survey advanced

slowly, especially during the Napoleonic Wars. The Ordnance Survey, ever short of money, supported itself like the Cassinis' company by publishing maps. By 1820, only one-third of England and Wales had been surveyed. The surveys of Ireland and Scotland were begun, respectively, in 1825 and 1837, in order to create maps at a scale of six inches to the mile, detailed enough for property and tax purposes. The entire project was finally completed in 1853. It then began again, for mapmaking never ends.[23]

Governments had long known that knowledge is power and that maps in particular are weapons of war, tools of administration, and incentives to development. Government-sponsored mapmaking spread far beyond France and Britain as most "enlightened" European states undertook great cartographic projects for purposes of taxation, military strategy, road building, or just to be modern. The most elaborate, and least valuable, was the *Josephinische Aufnahme* of Austria. In 1764, spurred by the loss of Silesia to Prussia, Empress Maria Theresa and her ministers decided to centralize their control over the provinces and therefore commissioned a comprehensive map of the entire empire in 5,400 sheets (compared with the Cassinis' 180 sheets). However, they had no unified plan and did not base their map on a trigonometric survey. In the best tradition of enlightened despotism, only three copies were made and kept as state secrets in the archives in Vienna. The *Aufnahme* was a triumph of detail over accuracy and of despotism over enlightenment.[24]

Nowhere was the power of knowledge more obvious than in the European penetration of other societies. When Napoleon invaded Egypt in 1798, he was accompanied by Colonel Jacotin of the Corps of Engineers and Geographers. After completing a trigonometric survey of the Nile Valley and the coast of the Sinai and Palestine, Jacotin drew a map on a scale of 1:100,000 on forty-seven sheets that were eighty centimeters high by fifty centimeters wide. It was engraved in 1808 and issued in 1818 in the famous thirty-six-volume *Description de l'Egypte,* published by Panckoucke. Two centuries later, cartographers admit that "the surveyed areas are characterized by such precision that there are relatively few discrepancies between Jacotin's and modern maps" (see fig. 4).[25]

What the French did for Egypt and Palestine, the British did for India, but on a much larger scale. The earliest maps of India were drawn by the Frenchmen Father Bauchet in 1719 and Bourguignon d'Anville in 1737 and 1752. After the Battle of Plassey in 1757, which gave the British possession of Bengal, the East India Company brought in surveyors to map the most important routes.

In 1767, Robert Clive, governor of Bengal, appointed Major Rennell the surveyor general of India, with orders to map all the territory under the East India Company's control. Between 1767 and 1777, Rennell took traverses

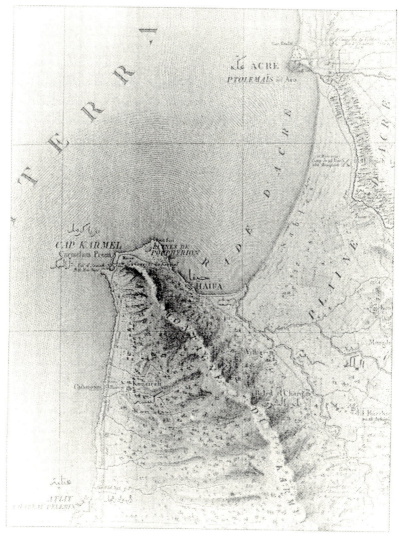

Figure 4. Colonel Jacotin, "Acre, Nazareth, le Jourdain" (detail), 1809–1828.

of the main roads and rivers, using a chain and a small theodolite, verified occasionally by astronomical observations; he filled in the intervening spaces by estimation, based on the oral reports of local inhabitants. In 1779, he published *The Bengal Atlas*, followed, three years later, by the *Map of Hindoustan* in four sheets. Rennell's maps were useful, but, lacking a base of triangles, they were still very inaccurate.[26]

In 1800, William Lambton (1753–1823), an officer who had fought in the American Revolutionary War, persuaded the government of the Madras Presidency to fund a trigonometric survey across the Indian peninsula.

Starting with a baseline near Madras, he ran a series of east-west triangles along the thirteenth parallel, showing that the Indian peninsula was forty-three miles narrower than on Rennell's map. Lambton then undertook an enormous project: to measure India along the seventy-eighth meridian from Cape Comorin in the south to Kashmir in the north. At the time, trigonometric surveys had been taken only in France and parts of England and Egypt. This method, though more accurate, was costly, for it required expensive instruments, educated surveyors and mathematicians, and a large staff to locate appropriate hilltops, clear trees, and build viewing targets every sixty miles or so. It was also slow work, for the surveyors could work only on clear days.[27]

Lord Moira, governor-general of India from 1813 to 1823, had previously served as master-general of Ordnance and was familiar with cartography and triangulation. In 1817 he founded the Great Trigonometric Survey of India (GTSI), with Lambton as its first superintendent. Gradually, the surveyors moved north from Cape Comorin along the meridian, reaching Bangalore in 1810 and the Central Provinces by 1820. When Lambton died in 1823, he was succeeded by Captain George Everest (1790–1866). Extending the chain of triangles across the Gangetic Plain to the Himalayas was especially difficult, for the crew had to erect fifty-foot towers at the apexes of the triangles. By 1843, when Everest retired, the Great Arc of India, at fourteen hundred miles the longest in the world, had reached the foothills of the Himalayas. It was followed by several secondary chains in southern and northeastern India.[28]

Mapping the Sea

Mapping the seas and their coasts and islands presented a very different challenge from mapping the land. At sea, one could not draw triangles or measure the arc of the meridian. Instead, the problem was knowing where one was in relation to the imaginary grid of latitudes and longitudes.

Latitude could be determined quickly with a sextant from the deck of a ship at sea, but longitude presented problems even for astronomers equipped with the finest instruments. Navigators who guessed their longitude by dead reckoning or by compass variation (the angle between magnetic north and true north) made stupendous errors. Christopher Columbus's estimate of the width of the Atlantic Ocean was off by eighteen degrees, or over 300 miles. Ferdinand Magellan, after crossing the Pacific, placed the Philippine Islands fifty-three degrees, or almost 4,000 miles, too far to the east. Cartographers who relied on the reports of travelers and navigators for their information published maps with very approximate (not to say fanciful) longitudes. Seventeenth-century maps showed the

Mediterranean Sea as fifteen degrees (825 miles) too long from east to west. Islands were discovered, then lost, then rediscovered somewhere else, and continents moved about in oceans that swelled or shrank with each new travel account.

Since ships' captains did not know their longitude, they navigated by going north or south to the latitude of their destination, then sailing east or west until they reached their goal. This worked only for large bodies of land, however; to find an island, a ship had to zigzag, sometimes for weeks, and still might miss its goal, especially if its maps were wrong, as they often were. Meanwhile, ships were always at risk of wrecking on an unexpected coast; in 1707, four warships were wrecked upon the Scilly Isles, almost within sight of England, losing two thousand men, because the captains had made an error in estimating their longitude.[29]

Navigators, astronomers, and cartographers had been obsessed with longitude since the sixteenth century. Governments were equally concerned, since an error in longitude could sink a fleet. In 1598, King Philip III of Spain offered a prize to anyone who could devise a method of determining longitude. The Dutch quickly followed suit. In the early eighteenth century, when England and France replaced Spain and the Netherlands as the leading naval powers, they too encouraged inventors. In France, the duke of Orleans offered 100,000 livres, while the English Parliament offered "a publick reward for such person or persons as shall discover the Longitude"—£10,000 for a method that could determine the longitude within one degree, £15,000 if within 40 seconds of a degree, and £20,000 if within half a degree—and created a Board of Longitude to study proposals and award prizes.[30]

At the end of the seventeenth century, astronomers knew of several ways to determine longitude in theory, but only one of these was practical. The first was the method of eclipses. Because eclipses could be predicted to the minute, observing an eclipse from a place of unknown longitude would automatically reveal the time at a "prime meridian" (i.e., the meridian that went through a place of known longitude such as Paris or Greenwich); subtracting local solar time from the prime meridian time gave the longitude. Unfortunately, eclipses of the sun and the moon happened too seldom to be of practical use.

The second method used the moons of Jupiter. As Galileo realized in 1610, the four satellites of Jupiter frequently passed in front of that planet (producing eclipses) or behind it (producing occultations). If one knew in advance when the eclipses of Jupiter's satellites would occur, one could determine longitude quite precisely. Jean-Dominique Cassini in France and John Flamsteed in England prepared the first accurate tables of the eclipses and occultations of the moons of Jupiter. Based on the tables Cassini published in 1690, European observatories were able to calculate their longitudes. Soon thereafter, expeditions to other parts of the world—Egypt, Siam, the Cape of Good Hope, Senegal, Madagascar, the West Indies—calculated their longitudes by the new method and reported them to the Paris Observatory. Cassini drew a planisphere (a circular map centered on the North Pole) on the floor of the observatory, on which he registered the new longitudes.

Cartographers and map publishers used the new data to draw corrected maps. The map that the Academy of Sciences produced in 1682, which showed France reduced by 20 percent, was one such result. Guillaume Delisle (1675–1726), the foremost French geographer of his time and a disciple of Cassini, published new world maps with corrected longitudes, showing the Mediterranean and the Atlantic much narrower from east to west and the Pacific much wider than on previous maps. In 1761, the cartographer Jean-Baptiste Bourguignon d'Anville (1697–1782) published a revised world map, with two hundred astronomical longitudes, twice as many as at the start of the century. Gradually, as more longitudes were determined, the map of the world that we know today emerged from the distortions and fantasies of the past.[31]

Alas, the moons-of-Jupiter method of determining longitude had two great drawbacks: it required an expert astronomer with a powerful telescope; and it did not work on board a ship. Hence, it did not qualify for any of the prizes, and the data it produced, while accurate, were rare and slow coming in. Clearly, something better was needed.

In the course of the eighteenth century, scientists developed a third astronomical method—the method of lunar distances—which worked by measuring the angle between the moon and a star. Since the moon moved across the sky faster than the stars, if one knew the angle and the local time and had a table giving the time for that angle at a prime meridian, one could calculate the longitude. This method required two innovations, both developed in the eighteenth century. The first was an instrument for measuring angles, the octant (later improved to become a sextant) introduced by John Hadley in 1731, with which one could read the angle formed by the moon and a star. The second, a table of lunar distances at a prime meridian, was more problematic; Isaac Newton remarked that devising a table of the moon's motions "is the only problem that ever made my head ache." The problem was finally solved by the German mathematician Tobias Mayer (1723–1762). In 1763, the English astronomer royal Nevil Maskelyne (1732–1811) explained Mayer's method in *The British Mariner's Guide;* in 1766 he published the first full table of lunar distance in *The Nautical Almanac and Astronomical Ephemeris for the Year 1767,* using as the prime meridian the one passing through the Greenwich Observatory.[32]

With these two innovations and a method of calculation, it was now possible to determine one's longitude at sea; but the procedure was still extremely complicated. Four people armed with sextants had to make several observations in quick succession; these observations had to be averaged out, then corrected for parallax and refraction through the atmosphere, then compared with the tables in *The Nautical Almanac*. All in all, it took a good mathematician up to four hours of work.[33] Commodore Charles Morris of the U.S. Navy recalled that, in 1800, "The navigators who could ascertain the longitude by lunar observations were few in number, and the process of the calculation a mystery beyond ordinary attainments."[34]

Meanwhile, a rival method had appeared, based on the measurement of time. In 1522, the Dutch astronomer Gemma Frisius had suggested that if one knew the exact time at one's location and at the prime meridian, it would be easy to calculate the longitude.[35] Two centuries later, however, there was still no clock accurate enough to permit longitude calculations. As Newton told a parliamentary committee on longitude in 1714: "By reason of the Motion of a Ship, the variation of Heat and Cold, Wet and Dry, and the Difference in Gravity in Different Latitudes, such a watch hath not yet been made."[36]

The timepiece that won the prize was the work of John Harrison, the most celebrated clockmaker in history. But Harrison was not the only clockmaker to pursue the Holy Grail of accuracy. Several other clockmakers were approaching it using simpler methods. In France, Pierre Le Roy and Ferdinand Berthoud competed for prizes offered by the Academy of Sciences. Like Harrison's, both of these men's clocks were tested at sea. Le Roy won the prize in 1769, and Berthoud became official purveyor of chronometers to the French navy.[37]

From the 1780s on, the English clockmakers Thomas Mudge, Thomas Earnshaw, and John Arnold turned Harrison's technological tour de force into a commercial enterprise. Earnshaw produced chronometers based on Le Roy's designs, which were much simpler than the complex Harrison timepieces. His competitor Arnold developed ways of manufacturing precision timepieces in series, a prototype of mass production. Unlike the exquisite but costly French chronometers, English chronometers gradually came down in price until they were within the reach of ships' captains. By 1815, England had produced four or five thousand chronometers, compared with France's three hundred.[38]

This technical advance was slow in reaching the ordinary ship. In the 1790s, only the East India Company equipped its ships with the costly devices. The Royal Navy did not issue chronometers to all its ships until 1825. In 1833 the French navy had forty-four chronometers for its 250 ships, and the U.S. Navy had fifty-four in 1835. Not until the 1840s did the supply of chronometers catch up with the demand.[39]

Each of the three solutions to the longitude problem had an impact on cartography, improving its information content, its accuracy, and its precision. Cassini's moons-of-Jupiter method fixed the location of observatories manned by astronomers; these were far apart, but they provided both a rough outline of the world map and the basis for a more exact map of France. Maskelyne's lunar distances method was much simpler but still required skill, patience, and a calm sea or, better yet, land from which to observe the sky. But it was the chronometer that made it possible to fix one's longitude quickly and accurately, and thereby filled in the map of the Southern Hemisphere and the Pacific Ocean.

For almost three centuries, whenever Spain's Manila galleons crossed the Pacific, their captains sailed north or south to the latitude of Manila or Acapulco, then sailed west or east until they reached their destination. During the trip, the crew members were so terrified of wrecking on some unexpected coast that they furled their sails at night. For fear of losing their way completely, they seldom deviated from their chosen path, missing the many islands that dot that ocean. If on occasion they sighted an island, they knew they could never find it again.

The new longitude methods changed all that. When Captain James Cook (1728–1779) sailed the Pacific on the *Endeavour* in 1768–1771, he used Maskelyne's lunar distance method to pinpoint the longitudes of Tahiti, New Zealand, and Australia; his longitude of New Zealand was off by only half a degree, or twenty-nine miles. On his second voyage in 1776–1779, he took with him a copy of Harrison's Number 4, made by the watchmaker Larcum Kendall, and he used lunar distances to check its rate; in three years and eighteen days, it lost 26.5 seconds.[40] Later oceanic explorers like La Pérouse, Vancouver, Bligh, and d'Entrecasteaux brought along chronometers. Thanks to the new longitude methods, maps of the Pacific Ocean published in the 1780s and 1790s began to show, accurately, the Marquesas Islands, the Society Islands, the New Hebrides, the Hawaiian Islands, New Caledonia, and Norfolk Island, as well as the coasts of Australia, New Zealand, and the Pacific Northwest of North America.

Just as important, they ceased showing Terra Australis and the Northwest Passage, mythical products of centuries of wishful thinking by European cartographers and navigators.[41] As George Vancouver wrote in 1791:

> Notwithstanding that our survey of the coast of North West America has afforded to our minds the most satisfactory proof that no navigable communication exists between the north pacific and the north atlantic oceans, . . . yet . . . it is very difficult to undeceive, and more so to convince the human mind, when prepossessed of long-adopted notions.[42]

Since the thirteenth century, portolans—sailing instructions illustrated with rough charts and sketches—had helped captains navigate the Mediterranean. Even with portolans, however, captains approached unfamiliar coasts warily and hired pilots to guide them into harbors. The first published book for Atlantic seafarers was Lucas Janszoon Waghenaer's *Spiegel der Zeevaert* (1584–1585), translated into English as *Mariner's Mirror* (1588), which gave sailing directions and maps from the Baltic to southern Spain.

Not until a century later did France and Britain publish seafarers' manuals (nicknamed "waggoners"), namely, *Great Britain's Coasting Pilot* in 1691 and *Le Neptune françois* in 1693. Whereas the English manual was based on compass bearings and estimated distances with few latitudes and no longitudes, *Le Neptune françois* was the result of a trigonometric survey of the French coasts by the astronomers Gabriel de la Hire and Jean Picard, with accurate longitudes established by Cassini's moons-of-Jupiter method. It was a product of Colbert's Paris Observatory and its injection of scientific methods into cartography.[43]

France was also far ahead of other countries in establishing a depository of hydrographic information. The Dépôt des cartes et plans de la Marine, founded in 1720, collected observations, maps, sketches, and charts from navigators and astronomers and published coastal maps and updated editions of *Le Neptune françois*. The French example was followed by Spain's Observatorio de la Armada in 1753, Britain's Hydrographic Office in 1795, and the American Depot of Charts and Instruments in 1830.[44]

Mariners' observations, the hydrographers' main source of information, had to be carefully correlated with previous reports and, if possible, duplicated and verified. Eighteenth-century hydrographers tended to be conservative, for human lives depended on the quality of such information. The coasts of the British Isles were far more complex than the French, and the weather, especially off Scotland, more treacherous. Yet until the mid–eighteenth century, British seafarers had only the dubious charts in the *Coasting Pilot* and some Dutch, Spanish, and French charts, in which sextants and chronometers revealed huge errors. As the surveyor Murdoch Mackenzie Sr. (1712–1797) pointed out:

> Sailors dare not rely on them in time of danger and difficulty; seldom or never attempting a coast or harbour they are unacquainted with, till they have got a pilot aboard, unless in great necessity; and then draughts are laid aside, and their sole dependence on eye or lead.

The first reliable survey of a British coast was that of the Orkney Islands, which Mackenzie published in 1750 as *Orcades: or, a Geographic and Hydrographic Survey*. He noted that his method of surveying

> differs from the usual way of sailing along the land, taking the bearings of the headlands by a sea compass, and guessing at the distance by eye or log line; and also from a very common tho' less certain method of constructing charts, without either surveying, navigating or viewing the

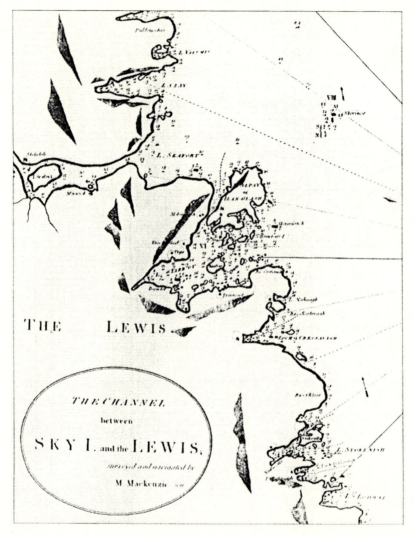

Figure 5. Murdoch MacKenzie Sr., hydrographic chart from *Orcades* (detail), 1776.

plans themselves; but only from verbal information, copied journals, or superficial sketches of sailors casually passing along the coast.[45]

Instead, he used triangulation, with apexes on shore and on nearby islands, a very tedious but accurate method, supplemented by soundings. On the basis of that work, the Admiralty commissioned him to survey the west coast of Britain and all of Ireland, resulting in two volumes of charts published in 1774 and 1776 (see fig. 5). Mackenzie also published *A Treatise of Maritim [sic] Surveying* as a guide to his successors.[46] His nephew Murdoch Mackenzie Jr., and the latter's cousin Graeme Spence went on to survey the southern coast of England in the years 1771 to 1804, taking regular soundings along the way. Like the Cassinis in France, the Mackenzie family brought scientific methods to bear on the hydrography of Britain.[47]

A family of surveyors, however assiduous, could not supply all the charts that British navigators needed. Since the middle of the century, the Admiralty had been urged to establish a hydrographic office to collect and publish charts and information on the French model. Finally in 1795, in the midst of war, it did so. To head the office, the Admiralty appointed Alexander Dalrymple (1737–1808), hydrologist to the East India Company, who had published charts of the Bay of Bengal.[48]

Hydrographic surveying was not limited to the coasts of Europe; in fact, some the most impressive surveys were done very far from European waters. In the 1760s, James Cook surveyed the coast of Newfoundland and the Saint Lawrence estuary. His charts and others of the east coast of North America were printed in *The Atlantic Neptune* in 1777–1781. On his several voyages to the Pacific, Cook always surveyed the coasts he encountered, in particular that of New Zealand.[49] From the 1790s on, navigators routinely used trigonometry to survey the coasts they sighted, from Bermuda to Korea. Matthew Flinders's survey of the Australian coast in 1802/03 was still in use a century and a half later. Under Dalrymple and his successors Thomas Hurd (1808–1829) and Francis Beaufort (1829–1855), the Hydrographic Office undertook extensive surveys of most of the world's coastlines and became the principal publisher of sea charts for the Royal Navy and the British merchant marine—in other words, for most of the world's ships.[50]

Above and below the Surface of the Earth

By the end of the eighteenth century, cartographers knew how to pinpoint the location and shape of surface features in relation to the imaginary grid of longitudes and latitudes. The next challenge was to represent on paper the bumps and dips of the earth, on land and underwater. Like geodesy, this also involved flattening a three-dimensional surface onto two-dimensional paper, a problem that was only beginning to be addressed in the eighteenth century.

Maps showing the depths underwater preceded topographical maps showing altitudes by almost a century. From the very beginning, mariners needed to know the position and depth of hidden rocks, reefs, sandbars, mudflats, and other features of the underwater landscape. Starting in the 1580s, sea charts showed not only harbors and coastlines but also soundings, that is, numbers to indicate the depth of the water. (For an example of an early nineteenth-century hydrographic map, see fig. 6.)

Drawing lines to join points of equal depth, or contour lines, did not

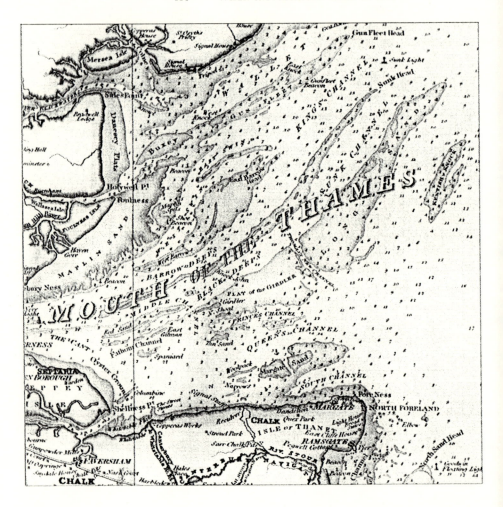

Figure 6. John Walker, hydrographic map from *Map of the Inland Navigation* (detail), 1830.

become common until the late eighteenth century. An early example of *isobath,* or underwater contour, lines is Count Luigi Marsigli's *Carte du Golfe du Lion* (1725), the first such map of a large area of the sea. Eight years later, Nicolas Cruquius published an isobath map of the Merwede estuary, a branch of the Rhine in the Netherlands, with contour lines for every ten feet in depth.[51] Contour lines were also used by the French cartographer Philippe Buache on a map of the English Channel published in 1737. These remained isolated efforts, however, and isobaths did not enter the vocabulary of hydrographers until the end of the century.[52]

On land, topographical maps were a necessity in forestry, geology, and land registries. They were also used in planning roads, canals, irrigation systems, and later railways.[53] Yet determining the altitude of land formations was considerably more difficult than sounding the depth of the sea.

Seventeenth-century maps of mountain areas showed mountains as little bumps, all of them of equal size (see fig. 7). The Cassini map was an improvement, for it showed hills and mountains as "molehills" or "centipedes" and valleys that looked like canyons carved into a flat plateau; their positions were correct, even if their altitudes and shapes were not (see fig. 3). Only rarely did figures indicate altitudes, and there was little beyond the letters D (*douce,* meaning easy) and F (*forte,* meaning steep) to indicate slopes.[54] Colonel Berthaut, a historian of French cartography, wrote:

> Where the map of France is most inconsistent, always mediocre, and often inferior to contemporary local maps is in the representation of relief. The hachures, presumably drawn according to the slopes, show neither the inclination, nor the differences in elevation, nor the shape of the ground. They only show the terrain, like a rough sketch, when a valley cuts into a plateau.[55]

Cassini IV even admitted: "We never pretended to make [topography] more than an accessory to the map of France. To make it more pleasant, we added, so to speak, a sketch, an outline of topography."[56] In 1786, Horace-Bénédict de Saussure gave the altitude of selected points in the margin of a map of Mont Blanc in his *Voyages dans les Alpes.*[57] In 1797–1799, Jean-Baptiste Ramond published *Carte physique et minéralogique de Mont Blanc,* showing altitude figures on the map itself.[58]

Since topography was of special importance to the military, the French army undertook its own surveys and drew its own maps. It began in 1748 with a survey of the Alps, followed by the Mediterranean coast and the eastern border provinces. The resulting maps were drawn on a scale of 1:14,000, with much more detail than the Cassinis' map, and showed elevations in numbers and pictured the terrain with hachures. The maps were never published.[59]

Hachures are lines that show, by their thickness, closeness, and length, the direction and shape of slopes. They first appeared in 1678 in the map of the environs of Paris. Gradually, the system was improved. Louis Capitaine, an associate of Cassini IV, published a map of France with hachures at a scale of 1:345,600; although based on the Cassini map, it showed relief much more clearly than the original.[60] By the end of the eighteenth century, cartographers like Jacotin could give "a fine plastic impression of relief forms" (see fig. 4).[61] A carefully drawn and engraved hachured map looked like a bird's-eye view of the terrain, lit by the oblique rays of the afternoon sun. It was art, even fine art, but it was not science.

The scientific method of showing elevation used contour lines that followed the terrain, each one at a given altitude, separated by equal differences in altitude. With contour lines, a trained map reader could determine not only the elevation of every point but also the gradients of

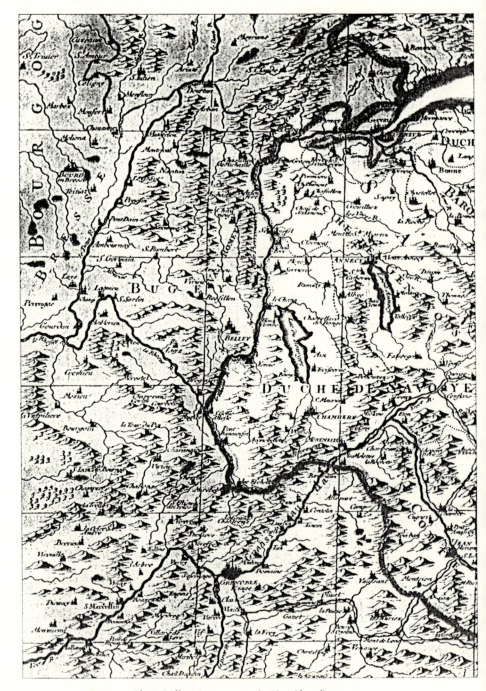

Figure 7. Alexis Jaillot, *Les montagnes de Alpes* (detail), 1692.

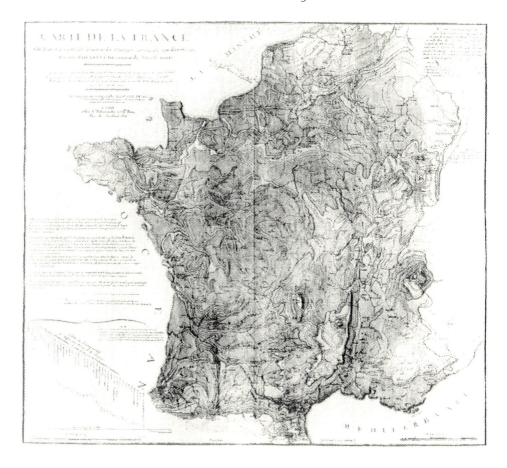

slopes, for the lines were far apart on gentle slopes and close together on steep ones.

The idea of contour lines on land was first proposed by the French surveyor Marcellin du Carla in a paper to the Academy of Sciences in 1771 and used by the map publisher Jean-Louis Dupain-Triel on two maps of France, one published in 1791, the other in 1798–1799 (see fig. 8).[62] Although these maps showed contour lines, much of the information was guesswork, for drawing contours above sea level meant taking hundreds of measurements of altitude by barometer or, better yet, by triangulation, a difficult and time-consuming process. The only systematic surveys of elevations were the secret military ones, and they covered only the border regions.[63]

The wars of the French Revolution and Napoleon merged the two French cartographic traditions, the Cassinis' map of France and the army's topographical maps. During the wars, French military cartographers were busy drawing maps of the rest of Europe for Napoleon's armies. In 1802 the Commission de topographie brought together all the official bodies that

Figure 8. Jean-Louis Dupain-Triel, contour map of France. 1791.

used maps, including the army, the forestry service, and the public works engineers, to establish guidelines for future maps. They agreed to adopt the metric system, mean sea level as the reference point for altitudes, and the use of contours for maps of towns and fortifications at scales of 1:1,000 to 1:10,000 and hachuring with oblique lighting for other scales.[64]

In 1815, Napoleon's military engineer–geographers returned to France. After considerable debate, the Commission royale de la carte de France, chaired by the mathematician Pierre Simon de Laplace, proposed a new map, to be drawn at a scale of 1:40,000, then engraved for publication at 1:80,000 and printed in 273 sheets of eighty by fifty centimeters. It was a military enterprise to be carried out by the Corps of Engineer-Geographers, placed under the command of the Etat-major, or General Staff, in 1830; as a result, the map was named *Carte d'Etat-major.* Handmade drafts contained contour lines to help engravers draw accurate hachures. Unlike the Cassini map, it was to show elevations, both in numbers and visually through the use of hachures and oblique lighting. A new triangulation of France was completed in 1845, and the topographical survey was finished in 1866. The first sheet, showing Paris, was published in 1833; the last, of Corsica, was published in 1880.[65] Almost all other European countries followed the French example and entrusted topographical mapping to military cartographers.[66]

There is a good reason nineteenth-century cartographers had difficulty reconciling the two ways of showing relief on a flat piece of paper. Contour lines were more accurate and scientific, if based on good topographical surveys, but they were hard to read; hachuring and oblique lighting gave an impression of relief but not an accurate representation.

The problem remains to this day, for it has no single solution. Every map is a compromise between clarity and detail, depending on its purpose and the scale to which it is drawn. Contour lines are preferred for large-scale maps of the kind used by engineers and hikers. For small-scale maps showing regions, countries, or whole continents, the best compromise first appeared in atlases of the 1830s and 1840s: contours, tinting in several colors between the contour lines, and hachuring with oblique lighting for visual effect.[67]

Geological mapping presented an even more complex challenge: how to depict an imaginary multilayered third dimension. The solution required a combination of cartography, sketching, and graphs. Before it could succeed, three cultural changes had to take place: the emergence of geology; a new system of symbolization called *stratigraphic sections;* and technical advances in engraving and printing to permit their dissemination. As Martin Rudwick has shown, it was not until the 1830s that all these changes coincided to produce the visual language of geology.[68]

A few eighteenth-century writers tried to show rocks and soil on maps or in sketches. Among the earliest were two maps in a paper presented in 1746 to the Academy of Sciences by Jean-Étienne Guettard (1715–1786).[69] Most authorities attribute the first geologic map to Johann Charpentier (1738–1805), whose *Petrographische Karte* (1778) used color washes to denote types of outcroppings, with boxes explaining the colors.[70] Meanwhile, since 1766, Guettard had been working with Antoine Lavoisier on *Atlas et description minéralogique de France.* When it was published in 1780, it contained thirty sheets, with symbols to indicate the location of mines, quarries, and outcroppings.[71] Neither of these maps showed any features below the surface.

Meanwhile, travelers who dealt with "geological" topics such as mountains or volcanoes occasionally illustrated their writings with sketches. But eighteenth-century artists, so adept at showing gentle landscapes, were not prepared to depict more dramatic formations. The engravings in Sir William Hamilton's *Campi Phlegraei: Observations on the Volcanoes of the Two Sicilies* (1776–1779) or Saussure's *Voyages dans les Alpes* were unconvincing and geologically uninformative.[72]

By the 1830s there had occurred, in Rudwick's words, "a remarkable change: the texts are now complemented by a wide range of maps, sections, landscapes and diagrams of other kinds."[73] The cause was the emergence of geology as a self-conscious discipline. In France, this development is identified with the *Essai sur la géographie minéralogique des environs de Paris* (1811) by the paleontologist Georges Cuvier (1769–1832) and the geologist Alexandre Brongniart (1770–1847).[74] In Britain, it was marked by the foundation of the Geological Society of London (GSL) in 1807 and the publication, from 1811 on, of its *Transactions.* By 1820, this journal was publishing accurate sketches of landscapes of geological interest. Unlike eighteenth-century works, in which illustrations were few and poorly executed, in the *Transactions* of the GSL, "the necessity of visual communication in geology first found institutional expression as part of the normal practice of that science."[75]

The technology of engraving and printing was instrumental in the emergence of geological illustration. Eighteenth-century illustrations had to be engraved on copper plates—a slow, costly process requiring skilled labor—and then printed separately from the text. For that reason, even expensive books like Hamilton's and Saussure's contained few illustrations beyond the frontispiece.

In the 1830s, publishers of natural history books such as Charles Lyell's *Principles of Geology* switched from copperplate to woodcuts. Wood engraving was cheap and could be incorporated into a page of text, but it could not show as much detail, and it wore out quickly. Colored maps and illustrations could be obtained only by hand coloring each copy.

Lithography, that is, etching on stone with acid, was faster and cheaper than copperplate and allowed tonal gradations and fine detail. It was invented in 1798 by Aloys Senefelder of Munich and promoted in England by Charles Hullmandel from 1818 on. Beginning in 1824, the Geological Society of London illustrated its articles with lithographs. Thanks to these changes, books and magazines began offering far more illustrations than they had previously.[76]

The emergence of geology and the development of better and cheaper illustration contributed to what Rudwick calls "the development of ever more abstract, formalized and theory-laden modes of representation" in an "integrated visual-and-verbal mode of communication."[77] Part of the new mode was the use of color washes, stippling, or shading to show surface rock and soil formations. More important was the geological section, a representation of an imaginary cliff, showing the nature of the underground geological formations along an imaginary line on the map. This method of representation was inspired by the illustrations on marine coastal charts that showed coastal cliffs as seen from shipboard. It took a mental leap to depict imaginary cliffs underground. Among the first to draw a geological section was John Whitehurst, whose *Inquiry into the Original State and Formation of the Earth* was published in 1778 (see fig. 9).[78] This book was followed by the works of Cuvier and Brongniart and the English geologists William Smith and Thomas Webster.[79]

The information about underground strata came from outcroppings, mines, and wells, which were few and far between. Hence, the early geological sections tended to show strata either perfectly parallel, like courses

Figure 9. John Whitehurst, geological section from *An Inquiry into the Original State and Formation of the Earth,* 1778.

of masonry, or smoothly curved. In the 1830s, with the enormous amount of cutting required by the new railroads, geologists recognized that strata were twisted and broken, and began to depict them accordingly. After 1830, such abstract representations gradually replaced landscapes in geological works, for "the geological community and their wider audience were able by this time to 'read' the still more formalized language of maps and sections."[80]

Statistical Graphs

As every newspaper reader knows, graphs are as much a part of our lives and culture as statistics. In business and the social sciences, they are a means of presenting quantitative data clearly and succinctly. In the natural sciences, they have an additional function: the instruments that observe natural phenomena, from recording barometers to atomic bubble chambers, often present their data in the form of graphs that scientists then analyze and turn into numerical data. In other words, information can travel in either direction between numbers and graphs. Historically, the two means of showing data—graphs and numbers—existed side by side for a century before they became firmly linked.

In this as in so many other respects, astronomy predated all the other sciences. As early as the tenth century, astronomers were showing planetary movements as cyclic lines on grids, with time as one of the axes.[81] Yet such representations were pictures, not true graphs. The mathematical foundation of graphs—the idea that the position of a point on a graph represents two numbers—had to await the theory of coordinates introduced by René Descartes (1596–1650) in the early seventeenth century.[82]

Cartesian coordinates spread slowly. Among the first to use them was the astronomer Christiaan Huygens in a letter to his brother Louis, dated November 21, 1669, showing the percentage of people surviving to different ages.[83] Edmond Halley included a graph in his article "On the Height of Mercury in the Barometer at Different Elevations above the Surface of the Earth; and on the Rising and Falling of the Mercury on the Changes of Weather," published in the *Philosophical Transactions of the Royal Society* in 1686. Others graphs followed, decades apart, in papers on capillary rise by Brook Taylor and Francis Hanksbee in 1712 and on barometric observations by Cruquius in 1724.[84] Meanwhile, scientists invented automatic recording devices, such as a wind speed recorder in 1726 and an anemometer in 1734. They did not publish the resulting graphs, however, but only the numerical tables derived from them.[85]

By the 1760s, graphs began to attract more attention from scholars. In the period 1765–1772, the mathematician Johann Heinrich Lambert (1728–

1777) published a three-volume work on applied mathematics. Most of it dealt with geometry and architectural drawing, but it also included a geometric figure representing a hypothetical life table (not a graph based on empirical data) and an essay on the theory of errors and on the technique of smoothing graphs.[86] In 1766, Philippe Buache included, on a map of the Seine basin, a bar graph showing monthly variations in the river's height in Paris from 1732 to 1766.[87] And in 1782, the German geographer August Crome (1753–1833) published an economic atlas of Europe with graphs showing comparative populations and productions.[88]

In the eighteenth century, only scientists understood and used graphs, and very infrequently at that. Not surprisingly, the first person to think of representing human beings by lines on a sheet of paper was a scientist, the chemist Joseph Priestley (1733–1804). Although he is now remembered as the "father of oxygen," Priestley possessed an encyclopedic mind and wrote works of history, grammar, theology, education, psychology, and much else. Most important (to history teachers, at any rate), he was the inventor of the time line.

In 1765, he published *A Chart of Biography,* a sheet three feet long by two feet wide, showing bars representing the lives of two thousand famous persons who lived between 1200 B.C. and A.D. 1750; it was accompanied by *A Description of a Chart of Biography,* a seventy-two-page index with dates.[89] The chart and its description were an instant success, going through dozens of editions, the last one in 1820. This inspired Priestley to issue *A New Chart of History* in 1769, along with *A Description . . . Containing a View of the Principal Revolutions of Empire that Have Taken Place in the World.*[90]

The idea of representing people and empires on a time line must have been so shocking to Priestley's contemporaries that he felt obliged to explain himself at great length, in the manner of his day:

> As no image can be formed of abstract ideas, they are, of necessity, represented in our minds by particular, but variable, ideas; and if an idea bear any relation to *quantity* of any kind, that is, if it admit of the modification of greater or less, though the Archetype, as it is called, of that idea be nothing that is the object of our senses, it is nevertheless universally represented in our minds by the idea of some sensible thing. Thus the abstract idea of TIME, though it be not the object of any of our senses, and no image can properly be made of it, yet because it has a relation to quantity, and we can say a *greater* or *less* space of time, it admits of a natural and easy representation in our minds by the idea of a measurable space, and particularly that of a LINE; which, like time, may be extended in length, without giving any idea of breadth or thickness. And thus a longer or a shorter space of time may be most commodiously and advantageously represented by a longer or a shorter line.[91]

In his *Chart of Biography,* Priestley addressed a philosophical question: How could an abstraction like time be represented by something as concrete as a line on a sheet of paper? In his *New Chart of History,* he explained the advantage of such a process:

> The capital use of any chart of this kind, that is, a most excellent mechanical help to the knowledge of history, impressing the imagination indelibly with a just image of the rise, progress, extent, duration and contemporary state of all the considerable empires that have ever existed in the world. If a person carries his eye horizontally, he sees, in a very short time, all the revolutions that have taken place in any particular country, and under whose power it is at present; and this is done with more exactness, and in much less time, than it could have been by reading. I should not hesitate to say, that a more perfect knowledge of this kind of history may be gained by an hour's inspection of this chart, than could be acquired by the reading of several weeks.[92]

In other words, the mind retains graphical data more efficiently than lists of words and numbers. Teachers owe this insight to Joseph Priestley.

Except for Priestley's charts, the first graphs were timid efforts, hidden away in scientific papers, mathematics texts, maps, or atlases. The creation of graphs as a major medium of communication was not the work of a scientist but of the self-taught publicist and adventurer William Playfair (1759–1823). As a youth, Playfair worked for a time as a draftsman for Boulton and Watt, manufacturers of steam engines. There, he may have learned of James Watt's "indicator," a device that plotted pressure-volume diagrams, which Watt kept secret. Later, when Playfair became interested in socioeconomic questions, his apprenticeship as a draftsman no doubt served him well.[93]

In 1786, he published *The Commercial and Political Atlas,* containing forty-four hand-colored graphs.[94] All but one of these were line graphs, with the horizontal axis representing time and the vertical axis showing English economic data, such as foreign trade or the national debt (see fig. 10). The sole exception was a bar graph of Scotland's imports and exports during the year 1785. Playfair's graphs were the first to use economic data. Unlike Priestley's charts, which were essentially linear, Playfair's were two-dimensional.

Like Priestley, Playfair was venturing into unexplored territory. In the introduction to his *Atlas,* he confronted the skepticism of readers who might question how money can be represented by a line:

> This method has struck several persons as being fallacious, because geometrical measurement has not any relation to money or to time; yet here it is made to represent both. The most familiar and simple answer

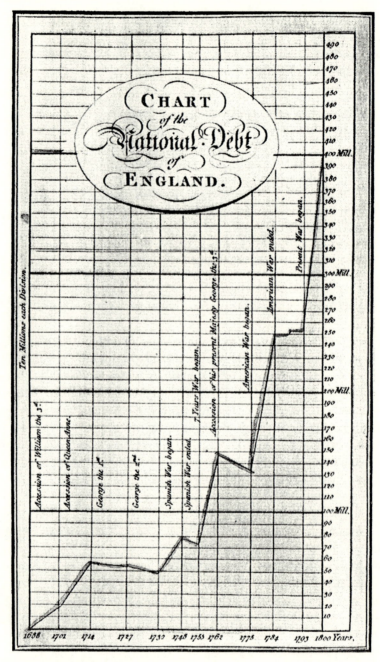

Figure 10. William Playfair, line graph from *The Commercial and Political Atlas*, 1801.

to this objection is by giving an example. Suppose the money received by a man in trade were all in guineas, and that every evening he made a single pile of all the guineas received during the day, each pile would represent a day, and its height would be proportioned to the receipts of that day; so that by this plain operation, *time, proportion,* and *amount,* would all be physically combined.

Lineal arithmetic then, it may be averred, is nothing more than those piles of guineas represented on paper, and on a small scale, in which an inch (suppose) represents the thickness of five millions of guineas, as in geography it does the breadth of a river, or any other extent of country.[95]

Playfair went on to give two reasons to present information in graphical form. The first was to improve the efficiency with which data were communicated: "As knowledge increases amongst mankind, and transactions multiply, it becomes more and more desirable to *abbreviate* and *facilitate* the modes of conveying information from one person to another, and from one individual to the many."[96] The second reason addressed a specific audience:

Men of high rank, or active business, can only pay attention to general outlines; nor is attention to particulars of use, any further than as they give a general information; it is hoped that, with the Assistance of these Charts, such information will be got, without the fatigue and trouble of studying the particulars of which it is composed.[97]

This, then, was the practical application of eighteenth-century rationalism: "men of high rank, or active business" needed economic information, and they needed to absorb it quickly and efficiently.

In 1801, Playfair published another book of graphs, the *Statistical Breviary,* which gave myriad statistics and brief narrative descriptions for each country in Europe, as well as Hindustan, and the population of the twenty-two largest cities of Europe.[98] It is of interest both because it attempted to show "the resources of every state and kingdom in Europe" in condensed fashion and because, to do so, Playfair introduced pie charts and circle graphs. On his "Statistical Chart shewing the Extent, the Population & Revenues of the Principal Nations of Europe," circles were proportional to the area of each country, and vertical tangents to these circles represented, on the left, the population and, on the right, the revenue of each country (see fig. 11).

Playfair used his graphics not only to show data but also to draw inferences. He drew dotted lines connecting the two tangents and stated that "the ascent of those lines being from right to left, or from left to right, shews whether in proportion to its population the country is burdened with heavy taxes or otherwise."[99] It did no such thing, since the slope was affected by the distance between the two tangents, that is, the area of the

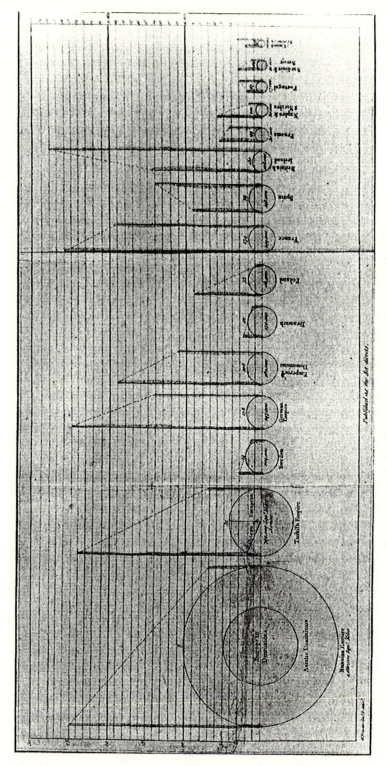

Figure 11. William Playfair, circle graphs from *Statistical Breviary*, 1801.

country in question. Thus, on his chart, the Russian government seemed less of a "burden" on its people than the English. Playfair was the first person to display demographic and economic data in graphical form. He was also the first—though far from the last—person to present overly complicated graphs and draw misleading conclusions from them.

Playfair seems to have been little appreciated in England. In the first fifty volumes of the *Journal of the London Statistical Society*, founded in 1837, graphs appear only fourteen times. Not until 1878 was Playfair mentioned in that journal, in a discussion by the economist William Stanley Jevons.[100]

Playfair had more influence on the Continent. In 1789, his *Atlas* was published in France, where it seems to have been better received than in England.[101] Denis-François Dounant, one of the founders of the Statistical Society of Paris, admired Playfair and translated his works.[102] In his report on his travels in South America, published in 1811, Alexander von Humboldt included bar graphs and superimposed squares, all clearly inspired by Playfair's *Statistical Breviary*.[103] He, too, stressed the efficiency of graphs: "Whatever relates to extent and quantity may be represented by geometrical figures. Statistical projections which speak to the senses without fatiguing the mind, possess the advantage of fixing the attention on a great number of important facts."[104]

Scientific journals began publishing graphs in the 1820s. As historian Laura Tilling has noted,

> By the 1830s data could be displayed in graphical form without straining the understanding of the reader; previously in the case of automatic recording devices, the tendency had been to convert the plotted data into tabular form to help the reader; now it was becoming increasingly common to display tabulated data graphically.[105]

Graphs soon spread to sociologists, economists, and engineers. André-Michel Guerry illustrated a sociological study with graphs showing the frequency of crimes at different ages and the percentage of crimes by age and by month.[106] Adolphe Quetelet used graphs in many of his works, starting in 1827.[107] By the 1830s, graphs and charts were regularly featured in scholarly journals.[108] In 1843, Charles-Joseph Minard, director of studies at the École des ponts et chaussées, France's most prestigious civil engineering school, published graphs analyzing railroad timetables and passenger traffic.[109]

By then, the use of graphs had become standard practice in Britain as well. The astronomer John Frederick William Herschel, the economist and philosopher William Whewell, and the philosopher of science J. D. Forbes popularized their use as tools of analysis.[110] Meanwhile, the epidemiologist William Farr published graphs showing the daily toll from cholera.[111]

In 1878, the French physiologist Etienne-Jules Marey wrote the first study of graphs as a medium of communication, filled with examples from natural science, medicine, economics, and other fields:

> Science is faced with two obstacles that impede its advance: the defects of our senses to discover truths, and the insufficiency of our language to express and transmit those that we have acquired. The purpose of scientific methods is to remove these obstacles; the graphic method has achieved this double goal better than any other.[112]

Graphs, a new medium of communication in the days of Priestley and Playfair, had entered the everyday language of educated people.

Thematic Mapping

A *thematic map* does not attempt to show the many features of the earth's surface, but generally only one. The feature in question can be a natural phenomenon, such as the distribution of palm trees, or a social one, such as the distribution of Buddhists. As a means of conveying information, a thematic map lies somewhere between a geographic map and a statistical graph. Just as many graphs show the variations of a given phenomenon over time, for instance, changes in the British balance of trade, so do thematic maps show variations of a phenomenon over space. Unlike geographic maps, thematic maps need not show shapes accurately but can represent them schematically, for instance, by showing countries as rectangles that are proportional to their population or wealth.

Since space occupies two dimensions on maps, a variable can only be shown as a third dimension. Hence, from the point of view of visual representation, thematic mapping required not only the necessary data but also a means of showing a third dimension on paper. As with three-dimensional geographic phenomena such as topography and soundings, cartographers could indicate the third dimension in various ways: with numbers, with circles or squares proportional to numbers, or with patterns, colors, or shading.

One of the difficulties confronting thematic cartographers was that statistics referred to given jurisdictions, such as departments, provinces, or states; hence, providing raw data on, say, crimes or education was misleading. What was needed was the ratio of a given phenomenon to the area or to the population—in other words, its density. Before thematic mapping could flourish, cartographer-statisticians had to become familiar both with the concept of density and with ways of representing it on paper by means of shadings, dots, or isolines (lines connecting points of equal density, technically isopleths). Both the data and the visual codes used to represent a third dimension schematically on paper were developed in the late eighteenth and early nineteenth centuries. As the cartographer Arthur Robinson pointed out:

> Although the roots of thematic cartography can be traced to the last half of the seventeenth century, the critical period of the most rapid growth and maturation occurred between approximately 1800 and 1860. As an event in the history of cartography this period ranks with that which occurred in the fifteenth century when Ptolemaic ideas were resurrected.[113]

Physical thematic maps predated social ones, since they are closer, conceptually, to geographic maps. The first person to conceive of them was that ingenious astronomer Edmond Halley, who published a map of the winds in *Philosophical Transactions of the Royal Society* (1686) and "A New and Correct Chart shewing the Variations of the Compass in the Western and Southern Oceans" (1701), with which he hoped (in vain, it turned out) that mariners could determine their longitude by the angle between magnetic north and true north. Then, in 1715, he published "A description of the passage of the shadow of the moon over England, in the total eclipse of the SUN, on the 22nd day of April 1715 in the morning."[114]

Thematic mapping was little used during the eighteenth century; an exception was Benjamin Franklin's map of the Gulf Stream in *Transactions of the American Philosophical Society* in 1786. The technique was revived in 1817 by Alexander von Humboldt, who published a map of the world with isothermal lines.[115] After that, isolines became a popular means of showing such meteorologic phenomena as barometric pressure (from 1827) and precipitation (from 1839). As a form of expression, thematic mapping came into its own with Heinrich Berghaus's two-volume *Physikalischer Atlas* (1845 and 1848), which included meteorologic, hydrographic, geological, botanical, and zoological maps.[116]

Thematic maps of social and cultural phenomena depended on the availability of data, statistical or otherwise. There were few such maps in the eighteenth century. The earliest was probably Gottfried Hensel's *Europa Polyglotta* of 1741, showing the distribution of languages, with Africa divided between the descendants of Japeth, Shem, and Ham.[117] Another, which became well known, was August Crome's "Neue Carte von Europa" of 1782, drawn to accompany his economic atlas of Europe, mentioned earlier. On it he placed symbols for different activities and commodities, but not their importance or quantity.[118]

Only after the end of the Napoleonic Wars did thematic mapping of social phenomena become popular, as statistics on population, crime, and education became available. In 1819, Charles Dupin published a map of "enlightened and obscure" France, showing illiteracy rates by department in

black-to-white shadings; he followed it eight years later with a map showing the ratio of persons per schoolboy in each department.[119] The study of
social phenomena—what was then called "moral statistics"—achieved
notoriety in France with the work of Guerry mentioned earlier. In both
Statistique comparée de l'instruction et du nombre des crimes, which he published in 1829
with Adrien Balbi, and *Essai sur la statistique morale de la France* (1833), Guerry presented maps showing the density of schoolchildren and of crimes, proving
that the crime rate did not fall but instead rose with the level of education,
a shocking revelation.[120] At the same time, Adolphe Quetelet's paper on
"propensity to crime" showed a similar correlation between crime and education in France, the Low Countries, and the Rhineland; widely publicized and translated, it aroused interest not only in social statistics but also
in the use of thematic maps as a way of presenting them.[121]

By the 1840s, thematic maps had become common and widespread.
Joseph Fletcher, barrister and social reformer, published a series of maps of
England and Wales, showing not only literacy and crimes but also improv-
ident marriages, bastardy, pauperism, and savings bank deposits.[122] A. K.
Johnson's *National Atlas* (1843) showed the peoples of Europe—"Celtic,"
"Teutonic," "Slavonian," and so on—by different colors, with "mixed peoples" by mixed colors.[123] Most amazing of all was Heinrich Berghaus's map
of the world, with different shadings showing the "spiritual constitution"
of different areas (see fig. 12); as he explained: "The maximum is in the
Christian lands, preferably of the Protestants; therefore these are shown as
light (white). The minimum or complete darkness of the soul is in the territory of the heathens, shown here as darkest, with the transition indicated
by shading."[124]

A final and more socially useful application of thematic mapping occurred in epidemiology. As described in chapter 3, the first statistics were
the sixteenth-century London bills of mortality giving the numbers and
causes of deaths each week by parish, and the first statistical study, John
Graunt's *Natural and Political Observations* (1662), was based on these bills. Yet it
was not until the 1830s that cartography and epidemiology joined forces to
produce maps of the incidence of deaths.

The proximate cause was the cholera epidemics that reached Europe
in waves after 1829, leading to a proliferation of epidemiological maps published with the hope of finding patterns that could help prevent the next
wave. Thus, in 1836, Dr. J. N. C. Rothenburg published *Die Cholera-Epidemie
des Jahres 1832 in Hamburg,* with shadings to indicate the severity of the disease
in the different districts of the city.[125] Most famous of all are Dr. John
Snow's maps of London. One showed the areas served by two water sup-
pliers, the Southwark and Vauxhall Company and the Lambeth Company,
indicating that cholera was a waterborne disease. The other, a map of the
Broad Street neighborhood, convinced him that the water drawn from the

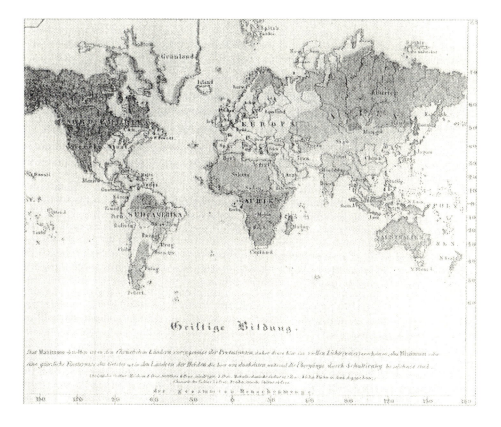

Broad Street pump was to blame for the disease.[126] It is thanks to these maps that clean water became a public responsibility.

Pictures, like other media of information, are in constant evolution. In aesthetic terms, no one would claim that there was "progress" between the late seventeenth and early nineteenth centuries. There was, however, much more and better information to be found in nineteenth-century maps and graphs than ever before, reflecting the greatly increased knowledge of the earth, the oceans, the subsoil, and the distribution of both natural and social phenomena that had accumulated in a century and a half. By the mid–nineteenth century, cartographers, geologists, and statisticians had found means of representing such information in more precise and accurate graphical forms than ever before. They represent a transition from a descriptive or narrative visual language—"elephants for want of towns"—to a scientific system of showing data visually.

Two centuries ago, engravings were costly, maps were rare, and most people saw few paintings in their lifetime. Today, in contrast, we are sur-

Figure 12. Heinrich Berghaus, map of "spiritual constitution," 1848.

rounded—some would say overwhelmed—by visual stimuli. Entirely new systems of displaying information visually were developed after 1850: photography, motion pictures, X rays, color printing, television, neon signs, and more.

Astonishing as they were, these media pale in comparison with the impact of computers on visual representations. In the two cases presented in this chapter—maps and graphs—computers have revolutionized the gathering, processing, and display of information. Computers are able to merge, compare, and analyze satellite images and data from remote sensing devices and from human observations to create not just maps but geographic databases that can hold as much information as thousands of maps and can be updated continuously. Computers can also easily turn digitized data and tables of numbers into graphical images of many different shapes. And static two-dimensional maps and graphs are only the beginning. Very soon our visual world will be flooded with motion maps, three-dimensional graphs, and other marvels as yet unimagined.

But computers do only what they are told. If they do astonishing things, it is because they have been programmed to do quickly what human beings could do by hand, but much too slowly to be worth trying. So it is not really computers that have revolutionized the visual presentation of information. It is the demand for accurate and efficient displays, which can be traced back to the Age of Reason, that led to the machines that we find so amazing.

Notes

1. Monique Pelletier, *La carte de Cassini: L'extraordinaire aventure de la carte de France* (Paris: Ecole nationale des ponts et chaussées, 1990), 45; John Noble Wilford, *The Mapmakers* (New York: Random House, 1981), 111–15.

2. The story of Harrison and his timekeepers has been told many times, most recently in a charming popular biography by Dava Sobel, *Longitude: The True Story of a Lone Genius Who Solved the Greatest Scientific Problem of His Time* (New York: Penguin, 1995).

3. Rupert Gould, *The Marine Chronometer: Its History and Development* (London: Potter, 1923), 8.

4. See Eugene S. Ferguson, *Engineering and the Mind's Eye* (Cambridge, Mass.: MIT Press, 1992).

5. Arthur Howard Robinson, *Early Thematic Mapping in the History of Cartography* (Chicago: University of Chicago Press, 1982), 15.

6. Unfortunately, some map historians, fascinated by the earlier "expansion of Europe," have ignored the contributions of the eighteenth and later centuries to the accuracy and precision of mapmaking; see, for example, Leo Bagrow, *History of Cartography,* trans. D. L. Paisley, revised by R. A. Skelton (Cambridge, Mass.: Harvard University Press, 1964), which ends the story of maps in 1700.

7. Numa Broc, *La géographie des philosophes: Géographes et voyageurs français au XVIIIe siècle* (Paris: Ophrys, 1975), 15; Lloyd A. Brown, *The Story of Maps* (Boston: Little, Brown, 1949), 212–14; Gerald Roe Crone, *Maps and Their Makers: An Introduction to the History of Cartography*, 5th ed. (Folkestone, England: W. Dawson, 1978), 128; Josef W. Konvitz, *Cartography in France, 1660–1848: Science, Engineering, and Statecraft* (Chicago: University of Chicago Press, 1987), 4; Robinson, *Early Thematic Mapping*, 18–19; Marc Duranthon, *La carte de France: Son histoire, 1678–1978* (Paris: Solar, 1978), 5.

8. David D. Landes, *Revolution in Time: Clocks and the Making of the Modern World* (Cambridge, Mass.: Harvard University Press, 1983), 160–61.

9. Mary S. Pedley, *Bel et Utile: The Work of the Robert de Vaugondy Family of Mapmakers* (Tring, Hertfordshire.: Map Collectors Publications, 1992), 17; Broc, *La geographie des philosophes*, 37–38; Pelletier, *La carte de Cassini*, 50–62; Wilford, *Mapmakers*, 99–101.

10. Mary Terrall, "Representing the Earth's Shape: The Polemics Surrounding Maupertuis's Expedition to Lapland," *Isis* 83 (1992): 218–37; H. Bentley Glass, "Maupertuis: A Forgotten Genius," *Scientific American*, October 1955, 100–110; Wilford, *Mapmakers*, 101–9; Broc, *La geographie des philosophes*, 38–40; Pelletier, *La carte de Cassini*, 67–71.

11. Pelletier, *La carte de Cassini*, 11–12, 62–67; Konvitz, *Cartography in France*, 9–16; Wilford, *Mapmakers*, 116.

12. Henri Marie Auguste Berthaut, *La carte de France, 1750–1898: Etude historique par le Colonel Berthaut, chef de la Section de cartographie*, 2 vols. (Paris: Service géographique de l'Armée, 1898–1899), 1:48.

13. Pelletier, *La carte de Cassini*, 192.

14. Berthaut, *La carte de France*, 1:56–57, 135–37.

15. Pelletier, *La carte de Cassini*, 6–14, 91–146, 197; Konvitz, *Cartography in France*, 16–44; Crone, *Maps and Their Makers*, 130–31; Berthaut, *La carte de France*, 1:59.

16. Charles Frederick Arden-Close, *The Early Years of the Ordnance Survey* [reprint from *Royal Engineers' Journal*, 1926] (New York: Kelley, 1969), 37.

17. Ibid., 2–3.

18. G. F. Heaney, "Rennell and the Surveyors of India," *Geographical Journal* 134 (September 1968): 318–19; Arden-Close, *Early Years of the Ordnance Survey*, 37.

19. Sven Widmalm, "Accuracy, Rhetoric, and Technology: The Paris-Greenwich Triangulation, 1784–1788," in *The Quantifying Spirit in the Eighteenth Century*, ed. Tore Frängsmyr, John L. Heilbron, and Robin E. Rider (Berkeley: University of California Press, 1990), 179–206.

20. Arden-Close, *Early Years of the Ordnance Survey*, 14.

21. Tim Owen and Elaine Pilbeam, *Ordnance Survey: Map Makers to Britain since 1791* (London: HMSO, 1992), 5–7; R. A. Skelton, "The Origin of the Ordnance Survey of Great Britain," *Geographical Journal* 128 (December 1962): 419–20; Wilford, *Mapmakers*, 118–23; Arden-Close, *Early Years of the Ordnance Survey*, 4–21.

22. Arden-Close, *Early Years of the Ordnance Survey*, 25–44; Owen and Pilbeam, *Ordnance Survey*, 3–12; Skelton, "Origin of the Ordnance Survey," 416–21.

23. J. H. Andrewes, *A Paper Landscape: The Ordnance Survey in Nineteenth-Century Ireland* (Oxford: Clarendon, 1975); Arden-Close, *Early Years of the Ordnance Survey*, 33–72; Owen and Pilbeam, *Ordnance Survey*, 15–37.

24. James Vann, "Mapping under the Austrian Hapsburgs," in *Monarchs, Min-*

isters, and Maps: The Emergence of Cartography as a Tool of Government in Early Modern Europe, ed. David Buisseret (Chicago: University of Chicago Press, 1992), 153–67.

25. *Atlas of Israel* (Jerusalem: Survey of Israel; Amsterdam: Elsevier, 1970), 1/4; Pelletier, *La carte de Cassini,* 197–200.

26. Satpal Sangwan, *Science, Technology and Colonisation: An Indian Experience, 1757–1857* (Delhi: Anamika Prakashar, 1991), 22–24; Matthew H. Edney, *Mapping and Empire: The Geographical Construction of British India, 1765–1843* (Chicago: University of Chicago Press, 1997), 5–17, 91–96.

27. Edney, *Mapping and Empire,* 21–22, 104–18.

28. Sangwan, *Science, Technology and Colonisation,* 24–26; Edney, *Mapping and Empire,* 20–22, 210–12, 237–63.

29. Wilford, *Mapmakers,* 128–29; Broc, *La geographie des philosophes,* 16, 281.

30. Rupert T. Gould, "The History of the Chronometer," *Geographical Journal* 57 (April 1921): 254–55; Gould, "John Harrison and His Timekeepers," *Mariner's Mirror* 21 (April 1935): 118; William J. H. Andrewes, ed., *The Quest for Longitude: Proceedings of the Longitude Symposium, Harvard University, Cambridge, Massachusetts, November 4–6, 1993* (Cambridge, Mass.: Collection of Scientific Instruments, Harvard University, 1996). See also Broc, *La geographie des philosophes,* 282; Landes, *Revolution in Time,* 112, 146; and Wilford, *Mapmakers,* 129.

31. Frédéric Philippe Marguet, *Histoire de la longitude à la mer au XVIIIe siècle, en France* (Paris: Auguste Challamel, 1917), 127–31; Charles H. Cotter, *History of Nautical Astronomy* (New York: American Elsevier, 1968), 182–89; J. B. Hewson, *A History of the Practice of Navigation* (Glasgow: Brown, Son and Ferguson, 1951), 223–50; Broc, *La geographie des philosophes,* 16–33; Brown, *Story of Maps,* 209–20; Pedley, *Bel et Utile,* 16–19.

32. Gould, *The Marine Chronometer* 8–9.

33. Derek Howse, *Greenwich Time and the Discovery of Longitude* (Oxford: Oxford University Press, 1980), 62–69; Marguet, *Histoire de la longitude,* 185–94; Landes, *Revolution in Time,* 151–55; Cotter, *History of Nautical Astronomy,* 188–237.

34. Steven J. Dick, "Centralizing Navigational Technology in America: The U.S. Navy's Depot of Charts and Instruments, 1830–1842," *Technology and Culture* 33 (July 1992): 491.

35. Mary Blewitt, *Surveys of the Seas: A Brief History of British Hydrography* (London: MacGibbon and Kee, 1957), 19.

36. Wilford, *Mapmakers,* 131.

37. Frédéric Philippe Marguet, *Histoire générale de la navigation du XVe au XXe siècle* (Paris: Société d'éditions géographiques, maritimes et coloniales, 1931), 148–57; Marguet, *Histoire de la longitude à la mer,* 158–84; Landes, *Revolution in Time,* 161–70; Howse, *Greenwich Time,* 75–77; Broc, *La geographie des philosophes,* 282–84.

38. Eric Gray Forbes, "The Origin and Development of the Marine Chronometer," *Annals of Science* 22 (March 1966): 14–20; Gould, "History of the Chronometer," 262–65; Landes, *Revolution in Time,* 171–86.

39. Dick, "Centralizing Navigational Technology," 469–95; Howse, *Greenwich Time,* 72; Gould, *Marine Chronometer,* 213.

40. Forbes, "Origin and Development of the Marine Chronometer," 10–12;

Gould, "John Harrison," 117, 126; Howse, *Greenwich Time*, 71; Blewitt, *Surveys of the Seas*, 23.

41. Wilford, *Mapmakers*, 148–52.

42. Quoted in Blewitt, *Surveys of the Seas*, 32.

43. Alexis Hubert Jaillot, *Le Neptune françois, ou atlas des cartes marines. Levées et gravées par ordre exprès du roy. Pour l'usage de ses armées de mer*, 2 vols. (Paris: Jaillot, 1693). See Derek Howse and Michael Sanderson, *The Sea Chart: A Historical Survey Based on the Collections in the National Maritime Museum* (Newton Abbot: David and Charles, 1973), 11–12; Blewitt, *Surveys of the Seas*, 17–21; Pelletier, *La carte de Cassini*, 56–57.

44. Archibald Day, *The Admiralty Hydrographic Service, 1795–1919* (London: HMSO, 1967), 11–12; Dick, "Centralizing Navigational Technology," 474; Konvitz, *Cartography in France*, 73–77; Howse and Sanderson, *Sea Chart*, 12, 91–93.

45. Murdoch Mackenzie, *Orcades: or, a Geographic and Hydrographic Survey of the Orkney and Lewis Islands, in Eight Maps* (London, 1750), quoted in Blewitt, *Surveys of the Seas*, 21.

46. Murdoch Mackenzie, *A Treatise of Maritim [sic] Surveying, in Two Parts: With a Prefatory Essay on Draughts and Surveys* (London: E. and C. Dilly, 1774).

47. Adrian Henry Wardle Robinson, *Marine Cartography in Britain: A History of the Sea Chart to 1855* (Leicester: Leicester University Press, 1962), 60–69; Blewitt, *Surveys of the Seas*, 21–29; Howse and Sanderson, *Sea Chart*, 12, 105; "McKenzie, Murdoch" and "McKenzie, Murdoch, the younger" in *Dictionary of National Biography* (herefter *DNB*) 12:604–5.

48. Blewitt, *Surveys of the Seas*, 29–36; Robinson, *Marine Cartography*, 97–127; "Dalrymple, Alexander," in *DNB* 5:402.

49. Joseph Frederick Wallet Des Barres, *The Atlantic Neptune, Published for the Use of the Royal Navy of Great Britain*, 2 vols. (London, 1777–1781). See Blewitt, *Surveys of the Seas*, 25–28, 86–87; and Howse and Sanderson, *Sea Chart*, 89–99.

50. Blewitt, *Surveys of the Seas*, 12–36; Robinson, *Marine Cartography*, 104–11; Howse and Sanderson, *Sea Chart*, 12.

51. François de Dainville, "De la profondeur à l'altitude: Des origines marines de l'expression cartographique du relief terrestre par cotes et courbes de niveau," *Internationales Jahrbuch für Kartographie* 2 (1962): 151–53.

52. Konvitz, *Cartography in France*, 67–75; Robinson, *Early Thematic Mapping*, 87–88; Crone, *Maps and Their Makers*, 138.

53. Francesc Nadal and Luis Urteaga, "Cartography and State: National Topographic Maps and Territorial Statistics in the Nineteenth Century," *GeoCritica* 88 (July 1990): 9–10.

54. Berthaut, *La carte de France*, 1:52.

55. Ibid., 2:146.

56. Quoted in Dainville, "De la profondeur," 151.

57. Horace-Bénédict de Saussure, *Voyages dans les Alpes, précédés d'un essai d'histoire naturelle des environs de Genève* (Neuchatel, 1779–1796).

58. Dainville, "De la profondeur," 151–55.

59. Berthaut, *La carte de France*, 1:57–58; Konvitz, *Cartography in France*, 34–39, 82–97; Duranthon, *La carte de France*, 10; Pelletier, *La carte de Cassini*, 86–87, 141–42.

60. Berthaut, *La carte de France,* 1:66.

61. *Atlas of Israel,* 1/4; Brown, *Story of Maps,* 247; Pelletier, *La carte de Cassini,* 56.

62. Marcellin du Carla, *Expression des nivellements, ou Méthode nouvelle pour marquer rigoureusement sur les cartes terrestres et marines les hauteurs et les configurations des terreins* (Paris, 1782); Jean-Louis Dupain-Triel, "La France considérée dans les différentes hauteurs de ses plaines, ouvrage spécialment destiné à l'instruction de la jeunesse," map (Paris, 1791), and "Carte de la France où l'on a essayé de donner la configuration de son territoire par une nouvelle méthode de nivellements," map (Paris, 1798–1799).

63. Konvitz, *Cartography in France,* 77–80; Arden-Close, *Early Years of the Ordnance Survey,* 141–42; Crone, *Maps and Their Makers,* 139; Duranthon, *La carte de France,* 34; Robinson, *Early Thematic Mapping,* 94.

64. François de Dainville, *Le Langage des géographes: Termes, signes, couleurs des cartes anciennes, 1500–1800* (Paris: Picard, 1964), x–xi; Dainville, "De la profondeur," 157; Berthaut, *La carte de France,* 1:137–41.

65. Dainville, "De la profondeur," 152; Berthaut, *La carte de France,* 1:184–232, 2:1–92; Duranthon, *La carte de France,* 31–44; Konvitz, *Cartography in France,* 60–61, 98–101.

66. Nadal and Urteaga, "Cartography and State," 24–28.

67. Robinson, *Early Thematic Mapping,* 97; Crone, *Maps and Their Makers,* 139.

68. This section is based on a remarkable article by Martin Rudwick, "The Emergence of a Visual Language of Geology, 1760–1840," *History of Science* 14 (1976): 149–95.

69. Jean-Étienne Guettard, "Mémoire et carte minéralogique sur la nature & la situation des terreins qui traversent la France et l'Angleterre," *Mémoires de l'Académie royale des sciences* (1746), also published separately in 1746; see Robinson, *Early Thematic Mapping,* 52–53.

70. Johann Friedrich Wilhelm Toussaint von Charpentier, *Mineralische Geographie der chursächsischen Lände* (Leipzig: Crusius, 1778), cited in Rudwick, "Visual Language of Geology," 161.

71. Jean-Étienne Guettard, *Atlas et description minéralogique de la France* (Paris, 1780); see Rudwick, "Visual Language of Geology," 160–61; Konvitz, *Cartography in France,* 87.

72. Sir William Hamilton, *Campi Phlegraei: Observations on the Volcanoes of the Two Sicilies, as They Have Been Communicated to the Royal Society of London* (Naples, 1776–1779).

73. Rudwick, "Visual Language of Geology," 150.

74. Georges Cuvier and Alexandre Brongniart, *Essai sur la géographie minéralogique des environs de Paris, avec une carte géognostique, et des coupes de terrain* (Paris: Baudouin, 1811); see Robinson, *Early Thematic Cartography,* 57–59.

75. Rudwick, "Visual Language of Geology," 158.

76. Ibid., 151–58; Robinson, *Early Thematic Mapping,* 57, 110.

77. Rudwick, "Visual Language of Geology," 152.

78. John Whitehurst, *A Inquiry into the Original State and Formation of the Earth; Deduced from Facts and the Laws of Nature* (London: Robinson, 1788).

79. William Smith, *Delineation of the Strata of England and Wales* (London, 1815); Thomas Webster, "On the Freshwater Formations in the Isle of Wight," *Transactions of the Geological Society of London* 2 (1814): 161–254.

80. Rudwick, "Visual Language of Geology," 164–77; quote on 177.

81. James R. Beniger and Dorothy L. Robyn, "Quantitative Graphics in Sta-

tistics: A Brief History," *American Statistician* 32 (February 1978): 1–11. See also Howard Gray Funkhouser, "Historical Development of the Graphical Representation of Statistical Data," *Osiris* 3 (November 1937): 269–404. Alfred Crosby makes the interesting point, however, that musical notation, which dates from the Middle Ages, is a graph showing time from left to right and pitch from bottom to top; see *The Measure of Reality: Quantification and Western Society, 1250–1600* (Cambridge: Cambridge University Press, 1997), 144.

82. Laura Tilling, "Early Experimental Graphs," *British Journal for the History of Science* 8-3, no. 30 (November 1975): 193–94.

83. Jacques Dupâquier and Michel Dupâquier, *Histoire de la démographie: La statistique de la population des origines à 1914* (Paris: Perrin, 1985), 210–11.

84. Tilling, "Early Experimental Graphs," 194–95.

85. Ibid., 195–97.

86. Johann Heinrich Lambert, *Beyträge zum Gebrauche der Mathematik und deren Anwendung*, 3 vols. (Berlin: Buchladens der Realschule, 1765–1772); Lambert, "Theorie der Zuverlässigkeit der Beobachtungen und Versuche," in vol. 1, pp. 424–88.

87. Konvitz, *Cartography in France*, 110.

88. August Frederik Wilhelm Crome, *Produkten-Karte von Europa* (Dessau: Der Verfasser, 1782).

89. Joseph Priestley, *A Chart of Biography* and *A Description of a Chart of Biography, with a Catalogue of all the Names Inserted in it, and the Dates Annexed to them* (London: J. Johnson, 1765).

90. Joseph Priestley, *A New Chart of History* and *A Description of a New Chart of History, Containing a View of the Principal Revolutions of Empire that Have Taken Place in the World* (London: J. Johnson, 1769).

91. Joseph Priestley, *Description of a Chart of Biography*, 7th ed. (London: J. Johnson, 1778), 6.

92. Joseph Priestley, *A Description of a New Chart of History*, 6th ed. (London: J. Johnson, 1786), 11–12.

93. Howard Gray Funkhouser and Helen M. Walker, "Playfair and His Charts," *Economic History* 3, no. 10 (February 1935): 103–9; Tilling, "Early Experimental Graphs," 212 n. 15.

94. William Playfair, *The Commercial and Political Atlas, Representing, by Means of Stained Copper-Plate Charts, the Progress of the Commerce, Revenues, Expenditure, and Debt of England, during the Whole of the Eighteenth Century* (London: J. Wallis, 1786); a second edition followed in 1787 and a third in 1801. On Playfair's contribution to statistical graphing, see Edward R. Tufte, *The Visual Display of Quantitative Information* (Cheshire, Conn.: Graphics Press, 1983), 32–34, 91.

95. Playfair, *Commercial and Political Atlas*, 3d ed. (London: J. Wallis, 1801), ix.

96. Ibid., vii.

97. Ibid., xiv–xv.

98. William Playfair, *Statistical Breviary: Shewing, on a Principle Entirely New, the Resources of Every State and Kingdom in Europe* (London: J. Wallis, 1801).

99. Ibid., 2.

100. Funkhouser, "Graphical Representation of Statistical Data," 293; Tilling, "Early Experimental Graphs," 200.

101. Funkhouser, "Graphical Representation of Statistical Data," 285; Funkhouser and Walker, "Playfair and His Charts," 107.

102. Konvitz, *Cartography in France*, 130.

103. Alexander von Humboldt, *Essai politique sur le royaume de la Nouvelle-Espagne, avec un atlas physique et géographique* (Paris: Schoell, 1811).

104. Quoted in Funkhouser, "Graphical Representation of Statistical Data," 269.

105. Tilling, "Early Experimental Graphs," 207.

106. André-Michel Guerry, *Essai sur la statistique morale de la France* (Paris: Crochard, 1833).

107. Adolphe Quetelet, *Recherches sur la population, les naissances, les décès, les prisons, les dépôts de mendacité, etc., dans le royaume des Pays-Bas* (Brussels: Tarlier, 1827); Quetelet, "Recherches sur le penchant au crime aux différens âges," *Nouveaux mémoires de l'Académie royale des Sciences et Belles-Lettres de Bruxelles* 7 (1832): 1–87.

108. Beniger and Robyn, "Quantitative Graphics in Statistics," 4.

109. Charles-Joseph Minard, *Second mémoire sur l'importance du parcours partiel sur les chemins de fer* (Paris: Fain et Thurnot, 1843).

110. Tilling, "Early Experimental Graphs," 207–11.

111. Muriel Nissel, *People Count: A History of the General Register Office* (London: HMSO, 1987), 81.

112. Etienne-Jules Marey, *La méthode graphique dans les sciences expérimentales et principalement en physiologie et en médecine* (Paris: G. Masson, 1878), 3.

113. Robinson, *Early Thematic Mapping*, x.

114. Funkhouser, "Graphical Representation of Statistical Data," 301; Robinson, *Early Thematic Mapping*, 46–51, 83–84.

115. Alexander von Humboldt, "Des lignes isothermes et de la distribution de la chaleur sur le globe," *Mémoires de physique et chimie de la Société d'Arcueil* 3 (1817): 462–606; and a map entitled "Sur les lignes isothermes," in *Annales de physique et chimie* 5 (Paris, 1817), 102–13; translated as "On Isothermal Lines, and on the Distribution of Heat over the Globe," *Edinburgh Philosophical Journal* 3 (1820). See Funkhouser, "Graphical Representation of Statistical Data," 301; Robinson, *Early Thematic Mapping*, 37, 81.

116. Heinrich Karl Wilhelm Berghaus, *Physikalischer Atlas* 2 vols. (Gotha: Justus Perthes, 1845–1848); English version: Alexander Keith Johnston, *The Physical Atlas; A Series of Maps and Notes Illustrating the Geographical Distribution of Natural Phenomena* (Edinburgh: Johnston, 1848). See Robinson, *Early Thematic Mapping*, 64–76.

117. Robinson, *Early Thematic Mapping*, 130–34.

118. On Crome, see Erica Royston, "Studies in the History of the Graphical Representation of Data," *Biometrika* 43 (December 1956): 241–47; Funkhouser, "Graphical Representation of Statistical Data," 199; Robinson, *Early Thematic Mapping*, 54–56.

119. Charles Dupin, "Carte de la France éclairée et de la France obscure" (Paris, 1819), cited in Funkhouser, "Graphical Representation of Statistical Data," 300; Dupin, "Carte figurative de l'instruction populaire de la France" (1827), cited in Robinson, *Early Thematic Mapping*, 156.

120. Funkhouser, "Graphical Representation of Statistical Data," 300; Robinson, *Early Thematic Mapping*, 62.

121. Quetelet, "Recherches sur le penchant au crime." See Robinson, *Early Thematic Mapping,* 160.

122. Robinson, *Early Thematic Mapping,* 164–66.

123. Ibid., 137.

124. Berghaus, *Physikalischer Atlas,* 2d section (1848), cited in Robinson, *Early Thematic Mapping,* 136.

125. J. N. C. Rothenburg, *Die Cholera-Epidemie des Jahres 1832 in Hamburg* (Hamburg: Perthes und Besser, 1836), cited in Robinson, *Early Thematic Mapping,* 170.

126. John Snow, *On the Mode of Communication of Cholera,* 2d ed. (London: Churchill, 1855); Robinson, *Early Thematic Mapping,* 176–89.

5

STORING INFORMATION

Dictionaries and Encyclopedias

I am the very model of a modern Major-General,
I've information vegetable, animal, and mineral,
I know the kings of England, and quote the fights historical,
From Marathon to Waterloo, in order categorical;
I'm very well acquainted too with matters mathematical,
I understand equations, both the simple and quadratical,
About binomial theorem I'm teeming with a lot o' news—
With many cheerful facts about the square of the hypothenuse.
I'm very good at integral and differential calculus,
I know the scientific names of beings animalculous;
In short, in matters vegetable, animal, and mineral,
I am the very model of a modern Major-General.

GILBERT AND SULLIVAN, *The Pirates of Penzance*

ENCYCLOPEDIAS AND DICTIONARIES ARE THE WORKHORSES OF CULTURE; almost everyone consults them from time to time, but almost no one studies them. These useful compendia of knowledge serve their purpose for a few years and then are shelved or pulped.

There are some notable exceptions to this rule, works whose significance transcends the time in which they appear. The most famous example of these is the *Encyclopédie, ou dictionnaire raisonné* of Diderot and d'Alembert. Denis Diderot (1713–1784) was one of the most prolific critics and essayists of the philosophes and a star of the French Enlightenment. His friend Jean Le Rond d'Alembert (1717–1783) was a mathematician, astronomer, and science writer. Together, they organized and edited the most ambitious work of their age. They planned it to be a universal compendium of all knowledge, organized in a coherent manner for the edification and enlightenment of the educated reading public. At the same time, they wanted it to be useful, practical, modern, and up-to-date. Despite its steep price, it enjoyed a huge popular success and became one of the best-selling works of the century.

Yet it left a poor legacy. Its sequel, the *Encyclopédie méthodique*, was a commercial and scientific failure that few people bought at the time and hardly anyone has looked at since. Today, intellectuals pay lip service to the original *Encyclopédie,* but no one goes out and buys a new edition.

Contrast this fate with that of two other encyclopedias that appeared a few years after Diderot and d'Alembert's: the *Encyclopaedia Britannica* and the *Brockhaus.* The first edition of the *Britannica,* which appeared in 1771, was a modest work, hastily put together by a printer, an engraver, and a penurious scribbler. The German *Conversations-Lexicon* was the creation of the publishing entrepreneur Friedrich Arnold Brockhaus (1772–1823), who bought up an unfinished encyclopedia, hired writers to complete it, and issued the first edition in 1809–1811. These were no masterpieces of erudition or compendia of all knowledge, but simple reference works. And yet they are still being issued, two centuries and many editions later.

Why the difference? The educated public admires erudition and intellectual sophistication, but what it buys is access to current information organized for efficient retrieval. The *Encyclopédie* symbolized the Enlightenment, and its influence has resonated through the centuries as a cultural monument; but as a practical and up-to-date reference work, it quickly became obsolete. Culture persists for ages, but most information is ephemeral, as those purveyors of information the Britannica and Brockhaus companies recognized from the start.

The eighteenth century produced a flood of compendia, printed matter in which information was presented in a logical, accessible manner: dozens of encyclopedias, hundreds of dictionaries, and thousands of almanacs, directories, stagecoach schedules, and other reference works.[1] This chapter deals with two essential reference works—encyclopedias and dictionaries—as information systems.

To analyze reference works as information systems, we use three criteria: storage, retrieval, and dissemination. To judge dictionaries and encyclopedias as information storage systems, we need to consider their length, their choice of topics, and the quality of their coverage. The arrangement of the entries, whether thematic or alphabetical, and such tools as indexes and cross-references determine the value of a reference work as an information retrieval device. Finally, we can judge the dissemination of the information contained in a reference work by the number of subscriptions or copies sold, by the number of subsequent editions, and by the number of imitations and pirated editions.

The Evolution of Dictionaries

In theory, it is easy to distinguish between dictionaries and encyclopedias, but in practice there is no clear way to differentiate them. As lexicographer Allen Read explains:

The distinction between a dictionary and an encyclopaedia is easy to state but difficult to carry out in a practical way: a dictionary explains words, whereas an encyclopaedia explains things. Because words achieve their usefulness by reference to things, however, it is difficult to construct a dictionary without considerable attention to the objects and abstractions designated.[2]

That is why so many reference works, such as Diderot and d'Alembert's *Encyclopédie, ou dictionnaire raisonné,* and the *Encyclopaedia Britannica; or a Dictionary of Arts and Sciences,* called themselves by both names. Some even explained why they included both concepts. In the subtitle of his *Lexicon technicum,* for example, John Harris promised to explain "not only the terms of art, but the arts themselves,"[3] while his successor Ephraim Chambers's *Cyclopaedia* claimed to offer "an explication of the terms and an account of the things signified thereby."[4]

Dictionaries and encyclopedias were ancient forms of expression, but the Age of Reason contributed much to their evolution. It was in the eighteenth century that dictionaries evolved from lists of words with simple definitions to works of scholarly erudition about languages, and that encyclopedias evolved from didactic "trees of knowledge" into the fact-filled, up-to-date ready reference works we know today. Also characteristic of that age was the proliferation of new works, ever-larger new editions of older works, and sales in the tens of thousands.

Some of this evolution occurred in response to a growing market for information, the result of general prosperity and the spread of education in the countries bordering on the North Atlantic; a scholar of eighteenth-century culture calls it "the ever-growing thirst for knowledge among the educated classes."[5] But new forms of presentation were also responsible for the success of reference works: the victory of vernacular languages and of the alphabetical order, improved typography, and the refinement of copperplate illustrations.

The earliest ancestors of dictionaries were medieval interlinear *glossa,* or explanations of difficult terms found in Latin texts, followed by *glossae collectae,* or lists of difficult Latin terms. By the sixteenth century, these had evolved into bilingual Latin-vernacular dictionaries, some arranged by topic, like John Withals's *Short Dictionarie of English and Latin for Yonge Beginners* (1554), others in alphabetical order, like Richard Huloet's *Abecedarium Anglo-Latinum* (1552).[6]

Monolingual dictionaries appeared in the seventeenth century and took two forms: "hard word" dictionaries and literary ones. The literary dictionary, one that explained words common to works of literature, was characteristic of countries of Romance languages. The genre originated in Italy with the *Vocabolario* of the Florentine Accademia della Crusca, published in 1612,[7] and was adopted by the French Academy, which launched

the project for an "official" dictionary in 1637. Unlike their Italian counter-
parts, the French academicians did not illustrate their definitions with quotations from the classics; instead, fancying themselves classical authors in
their own right, they made up examples. Yet so dilatory was their approach
that their dictionary was not published until 1694, by which time it was quite
out of date.[8]

By the end of the seventeenth century, the demand for a serious literary dictionary inspired several individuals to write their own. Pierre
Richelet based the entries in his *Dictionnaire de la langue françoise* (1680) on the
classic writers of his century:

> I wrote a French dictionary in order to serve the honest persons who love
> our language. To that end, I read our most excellent authors, and all
> those who have written about the arts with reputation. I composed my
> book with their most well-received words as well as their most beautiful
> expressions.[9]

Since the Academy had been granted the royal privilege of producing a dictionary, Richelet had to publish his in Geneva. Later editions, however,
were published in France.

Antoine Furetière ran into the same difficulty. As a member of the
Academy, he collaborated on the official dictionary but then decided to
strike out on his own. For this, he was expelled from the ranks of the "im-
mortals." His *Dictionnaire universel* (1690), like Richelet's, lacked the royal privilege and thus had to be smuggled into France from the Netherlands.
Nonetheless, it became the best-selling French dictionary of the early eighteenth century, with nine editions to 1727.[10]

Throughout this period, lexicographers debated the purpose of a dictionary. The French Academy spelled out the normative view of dictionaries in these words:

> One may perhaps say that one cannot be certain that a living language
> has reached its ultimate perfection. But that was not the feeling of Cicero
> who, after having reflected for a long time on this question, had no trou-
> ble claiming that in his day the Latin language had arrived at a degree of
> excellence to which one could add nothing. . . . This is the state in which
> the French language finds itself today and in which this dictionary has
> been composed.[11]

The French academicians were very selective in their choice of entries, rejecting archaic and newfangled words, as well as technical terms other
than those that referred to such noble pursuits as hunting, fencing, heraldry, falconry, and military strategy.

In contrast to the Academy's normative and literary view of language,
Furetière's dictionary contained entries that the academicians had ignored,

including terms of science, medicine, trade, and other forms of "bon us-age." This concept was defined as follows by Dumarsais in 1730:

> Good usage is the ordinary manner of speech of the honest persons of the nation . . . by which I mean persons whose condition, fortune, or merit raises them above the vulgar, and whose minds are cultivated by reading, by reflection, and by interactions with other persons who have the same advantages.[12]

What the academicians called "perfection" and "excellence" and what Dumarsais called "good usage" were clearly the linguistic representations of the social structure of the Old Regime. The fact that Dumarsais spoke of fortune and merit as well as "condition" left an opening for change, both social and linguistic. An early indication of this change was the inclusion in Furetière's dictionary of scientific, medical, and commercial terms, which contributed to the work's popularity. It was also arranged alphabetically rather than by the roots of words like the Academy's. In response to Furetière's challenge, the Academy commissioned one of its members, Thomas Corneille, to put together a supplement to its own dictionary, to contain terms of "arts and sciences." Published at the same time as the dictionary of the Academy, this "supplement" became a successful dictionary in its own right.[13]

The academicians, possessed of official "immortality" and royal privilege, maintained for many years the fiction that their choice of words represented "ultimate perfection." Finally, in the fourth edition of their dictionary in 1762, they caved in to the swelling demand for scientific and technological terms:

> Sciences and the arts having become more cultivated and widespread in the past century than they were before, it is now common to write in French about these matters. Consequently, several terms which are specific to them and which were formerly known only to a small number of people, have passed into the common language. Would it have been reasonable to refuse a place in our Dictionary to words which are nowadays in almost general use? We therefore had to admit into this new edition elementary terms of science and the arts, and even those of the crafts, which an educated man is likely to find in works which do not deal exclusively with the matters to which these terms belong.[14]

In England, which lacked a royal academy of letters, the evolution of dictionaries followed a very different path from the French. Seventeenth-century English dictionaries were of the "hard word" variety, that is to say, they defined only difficult and unusual words, generally "inkhorn terms" of foreign origin. The first in this genre was Robert Cawdrey's *Table Alphabeticall*, published in 1604. It was a small list of twenty-five hundred words defined as succinctly as possible, often using a synonym.[15] It was soon followed by a host of imitators: John Bullokar's *English Expositor* (1616),[16] Henry Cockeram's *English Dictionarie* (1623),[17] Thomas Blount's *Glossographia* (1656),[18] Edward Phillips's *New World of English Words* (1658),[19] and Elisha Coles's *English Dictionary* (1676).[20] According to lexicographer Jonathan Green, such works were aimed at "the educationally insecure: non-scholars, the *nouveau riche* aspirants to a higher class . . . and the wives of already established gentry. . . . They were, one might suggest, not so much works of reference as the linguisitic etiquette books of their period."[21]

In the early eighteenth century, two professional lexicographers, John Kersey and Nathan Bailey, created popular works that included both common and hard words. John Kersey's first work, *A New English Dictionary* (1702), contained twenty-eight thousand entries, many of them common words. The title page announced that the book was "chiefly designed for the benefit of Young Scholars, Tradesman, Artificers, and the Female Sex, who would learn to spell truly; being so fitted to every Capacity, that it may be a continual help to all that want an Instructor."[22] Kersey's definitions were often sloppy: "An *Apron*, for a Woman, &c."; "A *Elephant*, a Beast"; "A *Goat*, a Beast"; or "*May*, the most pleasant Month of the Year."[23] Yet his *New English Dictionary* was simple and inexpensive, and it stayed in print for over seventy years.

Strengthened by this success, Kersey undertook to revise Edward Phillips's *New World of English Words*, first published in 1658. In the process, he more than doubled the number of entries to thirty-eight thousand. His *New World of English Words*, or "Kersey-Phillips," as it was known, appeared in 1706.[24] Two years later, Kersey issued an abridged edition under the title *Dictionarium Anglo-Britannicum*, which contained the same entries as its predecessor but with shorter definitions and fewer cross-references.[25]

Kersey's successor, Nathan Bailey, was the most successful lexicographer of the eighteenth century, even if he has not been admitted into the literary canon. He established his reputation with his *Universal Etymological English Dictionary* of 1721. It contained forty thousand entries, more than any previous dictionary, including most common words (e.g., "*Man*, a Creature endued with Reason") and their etymologies. Yet it was printed inexpensively in a one-volume octavo (5 × 8–inch) edition and went through thirty editions until 1802, excluding reprints.[26] Editions published after 1755, when Johnson's *Dictionary* appeared, contained sixty-five thousand entries in one volume (compared with Johnson's forty thousand in two volumes).

Bailey followed the common tendency to increase the size and complexity of his work from one edition to the next. This left a niche for a "people's dictionary," one that was intended not to delight the educated but to instruct those whose "Education, Reading and Leisure are bounded within a narrow Compass." That niche was filled by Thomas Dyche and William Pardon's *New General English Dictionary*, first published in 1735. It was very short, with only twenty thousand entries, and measured only five by eight inches.

(In comparison, Johnson's dictionary occupied two folio, or ten-by-seventeen-inch, volumes.) It was also poorly written, with no cross-references, many errors, and very uneven editing. But it included vulgar terms and "cant," or slang, words no refined dictionary would touch, and it was cheap. Thus it went through twenty-one editions by 1794, plus translations into French.[27]

The success of Bailey's *Universal Etymological Dictionary* led him to issue an expanded version in 1730 entitled *Dictionarium Britannicum.*[28] A folio volume with forty-eight thousand entries, it was the most comprehensive dictionary in the English language up to that time, marked by advances in definitions, etymologies, and—for the first time—the pronunciation of words. This was the source for Johnson's choice of words and for many of his definitions.[29]

Despite the popularity and usefulness of Kersey's, Bailey's, and Dyche and Pardon's works, Samuel Johnson is the only lexicographer still remembered two centuries later. That is because Johnson aimed much higher: he sought to do single-handedly and well in eight years what the French academicians had done poorly in sixty. And he succeeded.

What set Johnson's dictionary apart from others and has endeared him to literary critics ever since was his definitions and quotations. Most of his definitions are succinct and pithy. *Excise,* for example, is "a hateful tax levied upon commodities, and adjudged not by the common judges of property, but wretches hired by those to whom excise is paid." *Lexicographer* means "a harmless drudge, that busied himself in tracing the original, and detailing the signification of words." Most important of all were the 118,000 quotations, most of them from English literature of the period 1590–1660, that he used to illustrate his 43,500 entries.[30]

In his *Plan of a Dictionary of the English Language,* written in 1747, Johnson had proposed that "one great end of this undertaking is to fix the English language." Like others, he believed that English had reached a state of perfection, like Cicero's Latin or Plato's Greek, from which it could only decline, unless it were rescued by a dictionary like those of the Accademia della Crusca or the French Academy.[31] Yet by the time his dictionary was completed eight years later, Johnson had recognized the futility of that aim:

> When we see men grow old and die at a certain time one after another, from century to century, we laugh at the elixir that promises to prolong life to a thousand years; and with equal justice may the lexicographer be derided, who . . . shall imagine that his dictionary can embalm his language, and secure it from corruption and decay.[32]

Johnson's dictionary represents the last gasp of the classical tradition, the belief that "we retard what we cannot repel, . . . we palliate what we cannot cure."

Less than a generation later, lexicography was thrown wide open not by English literati but by events in France. Presaging the Revolution was the three-volume *Dictionnaire critique* of Jean-François Féraud, published in 1787–1788.[33] Rejecting the normative view of lexicography, Féraud declared his work open to new words and expressions, as well as the ever-growing technical vocabulary.[34] Change was in the air. The "classical" French authors of the seventeenth century—Molière, Racine, Corneille, Fénelon, and others—were falling out of fashion. Moreover, the permanence of words was undermined by the philosophe Condillac, for whom words not only expressed ideas that already existed but also developed in symbiosis with new ideas. Linnaeus had shown the way with his system of naming plants, and Lavoisier was doing the same with the vocabulary of chemistry.

The French Revolution brought not only new social groups into power but also their vocabulary into common use. New words such as *anarchiste, amendement, démocratie,* and *département* entered into everyday use.[35] Besides politics, romanticism and industrialization also spawned new vocabularies, and such pressures of change broke the resistance of lexicographers. As Jean-Charles Laveaux explained in the preface to his *Dictionnaire de la langue française* (1820):

> The dictionary of a language must form itself, increase, and improve at the same pace that the language it represents forms itself, increases, and improves. The lexicographer must neither propose nor invent new words and expressions. The secretary of usage, he must strive to know it well, to follow it in its progress and variations, and to trace all its movements.[36]

Even more forcefully, the preface to A. de Rodier's *Nouveau dictionnaire français-espagnol* (1826) declared: "The dictionary, passive witness of all the revolutions of thought, must conserve even its aberrations. He is not the judge, but the recorder of languages; he does not argue, he registers; he has but one law, and that is usage; he has but one arbiter, time."[37]

From Dictionaries to Encyclopedias

Even as dictionaries evolved from defining "hard words" to giving the origins and meanings of words, another change was taking place in reference works that explained "not only the terms of art, but the arts themselves." This evolution began with the appearance of historical and technical dictionaries in the late seventeenth and early eighteenth centuries and culminated, a century later, in the publication of popular and frequently revised "conversation" encyclopedias. This trend paralleled the publication of far larger and costlier "universal" encyclopedias, to which I will turn later. The competition between the two genres represents two distinct conceptions of information and the evolution from information-as-knowledge to information-as-data.

This process began toward the end of the seventeenth century with the historical dictionaries of Moréri and Bayle. Louis Moréri (1643–1680) first published his *Grand dictionnaire historique* in 1674. As the subtitle explained, it was a "curious mixture of sacred and profane history."[38] It quickly proved popular, for it contained biographical sketches of famous Catholic and aristocratic notables. Long after the author died in 1680, publishers continued to issue new and expanded editions, from the two-volume edition of 1681 to the twenty-fourth edition of 1759 in ten volumes.[39]

Some years later, Pierre Bayle (1647–1706), a French Calvinist living in exile in Holland, began writing a refutation and correction of Moréri's work, but he soon expanded the project into a biographical dictionary of Protestant notables entitled *Dictionnaire historique et critique* (1697). Although Bayle carefully backed up his ideas with facts and sources, his skeptical view of religion got him in trouble with both Protestants and Catholics. Perhaps for this reason, his work proved enduringly popular. It was reissued many times after his death, growing from its original two volumes until it reached sixteen volumes in its eleventh and last incarnation in 1820.[40]

The earliest technical dictionary was John Harris's *Lexicon technicum*, which first appeared in 1704. Despite its Latin title, it was, as its subtitle indicates, "an Universal English Dictionary of Arts and Sciences."[41] It was a short work, with eighty-two hundred entries in one volume; later editions expanded it to two volumes and twelve thousand entries. It was the first book in English to deal systematically with the physical sciences, navigation, mathematics, and commercial arithmetic, along with short entries on grammar and philosophy. Unlike Moréri and Bayle, Harris avoided biographies and theology. His dictionary achieved a modest commercial success: the first edition (1704) had nine hundred subscribers, and the supplement published in 1710 had twelve hundred. Its importance, however, lay in bringing technology and science into reference works.

Harris was soon followed by other technical encyclopedists, like Ephraim Chambers, whose *Cyclopaedia* appeared in 1728.[42] This work was considerably longer and more detailed than Harris's, beginning with a two-volume folio edition and eventually growing to five volumes. Chambers's *Cyclopaedia* was more than a dictionary but less than a general encyclopedia; it was a hybrid, an encyclopedic dictionary. It was especially strong in Newtonian science, in the philosophy of Locke, and in such technologies as dyeing, brewing, engraving, and candle making, but it was weak in history, geography, and biography. To illustrate its entries, it included many full-page and foldout engravings. Chambers's *Cyclopaedia* had another virtue besides its impressive coverage. It was the first work to make systematic use of cross-references, such as "Acoustics, see also Ear, Hearing, Phonics." It also included an index of terms that did not merit entries of their own. It was a handy and efficient reference tool.

Not surprisingly, the *Cyclopaedia* went through many editions, the last in 1795. It also inspired many later and more famous works. Diderot and d'Alembert's *Encyclopédie* began as a project to translate Chambers into French, and the first editions of two well-known English encyclopedias, the *Encyclopaedia Britannica* and Abraham Rees's *Cyclopaedia,* clearly imitated Chambers.

The idea of a practical and accessible reference work originated in Germany in the early eighteenth century. In 1704, the Leipzig bookseller Gleditsch pioneered a type of reference work aimed at meeeting the needs of the reading public rather than serving as a monument of scholarly erudition. In the words of Ernst Lehmann, the historian of this genre, its purpose was "to explain the most important contemporary problems . . . in a short, easily understood manner."[43]

The first such work was *Reales Staats- und Zeitungs-Lexicon* (Factual political and newspaper reference book; 1704), meant to explain words that appeared in newspapers. Though it was written by Philipp Balthasar Sinold von Schütz, the book became known as "Hübners" after Johann Hübner, who wrote the preface. One of the most successful eighteenth-century German publications, it went through thirty-one editions, the last one in 1824–1828, more than a century after the first.[44] By the fourth edition, published in 1709, the title had changed to *Reales Staats-, Zeitungs- und Conversations-Lexicon* (Factual political, newspaper, and conversation reference book), a compendium of knowledge useful in social conversations, at the time a popular bourgeois entertainment. In German the expression *Konversations-lexicon* is still used to designate a short, up-to-date encyclopedia.

The Hübners had many rivals throughout the eighteenth century, such as Marperger's *Curieuses Natur-, Kunst-, Berg-, Gewerk- und Handlungs-Lexicon* (1712), a practical reference book that explained commercial, scientific, and craft terms.[45] The best-known was Jablonski's *Allgemeines Lexicon,* first published in 1721.[46] It privileged scientific and technical subjects at the expense of theoretical ones; for instance, *Wein* (wine) got over five columns, and *Wallfisch* (whale) got three, while *Geometrie* received twenty-two lines and *Logick* only seventeen. Jablonski's position as first secretary of the Prussian Academy and tutor to Prince Frederick William of Prussia helped legitimize German as the language of the educated, on a par with Latin and French.[47] Another example of this genre with a revealing title was Roth's *Gemein-nütziges Lexikon,* or "Commonly Useful Lexicon for Readers of all Classes, Especially for the Uneducated."[48]

The German "conversational" encyclopedia became an institution in the early nineteenth century, thanks to the genius of Friedrich Brockhaus. In 1808, he bought the surplus copies of an unfinished and unsuccessful work by Renatus Löbel and Christian Franke entitled *Conversations-Lexicon* and hired writers to complete it. The first six volumes appeared in 1809, and a two-volume supplement came out in the next two years.[49] It was aimed at a popular, not a scholarly, audience, and its short, up-to-date articles were tightly packed with information dealing with topics in the arts and sciences that might arise "in social conversation."

Although this edition sold only two thousand copies, that was enough to warrant a new edition. The second edition, in ten volumes, began appearing in 1812 and sold three thousand copies within a year. The later volumes of that edition were still being issued when Brockhaus decided to begin a third edition. From 1814 through 1819, volumes of the second, third, and fourth editions were being sold simultaneously, as printers struggled to keep up with the demand. To boost sales, Brockhaus offered rebates to customers who traded in their old editions for new ones. The fifth edition (1819–1820) sold twelve thousand copies within a year and twenty thousand more over the next three years. By the 1830s, Brockhaus was selling thirty thousand copies of each new edition and inspiring numerous imitators.[50]

The *Brockhaus* grew larger with each edition. The fifth edition, in ten volumes, was so large that Brockhaus, recognizing the transition to a new genre, named it *Real-Encyclopädie für die gebildeten Stände (Conversations-Lexicon)*, or "Factual Encyclopedia for the Educated Classes (Conversation-Lexicon)." To stay competitive in the low end of the market, he then published a smaller and cheaper *Deutsche Taschen-Encyklopädie oder Handbibliothek des Wissenswürdigsten* (German pocket encyclopedia or hand-library of the most useful knowledge).[51]

In its first edition of 1771, the *Encyclopaedia Britannica; or, a Dictionary of Arts and Sciences, Compiled upon a New Plan*, was an English-language analogue of the German *Konversations-lexicon* rather than a general encyclopedia.[52] Its beginnings were humble. Although its title page proclaimed that it was the work of "a society of gentlemen in Scotland," it was actually created by the printer Colin Macfarquhar and the engraver Andrew Bell, who hired an unemployed scholar, William Smellie, to write the text. Unlike his contemporary Diderot, Smellie did not rely on experts, a costly and time-consuming process, but compiled his information from a few well-known books. The result was a short work—three volumes, or 2,659 quarto pages—written in a mere three years. As the preface explains, the purpose of the book was as modest as its means: "Utility ought to be the principal intention of every publication. Whenever this intention does not plainly appear, neither the books nor their authors have the slightest claim to the approbation of mankind."

The "new plan" mentioned in the title was a compromise between the encyclopedic and the dictionary traditions. Forty-four "treaties or systems" dealt with themes that Smellie considered important, namely, the sciences, medicine, crafts, mathematics, and business. These entries could be quite long: "medicine" occupied 111 pages, "arithmetick" 58 pages, "surgery" 39 pages. Another thirty entries occupied three pages or more. Everything else was slighted. Apart from the long "treatises," the book was filled with very short dictionary-type entries, such as "WOMAN, the female of man. See HOMO," or "APIARY, a place where bees are kept."

The choice of topics probably reflected not only the interests of Smellie and his colleagues but also those of prospective readers. The first *Britannica* was sold both by subscription and in three-volume sets. It created no stir in the literary world, but the three thousand sets that were sold were enough to make the venture profitable and induce Macfarquhar and Bell to expand it into a larger "universal" encyclopedia.

The second *Britannica*, written by James Tytler and issued between 1778 and 1784, was approximately three times longer than the first. Some of the articles were expanded, such as "medicine" to 309 pages or "geography" to 195 pages. It also included history and biographies, two previously neglected areas, as well as botanical tables and a list of sources. Despite its length, it sold forty-five hundred copies, even more than the first.

As before, the publishers decided to issue a new edition. Unlike previous editions, the third *Britannica* (1794–1797) included articles by several contributors. It was twice as long as the second edition, filling eighteen volumes, or 14,579 pages, with 542 plates. It was even more successful than its predecessors, selling thirteen thousand copies and making a profit of forty-two thousand pounds.[53] Thus did the *Britannica* become an ongoing business producing periodically revised editions to serve a growing public of educated (and would-be educated) people.

Universal Encyclopedias

The same age that produced the *Cyclopaedia*, the *Britannica*, and the *Brockhaus* also created several enormous encyclopedias. The driving forces behind these ambitious attempts were seldom printers or booksellers but instead were men who believed that knowledge is finite and comprehensible. What is amazing is not that they failed to encompass all knowledge in one great work but that some are still remembered and revered, and occasionally consulted.

The first of the new encyclopedists of the Age of Reason was the Franciscan friar Vincenzo Marco Coronelli, an ambitious ecclesiastic who befriended kings and aristocrats and got elected minister-general of the

Franciscan order in 1701.[54] Before becoming an encyclopedist, he was already a famous cartographer, a globe maker, and the author of hundreds of books on a wide variety of subjects. Yet these achievements did not fully absorb his prodigious energy, and he decided that creating an encyclopedia would enhance his reputation.

His inspiration came in part from the long-revered *Historia naturalis* of Pliny the Elder (A.D. 23–79) and in part from the success of contemporary works such as Moréri's, Bayle's, and Johann Jacob Hoffmann's *Lexicon universale historico-geographico-chronologico-poëtico-philologicum* (1677), with its biographies and genealogies of princely families. Coronelli had a more ambitious goal, however: to write a complete encyclopedia in forty-five volumes, the first such work in Italian with entries in alphabetical order, to be entitled *Biblioteca universale.* He chose the Tuscan form of Italian instead of Latin to make the work accessible to the less educated, including lower-ranking Franciscan friars.

In order to produce an encyclopedia efficiently—for he was involved in dozens of other projects at the same time—Coronelli devised an elaborate plan. First he would gather his historical and biographical data from Moréri, as corrected by Bayle, and his geographic information from Baudrand's *Geographia,* as corrected in Sanson's *Disquisitiones geographicae.*[55] As his biographer James Fuchs explained:

> The idea of absorbing these two works [Moréri and Bayle] into his own was an extremely attractive one; and because Coronelli also had Bayle and Sanson at his side, he had the means of improving upon the two masters, Moréri and Baudrand, without having to do any research.[56]

Better yet, he found a way to get others to do the writing for him. As minister-general of the Franciscan order, he ordered Franciscan monasteries to subscribe to his encyclopedia. He also insisted that the friars contribute entries and that they educate the lower ranks of the order, so they could contribute too. He also solicited information and articles from the many well-placed individuals he knew throughout Europe, asking all contributors to subscribe to earlier volumes and subscribers to contribute to future ones. According to Fuchs, "For the more people there were who contributed, the more information there was to be shared; and the more diverse this group of contributors and subscribers was, the more opportunities there were for people to learn from each other, and to expand each other's horizons."[57] Only seven of the planned forty-five volumes were published.[58] Not surprisingly, his work was especially strong on geography, with multipage articles on such topics as Bavaria, England, Alexandria, Brindisi, and—naturally, for a Franciscan—Assisi. He also treated foreign cultures, languages, and religions, especially those of the Middle East.

In going ahead with such a bold project, Coronelli took some ideological risks. Unlike previous minister-generals, he was not a church
scholar but a modern, almost secular, man imbued with ideas about universal (as opposed to doctrinal) truth. His admiration for the Calvinist and
freethinker Bayle brought him to the attention of the Inquisition. Some
Franciscans disliked being forced to subscribe and resented having to inte-
grate the lower and upper ranks of the order. And so in 1704, Pope Clement
XI suspended Coronelli from the leadership of the order, putting an end to
the *Biblioteca universale.*

When Johann Heinrich Zedler began publishing his *Grosses vollständiges
Universal-Lexicon* in 1732, he intended it to be twelve volumes long.[59] Zedler
and his successor, the philosopher Carl Günther Ludovici, persuaded professors at the University of Halle and the University of Leipzig to contribute entries. As a result, the work grew ever longer until, in the words
of lexicographer Ernst Lehmann, "it stands before us like a proud baroque
building."[60] The first half of the alphabet (*A* through *L*) took up eighteen
volumes, but *M* through *Z* took forty-six, with the letter *U* alone occupying six volumes and the letter *S* occupying nine. As a result, when it was
finished in 1754, it filled sixty-four volumes plus a four-volume supplement.

The *Universal-Lexicon* was "universal" in that it covered all topics, even,
after the letter *M,* the biographies of living persons. Though it featured entries on tiny villages and obscure mountains and rivers, its geography was
very biased; the city of Leipzig received 159 columns (79 pages), while Berlin
got only 2; Lapland took up 64 columns, but France only 10; and information about faraway places like Africa and America was very out of date. The
entries on philosophy were also very local, with the philosopher Christian
Wolf getting 128 columns and "Wolfische Philosophie," 349.

Science occupied a large part of the *Universal-Lexicon,* but it was still
largely pre-Newtonian, even pre-Galilean. In Zedler's opinion, "The purpose of the study of science . . . is nothing more nor less than to combat
atheism, and to prove the divine nature of things." Many entries dealt with
such arcana as necromancy, chiromancy, witchcraft, and perpetual motion. While Johann Sebastian Bach rated only a single column, alchemical
concepts such as vitriols got 234 and powders, 282. So obsolete were the entries that Ludovici, who inherited the work from Zedler, published a four-
volume supplement to correct the errors in the previous sixty-four.
Although the work had fifteen hundred subscribers and sold fifty-five hundred copies, no one thought of producing a second edition, for the attention of the educated public had turned to a much more exciting work, the
Encyclopédie.

If the *Encyclopédie* is still fondly remembered, it is because of Diderot and d'Alembert's radical philosophy. In the article "Encyclopédie," Diderot announced that his goal was "to assemble all knowledge scattered on the surface of the Earth, to expose its general system to the men with whom we live, and to transmit it to the men who will come after us." The "general system" in question was based on a schematic "tree of knowledge" that Francis Bacon (1561–1626) had proposed a century earlier, which placed man at the center, with philosophy as the trunk. Religion was but one of the branches, on a par with superstition and magic. Knowledge could come only from observation and inductive reasoning, not from revelation or traditional authorities.[61]

To a cultured class that was losing its passion for religious faith but had not yet surrendered to the passions of secular ideologies, secular humanism was clearly subversive and, for that reason, exciting, dangerous, and seductive. Though we can extol (or excoriate) the philosophy that inspired this monumental work, we must not forget that it was not only philosophy disguised as an encyclopedia but also an actual working encyclopedia.

The *Encyclopédie* was, after Zedler's, the longest and most complete compendium of information ever published up to that time. In its original folio edition, it contained seventeen volumes of text plus eleven volumes containing 2,885 clear, detailed engravings. To write its 71,818 entries, Diderot and d'Alembert recruited some 135 collaborators. Some, like Buffon and Voltaire, were already famous, while others—Rousseau, Turgot, and Necker—were soon to be. Diderot is said to have written five thousand entries himself.

The most radical innovation, after the philosophy itself, was the editors' insistence on covering the *métiers,* or crafts, by describing and illustrating them profusely. Here, especially, their method was inductive, as the prospectus explains:

> We turned to the most skilled workers of Paris and of the kingdom. We went to the trouble of visiting the workshops, of questioning them, of writing under their dictation, of developing their thoughts, of finding the appropriate terms of their professions, of listing and defining them.[62]

They devoted forty-four pages to glassmaking, thirty-three to masonry, and twenty-five to mills. To the readers of the *Encyclopédie,* perusing such articles and engravings constituted intellectual voyeurism. To posterity, however, they are a precious document in the history of preindustrial technology. No subsequent encyclopedia has dared present radical ideas, yet all of them offer articles on various technologies with illustrations of machines and devices.

Not surprisingly, given its fame, the *Encyclopédie* has long attracted the attention of historians. Most have concentrated on its notoriety, the protests of the church, and its political troubles. In addition, we now have, thanks to Robert Darnton, a clear picture of the business history of the *Encyclopédie*, which describes the various editions and how many copies were sold.[63] Because of the enormity of the task and the various political obstacles it had to overcome, the original folio edition came out in spurts between 1751 and 1772. Although it cost 980 livres—a small fortune—it nonetheless attracted four thousand subscribers from the wealthiest and most cultured classes of Europe. It also proved to be extremely profitable to its original publisher, André-François Le Breton, and to his successor, Charles-Joseph Panckoucke.

This commercial success caught the attention of printers in Switzerland and Italy, who could turn out cheaper copies and smuggle them into France. The first of these pirated editions were also in the large folio size. One printed in Lucca between 1758 and 1776 sold three thousand copies at 737 livres; another, from Geneva (1771–1776), sold two thousand copies at 840 livres; a third, from Leghorn (1770–1778), sold fifteen hundred copies at 574 livres. Then came several smaller versions: the Geneva and Neuchâtel quarto editions (1777–1778), which sold over eight thousand copies at 384 livres, and the Lausanne and Bern octavo editions (1778–1782), selling six thousand copies at 225 livres, or one-quarter the price of the original.[64] Between the original and the pirated editions, the *Encyclopédie* sold twenty-five thousand sets at an average of thirty volumes per set, or three-quarters of a million books in all. Without a doubt, the *Encyclopédie* was the best-selling work of its age, reaching educated readers—lawyers, priests, doctors, and other professionals—throughout Europe. As Darnton explains: "A quarto on the shelf would proclaim its owner's standing as a man of knowledge and as a philosophe."[65]

The success of the *Encyclopédie* inspired not only plagiarists but also writers and publishers who believed they could improve on it. The first of these was Panckoucke, the wealthiest and most successful publisher in Europe, who had bought the rights to the *Encyclopédie* from Le Breton in 1768. Panckoucke decided that the *Encyclopédie* had neglected too many topics, that it contained too many duplications and awkward cross-references, and that the plates were poorly integrated with the text. In 1782 he therefore announced a work to be called *Encyclopédie méthodique, ou par ordre de matières* (Methodical encyclopedia in thematic order). Instead of containing entries on every subject arranged alphabetically, as in the original *Encyclopédie*, this work would be composed of twenty-six "dictionaries," each one to include "everything that is true and real in the science or the art that it deals with."[66] Each dictionary would contain an analytical table "indicating the order in which the main entries should be read in order to transform them into coherent didactic treatises."[67] Finally, the *Vocabulaire universel* would combine a "supreme repertory of every idea and every word in the French language" with an index to the articles in the other twenty-six volumes.[68] The entire work would occupy forty-two volumes of text and seven of plates, or 50 percent more text than Diderot's, but at a lower price.

Panckoucke aimed at a market that publishers had only recently discovered: "not an elite already informed of scientific and philosophical discoveries, but a growing public opinion coming essentially from the bourgeoisie, whose members have not always had a very careful and modern education, but whose curiosity, as adults, has not died out."[69]

"If we carry out our plan exactly," he wrote to his subscribers in 1787, "you will find everything that men have conceived, imagined, and created since the art of writing was invented. There will not be a single word, a single object of human knowledge about which you will not find satisfying details."[70] The result would be "a complete and universal library of all human knowledge," "one of the most beautiful monuments that men in any age have ever raised to the glory of letters, sciences, and arts," "the richest, the largest, the most interesting, the most exact, the most complete and the best organized anthology that anyone might desire," and "the greatest and the most useful of enterprises ever undertaken since books have been printed."[71]

To achieve this exalted result, Panckoucke had clerks cut apart two copies of the *Encyclopédie* and file the articles under his twenty-six rubrics. He then recruited the most famous academic specialists he could find, gave them the clippings, and asked them to bring the text up to the highest standards.

Unfortunately, academicians were well paid by the state and had no reason to respect limits of time or space.[72] Some procrastinated for years and produced nothing. Others produced works that were complete, up-to-date, and gigantic. Jean-Baptiste de Lamarck, asked to write a two-volume work on botany, produced eight volumes of text plus a five-volume supplement and five volumes of plates. Gaspard Monge wrote not one but five volumes on physics. Guyton de Morveau's dictionary of chemistry grew from one to five and a half volumes.

Panckoucke contributed to this inflation by adding ever more dictionaries: mathematical amusements, gardening, "academic arts" (horseback riding, fencing, dancing, and swimming), hunting, fishing, trees and forestry, artillery, music, police and municipalities, even separate dictionaries for worms, arachnids, and zoophytes.[73]

By 1788, it was clear that the *Encyclopédie méthodique* would be far larger and take many years longer than anticipated. The work grew, first to thirty-six dictionaries in 60 or more volumes, then to fifty-one dictionaries in 124 or more volumes. Needing money, Panckoucke wrote to his five thousand subscribers:

If we had limited ourselves to give only 57 to 60 volumes as we assumed we would in the Prospectus, the *Encyclopédie* would have once again been a failure. . . . To reduce today the number of volumes that the Authors have judged necessary to complete this great work would be to mutilate it, to cause its ruin. The *Encyclopédie* would become a monster that we would regret having produced.[74]

Then came the French Revolution. Panckoucke's print shops, which previously had turned out ten volumes per year, now found more lucrative work printing pamphlets and broadsheets. Authors became distracted by politics. Subscribers dropped out. Panckoucke tried to keep his project alive by adding a volume on the Constituent Assembly. But in 1794, age and impending financial ruin forced him to hand over the business to his son-in-law. Volumes continued to appear one by one until 1832, long after Panckoucke and most of his original authors and subscribers had died.

The *Encyclopédie méthodique* ended up with $166\frac{1}{2}$ volumes of text, plus supplements, atlases, and plates, bringing the total to around 200 volumes. About half the work was devoted to the sciences, reflecting the enthusiasm of the French reading public. These volumes summed up the state of the sciences at the time they were written, but new discoveries quickly rendered them obsolete. The same was true of the sections on philosophy, jurisprudence, and even the arts.

It is no surprise that encyclopedias, like other works of erudition, become obsolete in time; the publishers of the *Britannica* and the *Brockhaus* knew this, too. Panckoucke, however, believed that all knowledge could be captured in one work, if only it were long enough. Unfortunately, the *Encyclopédie méthodique* lacked the redeeming qualities of Diderot's *Encyclopédie*. It was neither polemical nor radical, and its engravings were no match for Diderot's. It now occupies yards of library shelf space, all but forgotten by scholars.

The success of the *Encyclopédie* and the flood of new information also inspired German intellectual entrepreneurs to dream of capturing all of human knowledge in a single all-encompassing work. The results were, along with Panckoucke's, among the longest works ever published.[75]

When Johann Georg Krünitz began publishing his *Oeconomisch-technologische Encyklopädie* in 1773,[76] the letter *A* took up two and a half volumes, each one six to eight hundred pages long. As he continued writing, the amount of economic, technological, and scientific information that came his way increased exponentially. Thus the letter *K* occupied twenty-six volumes and took nine years to write; the letter *L* occupied twenty-four and a half volumes and took sixteen years. By the time he died, Krünitz had written seventy-three volumes, or fifty-one thousand pages, and the work was only half finished. His successors labored on, taking twenty-one years to write the fifty volumes of the letter *S*. The last volume, number 242, appeared in 1858, eighty-five years after the first.

In 1818, Samuel Ersch and Johann Gottfried Gruber issued the first volume of their *Allgemeine Enzyklopädie der Wissenschaften und Künste*. By the time they completed the letter *G*, they had reached volume 99. The article "Griechenland" (Greece) alone occupied eight volumes, or 3,668 pages. The publisher, Brockhaus, continued to issue volumes long after the original authors had died but finally ended the project, still incomplete at volume 167, in 1889.[77]

The Alphabetical versus the Thematic Order

The way in which information is arranged in a reference work—whether in short or long entries, in thematic or alphabetical order, with cross-references or indexes—reveals a great deal about how the authors intended it to be used. The Age of Reason was characterized by an ongoing tension between two conflicting views: whether to regard encyclopedias as works of reference designed to help the reader retrieve specific information efficiently or as works of erudition aimed at educating the reader. Behind this tension lay divergent views of information (as knowledge or as data) and of readers (as persons of leisure seeking general knowledge or as people in a hurry needing specific information). The alphabetical order emerged as the key characteristic of compendia designed for efficient information retrieval, while the thematic arrangement characterized works of didactic erudition. The tension between the two systems ran through the entire period under consideration here and has by no means been resolved two centuries later.

The alphabet dates back thousands of years. From the beginning, the letters have always been arranged in the well-known "alphabetical" order, and thus it is surprising to note how many seventeenth- and eighteenth-century works have the word *alphabet* in the title: Cawdrey's *Table Alphabeticall*, Coronelli's *Biblioteca . . . con ordine alfabetico*, the *Encyclopaedia Britannica . . . in the order of the alphabet*, Ersch and Gruber's *Allgemeine Encylopädie . . . in alphabetischer Folge*, Rees's *Cyclopedia . . . in one Alphabet*, Krünitz's *Oeconomisch-technologische Encyklopädie . . . in alphabetischer Ordnung*, Roth's *Gemeinnütziges Lexikon . . . in alphabetischer Ordnung*, and many others. How could this familiar order have been such a novelty in the seventeenth and eighteenth centuries that it merited a mention in the titles of reference works?

The idea of arranging words (not just letters) alphabetically occurred many times. The ancient Greeks used it sporadically, as did the Romans; but as the philologist Lloyd Daly pointed out, "For each example cited, there are hundreds of documents where the principle might have been used but was not."[78] Pliny the Elder, in his *Historiae naturalis,* listed alphabetically only those plants that he could not classify botanically.[79]

In the Middle Ages, human science was seen as an attempt to approach God's science. Some medieval encyclopedists organized their works to follow the pattern of Creation, as in Genesis, others according to the Bible and the church fathers, to help priests composing sermons. In the twenty parts in Isidore of Seville's *Etymologiae* (636), only one—a dictionary—was in alphabetical order.[80] Medieval glossaries were often arranged alphabetically by the first letter or two of each word, but seldom more.[81] In his glossary *Elementarium doctrinae erudimentum* (c. 1053), Papias explained:

> Anyone who wishes to find anything quickly must also notice that this whole book is composed according to the alphabet not only in the first letters of the parts but also in the second, third and sometimes even in the further determinative arrangement of the letters.[82]

Papias's system was soon forgotten, however. One hundred forty-six years later, Peter of Cornwall, having compiled a list of biblical terms in the order of their appearance in the Bible, added an alphabetical index, explaining that it would allow the reader "to find quite easily what is sought, according to a new method, alphabetical order."[83]

By the thirteenth century, first-letter alphabetical order was commonly used for such scholastic tools as concordances to the Bible, interpretations of Hebrew names, indexes to law books and to the works of Aristotle and the church fathers, and the occasional library catalog. But it was never used in the vernacular, for popular usage, or for administrative purposes such as tax rolls or lists of tenants.[84]

Thus, in 1286, Giovanni di Genoa again felt the need to explain the system to the readers of his *Catholicon:*

> You may proceed everywhere according to the alphabet. So, according to this order you will easily be able to find the spelling of any word here included. For example I intend to discuss *amo* and *bibo.* I will discuss *amo* before *bibo* because *a* is the first letter of *amo* and *b* is the first letter of *bibo* and *a* is before *b* in the alphabet. . . . Now I have devised this order at the cost of great effort and strenuous application. Yet it was not I, but the grace of God working with me. I beg of you, therefore, good reader, do not scorn this great labor of mine and this order as something worthless.[85]

Giovanni's strenuous application notwithstanding, authors of glossaries and dictionaries preferred to list words by topic (say, birds on one page, four-legged creatures on another) or in the order in which they appeared in a well-known text, like the Bible.

The reason the alphabetical order was seldom used, though it was known and understood, is quite simple. Creating an alphabetical list of any length requires much time, effort, and costly parchment, and for texts that were intimately known or even memorized, such effort simply did not pay. Not until the advent of cheap paper and especially of printing, with its larger readership, was the effort justified.[86]

The first major reference work to be published in alphabetical order was Robert Cawdrey's *Table Alphabeticall*. In the preface, the author felt he needed to enlighten his readers:

> If thou be desirous (gentle Reader) rightly and readily to vnderstand, and to profit by this Table, and such like, then thou must learne the Alphabet, to wit, the order of the Letters as they stand, perfectly without booke, and where euery Letter standeth: as (b) neere the beginning, (n) about the middest, and (t) toward the end. Nowe if the word, which thou art desirous to finde, begin with (a) then looke in the beginning of this Table, but if with (v) looke towards the end. Againe, if thy word beginne with (ca) looke in the beginning of the letter (c) but if with (cu) then looke toward the end of that letter. And so of all the rest. &c.[87]

The alphabetical order finally became the norm in reference works in the last quarter of the seventeenth century. In 1677, Johann Jakob Hoffmann published the two-volume *Lexicon universale,* followed by the three-volume *Continuatio* in 1683, alphabetical but in Latin.[88] Moréri's *Grand Dictionnaire historique* came out in 1674, followed by Richelet's *Dictionnaire de la langue françoise* in 1680 and Furetière's *Dictionnaire universel* in 1690.

Their main competitor was the dictionary of the French Academy, in which words were arranged by their roots; thus under *faire* it defined not only *facile* and *façon,* but also *affaire, défectueux,* and *efficace,* while *s'acheminer* came under *chemin.* As the academicians explained:

> As the French language contains primitive words as well as derived and composite words, we judged that it would be pleasant and instructive to arrange the Dictionary by roots, that is, listing all the derived words under the primitive words from which they descend, whether these primitive ones are of purely French origin, or come from Latin or any other language.[89]

The result was a work that was "pleasant and instructive" for the educated, but difficult for everyone else.

One reason the alphabetical order was so seldom used was that there was no accepted spelling. Nor could there be an accepted spelling until there were authoritative dictionaries. Germans did not distinguish between the letters *i* and *j* or the letters *u* and *v* until the eighteenth century; thus, the entry for "Verstand" came before "Urteil." Likewise, the French Academy did not differentiate those letters until 1740. Other spelling issues

made the alphabetical order problematic. Silent letters were sometimes included and sometimes omitted, as in *advocat* and *avocat*, or *blasmer* and *blâmer*.
And spelling had to adjust to a changing pronunciation, as in the shift from
françois to *français*. Such issues were not resolved until the 1830s.[90]

There were also mistakes. In Cawdrey's work, a random sample of 218
entries showed that 12 percent were out of order. Sometimes the author
preferred one spelling and the printer another, but made changes without
reordering the words; thus *tiranize* appeared between *turbulent* and *type*.
Elsewhere, roots preceded derivatives, as in *captiue* before *captiuate*; Blount's
Glossographia (1656) put *epidemy* before *epidemical*, and *nugatory* before *nugation*.
Such deviation from the strict alphabetical order continued to occur
throughout the seventeenth and eighteenth centuries, at a rate of 6 to 8
percent in most dictionaries.[91]

Then there were works by authors who simply did not understand the
system. A case in point is the *Table alphabétique des dictionnaires* (1758) by Jacques
Bernard Durey de Noinville.[92] Despite its title, this bibliography of dictionaries jumps back and forth between a thematic and an alphabetical
arrangement. Thus it begins with an entry for "Dictionarium abstrusorum
vocabulorum" (perhaps because *abstrusorum* begins with *a*) and ends with
"Nouveau Dictionnaire du Voyageur" (because *voyageur* begins with *v*). It
lists all English-language dictionaries under *a*, for *Anglois*, but does not al-
phabetize them.

In encyclopedias, the alphabetical order raised issues that were far more
unsettling than these technical problems, for it challenged the older thematic arrangement. A thematic arrangement, by definition, arranges concepts according to a preconceived plan. To place concepts in alphabetical
order is to assume that their order has nothing to do with their importance. In his study of the *Biblioteca universale*, James Fuchs argues that
Coronelli's choice of the alphabetical order was motivated by just such
thinking:

> The topical encyclopedia became for him a symbol of all the hierarchies
> on earth that he opposed, and correspondingly, he thought that by ar-
> ranging his encyclopedia alphabetically, he was striking a symbolic blow
> against them. The alphabet was the great leveler. Religious matters
> would not be ranked above secular ones, mechanical skills would not be
> placed below intellectual ones, and articles on princes would appear side
> by side with articles on peasants. . . . Protestants and heretics would be
> placed side by side with Catholics, and this rhetorical ecumenicalism re-
> flected the "spirit of ecumenicalism" that characterized Coronelli's ca-
> reer and that placed him in the context of Leibnitz and other seven-
> teenth-century ecumenicalists. What a wonderful justification for an
> alphabetical encyclopedia![93]

Coronelli's egalitarian and ecumenical views were no doubt important factors, but there is a more likely reason he chose the alphabetical order: he was in a hurry to publish texts he obtained from his many contributors, and this urgency precluded any grand topical scheme. As text came in, he sought headings under which he could print it, and if there was no appropriate word in Italian, he simply picked a foreign word: from Arabic, *aakrab* (scorpion) and *aar* (year); from Hebrew, *aalma* (virgin); from Greek, *aantha* (earrings); from Latin, *abalienare* (alienate); and so on.[94] As a result, his work was neither logically arranged nor convenient for readers.

If Coronelli used the alphabetical order for his own convenience, his successors adopted it for the convenience of their readers. In the preface to his *Cyclopaedia*, Ephraim Chambers explained: "If the system be an improvement upon the Dictionary, the Dictionary is some advantage to the System; and that this is perhaps the only way in which the whole circle, or body of knowledge, with all its parts and dependencies, can be well delivered."[95] This idea, that the alphabetical order permits knowledge to be "well delivered," appears time and again in the literature on lexicography.

By the mid–eighteenth century, the alphabetical order had become the norm, as historian Georges Matoré explains: "Dictionaries and encyclopedias are presented alphabetically, a system that surely suits a society that likes facility and that would rather inform itself quickly and efficiently than accumulate extended knowledge."[96]

The philosophes of the Age of Reason were never comfortable with the alphabet. Voltaire complained that the word *alphabet* meant nothing more than "AB." Dumarsais, who wrote the article "Alphabet" in the *Encyclopédie*, noted a lack of conformity between some letters, such as *c, k,* and *q,* and the sounds they were supposed to represent; he advocated a new, more phonetic, spelling.[97]

The alphabetical order was also disturbing, for it brought out the contradiction between logic and practicality. In planning their *Encyclopédie*, Diderot and d'Alembert struggled with the contradiction between extended knowledge and efficient information retrieval. Their original plan was to present knowledge as a coherent system, based on Francis Bacon's tripartite division into memory and history, reason and philosophy, and imagination and poetry. At the beginning of their first volume was a large foldout chart entitled "Système figuré des connoissances humaines," representing the three branches of knowledge and human activity in three columns: history, philosophy, and poetry. In each column, topics were arranged according to the importance the editors attached to them, in the schematic representation of their secular humanist philosophy. Yet they chose to arrange the articles alphabetically, as they explained in their prospectus: "We believe we had good reasons to follow the alphabetical order in this work. It seemed more convenient and easier for our readers who, wishing to learn the meaning of a word, will find it more easily in an alphabetical Dictionary than in any other." They had a new type of reader in mind: "No longer the old-fashioned sage, whether cleric or layman, locked in his study for long hours of study and meditation, far from the agitation of the world, but a man in a hurry who looks up rather than reads, seeking an immediate answer to a precise question."[98] But how to connect the "immediate answer to a precise question" to their systematic chart of human knowledge? In the "Preliminary Discourse" they explain:

> It remains to show how we tried to reconcile in this Dictionary the encyclopedic order with the alphabetical order. For that we used three methods, the Systematic Chart at the beginning of this work, the Science to which each article refers, and the manner in which the article is treated. After the word which is the subject of the article, we normally put the name of the Science which this article is part of; one can simply see in the Systematic Chart the rank that this Science occupies to know the place that the article should have in the encyclopedia.[99]

To overcome the fragmentation of knowledge—what historian Pierre Rétat has called "the curse of the alphabetical order"—Diderot and d'Alembert used extensive cross-references, a system first introduced by Chambers in 1728 in his *Cyclopaedia*. However, they used the system poorly: many articles had no cross-references, while others sent the reader looking for nonexistent articles.[100]

Nonetheless, the tension remained between the encyclopedists' urge to write long, "encyclopedic" articles and the demands of the "man in a hurry" for "an immediate answer." To resolve this dilemma, Panckoucke published, without Diderot's permission, a two-volume *Table analytique*, or index, to the *Encyclopédie* by Pierre Mouchon.[101] Thus were born those indispensable tools needed to navigate long reference works: the cross-reference and the index.[102]

Objections to the alphabetical order arose soon after the *Encyclopédie* appeared. I have already described how Panckoucke presented his *Encyclopédie méthodique* as a more sensible arrangement than Diderot's original. The same logic motivated Samuel Taylor Coleridge to propose an alternative to the *Britannica*, to be called *Encyclopaedia Metropolitana*.[103] In his essay "On the Science of Method," Coleridge offered to provide:

> unity of design and of elucidation, the want of which we have most deeply felt in other works of similar kind, where the desired information is divided into innumerable fragments scattered over many volumes, like a mirror broken on the ground, presenting instead of one, a thousand images, but not entire.[104]

In an obvious reference to the *Britannica,* Coleridge denounced "a huge unconnected miscellany of the *omni scibile* [all that is knowable], in an arrangement determined by the accident of initial letters" and blamed it on "the
impudent ignorance of your Presbyterian booksellers."

While Coleridge blamed the alphabetical order on editors, others
pointed their fingers at readers. The Swedish classicist Adolf Törneros
complained that "Lexica, e.g. Conversations-Lexica, are like grocery stores,
where everybody can fetch his temporary or minute needs, like snuff for
two pence."[105] And as late as its *Dictionnaire's* seventh edition (1878), the
French Academy still yearned for the old arrangement by roots that it had
given up 160 years earlier:

> a more scientific arrangement, more pleasant for the reader who is curi-
> ous to know the genealogical history of words and to follow until our
> own time its successive generations, one that should perhaps have been
> kept, if dictionaries had what is called readers, but unfortunately too
> much trouble for the common public, which gets annoyed, when open-
> ing a Dictionary, if it does not immediately find the word it is seeking.[106]

The alternative, a compendium of knowledge organized along thematic lines, was appealing in theory but more problematic in practice.
Coleridge ran into the same problem that had troubled Panckoucke. He
had envisioned an encyclopedia as, in Robert Collison's words,

> an ordered form of education, in which an intelligent man might start
> at page 1 of volume One in a state of natural ignorance, and emerge at
> the end of the last volume with a balanced understanding of the world
> and its achievements. Coleridge, if he looked upon an encyclopaedia as
> a work of reference at all, regarded this aim as secondary to the main idea
> of the course of self-education which it was the encyclopaedia's duty to
> offer.[107]

The realities of a competitive publishing business soon undermined this
noble but quixotic ideal. The first publisher went bankrupt, the first volumes did not sell, and Coleridge withdrew from the project. A second
edition, issued between 1848 and 1858, consisted of forty-five volumes, each
on a different topic—for example, "History of the Ottoman Empire,"
"Manual of Electro-Metallurgy," or "Universal Grammar." Far from
offering a coherent education to an intelligent man in a state of natural ignorance, the *Metropolitana* ended up, like the *Encyclopédie méthodique,* as a series
of unrelated textbooks.[108]

The tension between integrated knowledge and efficient information
retrieval persists to this day. The fifteenth edition of the *Encyclopaedia
Britannica* (1987), with its *Propaedia* that attempts to organize knowledge thematically, its *Micropaedia,* with tens of thousands of short entries for quick
reference, and its *Macropaedia,* with four thousand in-depth articles, is a re-

cent attempt to have it both ways. Perhaps computers, with their hyper-
text links, will finally resolve the problem that Diderot, d'Alembert, and
all their followers have wrestled with for over two hundred years.

The Quantification of Reference Works

We should not gauge the value of a reference work by its reputation two
centuries later. The literary canon—how fondly a work is remembered by
intellectuals—measures its lasting influence but not its value to readers in
its own time. To know that, we need other criteria. As a crude approximation, let us look at some numbers.

In 1796, the English bibliographer William Marsden compiled the
Catalogue of Dictionaries, Vocabularies, Grammars, and Alphabets, listing every linguistic book in every language that he could find in the libraries of London,
Oxford, and Cambridge, as well as his own. A tabulation of the books in his
list by decade yields the information in table 1.

More recently, the lexicographer Bernard Quemada analyzed all
French-language reference works from the sixteenth through the mid–
nineteenth centuries, including subsequent editions of the more prominent ones and glossaries and specialized vocabularies. His list can be sum-
marized in table 2.

There is a remarkable parallel between the number of works cited by
Marsden and by Quemada (see fig. 13). In both cases the numbers stay approximately level throughout the seventeenth and early eighteenth centuries, then rise dramatically in the second half of the eighteenth century.
In the case of Quemada's French dictionaries, the numbers dropped in the
1780s and 1790s because of the Revolution, then soared again in the early
nineteenth century, reaching almost three hundred in the 1830s. Though
these figures may be incomplete, they nonetheless indicate a boom in the
supply of linguistic tools.[109]

The length of encyclopedias measures, very roughly, the amount of
information their editors thought important enough to print. This is not
the same as the amount of information that reached the public. A better
approximation of the demand for information is the popularity of a reference work, as measured by the number of editions. The most popular
books of the eighteenth and early nineteenth centuries were ephemera
such as almanacs and textbooks.[110] Yet reference works also did well. Some
reference works that originated in this period still exist, such as the
Dictionnaire de l'Académie française, first published in 1694; the *Encyclopaedia
Britannica,* which first appeared in 1771; *Brockhaus,* Germany's best-known series of dictionaries and encyclopedias, beginning with the *Conversations-
Lexicon* of 1809–1811; and, in the United States, the myriad "Webster's dictio-

TABLE 1. Number of Dictionaries, Vocabularies,
Grammars, and Alphabets in all Languages
Published by Decade, 1500–1789

Decade	Dictionaries
1500–1509	1
1510–1519	4
1520–1529	2
1530–1539	12
1540–1549	5
1550–1559	16
1560–1569	10
1570–1579	9
1580–1589	14
1590–1599	36
1600–1609	36
1610–1619	43
1620–1629	33
1630–1639	55
1640–1649	41
1650–1659	49
1660–1669	44
1670–1679	45
1680–1689	49
1690–1699	41
1700–1709	50
1710–1719	42
1720–1729	43
1730–1739	43
1740–1749	57
1750–1759	57
1760–1769	63
1770–1779	104
1780–1789	148

Source: William Marsden, A Catalogue of Dictionaries, Vocabularies, Grammars, and Alphabets (London, 1796).

naries" that trace their lineage back to Noah Webster's *American Dictionary of the English Language* of 1828.

Even within this period, there were some remarkable publishing successes. The *Vocabolario degli accademici della Crusca*, the first dictionary published by an academy, ran through twenty editions from 1612 to 1883. Moréri's *Grand dictionnaire historique*, first published in 1674, reached its twenty-fourth and last edition in 1759, not including eight German editions, six English ones, and one each in Spanish and Dutch. Antoine Furetière's *Dictionnaire universel* went through nine editions between 1690 and 1727. Pierre

TABLE 2. Number of French-Language Dictionaries
Published by Decade, 1540–1849.

Decade	Dictionaries
1540–1549	20
1550–1559	24
1560–1569	24
1570–1579	30
1580–1589	27
1590–1599	19
1600–1609	28
1610–1619	20
1620–1629	14
1630–1639	15
1640–1649	33
1650–1659	24
1660–1669	41
1670–1679	21
1680–1689	28
1690–1699	27
1700–1709	33
1710–1719	34
1720–1729	23
1730–1739	24
1740–1749	36
1750–1759	77
1760–1769	121
1770–1779	122
1780–1789	82
1790–1799	95
1800–1809	130
1810–1819	113
1820–1829	268
1830–1839	291
1840–1849	265

Source: Bernard Quemada, *Les dictionnaires du français moderne 1539–1863: Etude sur leur histoire, leurs types et leurs méthodes* (Paris: Didier, 1967), 567–634.

Bayle's *Dictionnaire historique et critique* remained popular throughout the eighteenth century; its eleventh and last edition (not including one German and four English translations) appeared in 1820.

In Germany also, encyclopedic dictionaries were often reprinted. The most successful of these was Hübner's *Reales Staats-, Zeitungs- und Conversations-Lexicon,* which went through thirty-one editions between 1704 and 1828.[111]

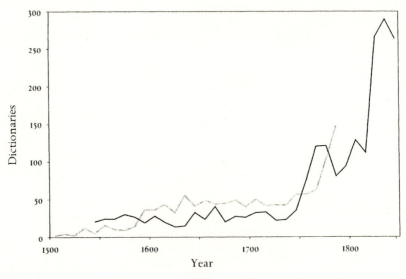

Figure 13. Number of dictionaries and other linguistic books, by decade, 1500–1849.

Three English works were also best-sellers, as measured by the number of editions and reprints. Nathan Bailey's *New Universal Etymological English Dictionary*, first published in 1755, reached its thirtieth edition by 1802.[112] Another popular work was Ephraim Chambers's *Cyclopaedia*, with twenty-three editions or reprints between 1728 and 1795, plus four Italian editions. The *New General English Dictionary*, by Thomas Dyche and William Pardon, had twenty-one English editions and four French translations between 1735 and 1794.

Finally, there is Diderot and d'Alembert's *Encyclopédie*. Although it was one of the longest works published up to that time and one of the most expensive books ever, it was nonetheless a best-seller. Besides the original edition and its many pirated copies, there were adaptations such as Felice's *Encyclopédie d'Yvernon* (1770–1780) and more distant translations and imitations such as the *Deutsche Encyclopädie* of 1778–1807, the *Edinburgh Encyclopedia* of 1808–1830, and the *British Encyclopaedia* of 1809.[113]

Yet another indicator of the demand for information is the increasing length of popular reference works in subsequent editions. Unlike works that started out enormous and were never reprinted (or, worse yet, never completed), the more popular reference works built on their reputation to keep up with the growth of knowledge and the public demand for information. Thus Moréri's *Grand dictionnaire historique* started out as a one-volume work, doubled in size in the second edition (1681), doubled again in 1692, and ended up, in its twenty-fourth and last edition in 1759, as a ten-volume compendium. Its rival, Bayle's *Dictionnaire historique et critique,* originally came out in two volumes, went through many editions as a four-volume work, and was reissued (or, more accurately, its name was used) as a sixteen-volume work in 1820. The first edition of the *Encyclopaedia Britannica* (1771) had three volumes and 2,659 pages. Its success emboldened its publishers to issue a ten-volume, 8,595-page edition in 1778–1784; then an eighteen-volume, 14,579-page third edition in 1797; a fourth edition of twenty volumes and 16,033 pages in 1801–1810; and so on. Finally, we might note the fastest-growing reference work of all, Abraham Rees's *Cyclopaedia,* which went from a five-volume work in 1778–1788 to a forty-five-volume work in 1819–1820.[114]

The most difficult question to answer is how many copies of a book were sold. Long encyclopedias were often sold by subscription, and the number of subscribers varied over the course of a publishing history that could take decades. In addition, in the absence of enforceable copyright laws, "official" editions had to compete with pirated ones; in the Netherlands, Switzerland, and northern Italy, publishers specialized in copies of French works, while American publishers flooded their newly independent country with pirated British works. Nonetheless, approximate as the numbers are, they still give a sense of the growing penetration of reference works.

In the early years of the eighteenth century, it took very few buyers to make a book popular. Harris's *Lexicon technicum* was considered a "commercial success" with nine hundred subscribers to the first edition (1704) and twelve hundred to the supplement (1710).[115] Similarly, the first edition of Chambers's *Cyclopaedia* had slightly under four hundred subscribers, yet it proved popular enough to warrant numerous later editions and translations.[116] Bayle's *Dictionnaire* (1697) was even more popular, with two thousand copies printed.[117]

By the midcentury, reference works were printed in greater volume. Zedler's *Universal-Lexicon* started out with fifteen hundred subscribers; fifty-five hundred copies were printed but not necessarily sold, which may explain why the enterprise went bankrupt.[118] In comparison, the Paris folio edition of Diderot's *Encyclopédie* had four thousand subscribers. Later pirated editions brought the total number sold to approximately twenty-five thousand.[119]

Another trend demonstrated the growing use of reference works among the middle class. This was the rising popularity of "portable" books in the quarto (approximately 7 × 10 inches), octavo (5 × 8 inches), or even smaller sizes, in place of the huge folio volumes of Johnson's *Dictionary* and the *Encyclopédie.*[120]

Reference works increased in popularity throughout the century. The first edition of the *Encyclopaedia Britannica* (1771) sold over three thousand sets at twelve pounds per set, a steep price for a three-volume work. The second edition (1778–1783), in ten volumes, sold forty-five hundred sets. The third edition (1787–1797), in eighteen volumes, sold thirteen thousand sets. The fourth edition, however, sold only four thousand sets, perhaps because it was really a reprint of the third with a two-volume supplement.[121]

In Germany, the gigantic works of Ersch and Gruber, Krünitz, and Zedler found few buyers. By the beginning of the nineteenth century, however, the German reading public was eager for an up-to-date and affordable encyclopedia, a demand that Friedrich Arnold Brockhaus knew how to satisfy. The first edition of his *Conversations-Lexicon,* in six volumes and a two-volume supplement (1808–1811), sold two thousand copies. The second edition (1812–1819) sold three thousand. The fifth edition in ten volumes, entitled *Allgemeine deutsche Real-Encyclopädie,* sold out twelve thousand copies within a year and another twenty thousand in the next three years. By the 1830s, Brockhaus was selling thirty thousand copies of each edition, some of which were published simultaneously. An encyclopedia had become one of the fixtures of a bourgeois household.[122]

This study of reference works of the Age of Reason is not an exercise in literary criticism but an attempt to investigate how the educated public of that age sought and used information. Three conclusions stand out. First, there was an unmistakable growth in the market for reference works, whether measured by the number of works published, their length, their growth, the number of editions, or the number of customers. Second, the reading public became increasingly interested in secular matters, especially science and technology, rather than theology. Third, the public favored works in alphabetical order designed for rapid reference, rather than didactic works arranged thematically. Erudition was being displaced by efficient information storage and retrieval systems.

Today, as computers make it easy to access and retrieve information, digitized reference works are proliferating. Traditional encyclopedias are marketed on CD-ROMs or on-line, with electronic indexes to find references instantaneously. Dictionaries reappear in software as spell-checkers and thesauruses. Databases, periodical indexes, and library catalogs are accessible anytime, from anywhere, and in any order.

No sooner have traditional reference works become digitized than the ground begins to shift under their feet. The Internet promises to engulf all public information, indiscriminately presented and easily accessible. Using search engines, keywords, and hyperlinks, it is possible to find almost anything. The World Wide Web is a universal encyclopedia taken to extremes: all the information in the world without any organizing principle, and every user his or her own encyclopedist. It would leave even Coronelli and Zedler breathless.

Notes

1. On eighteenth-century almanacs, see, for example, Gaston Saffroy, *Biblio-graphie des almanachs et annuaires administratifs, ecclésiastiques et militaires français de l'Ancien Régime* (Paris: G. Saffroy, 1959); and Victor Champier, *Les anciens almanachs illustrés: Histoire du calendrier depuis les temps anciens jusqu'à nos jours* (Paris, 1886). Good examples of stagecoach schedules are Daniel Paterson, *A New and Accurate Description of All the Direct and Principal Cross Roads of Great Britain* (London: T. Carnan, 1771); 14 subsequent editions to 1811; and *Paterson's British Itinerary, Being a New and Accurate Delineation and Description of the Direct and Principal Cross Roads of Great Britain*, 2 vols. (London: C. Bowles, 1785); later editions to 1807. The most popular compendium of natural history of the eighteenth century, perhaps of all time, was Noël-Antoine Pluche, *Le spectacle de la nature* (Paris, 1732), which went through eighteen editions in French and some thirty translations and editions in other languages.

2. Allen Walker Read, "Dictionary," *Encyclopaedia Britannica*, 15th edition, *Macro-paedia* 18:385–94.

3. John Harris, *Lexicon Technicum, or an Universal English Dictionary of Arts and Sciences: Explaining not only the Terms of Art, but the Arts Themselves* (London, 1704).

4. Ephraim Chambers, *Cyclopaedia: or, An Universal Dictionary of Arts and Sciences, Containing an Explication of the Terms and an Account of the Things Signified Thereby in the Several Arts, Liberal and Mechanical, and the Several Sciences, Human and Divine, Compiled from the Best Authors*, 2 vols. (London: James and John Knapton, 1728); later editions to 1795. See also Lael Ely Bradshaw, "Ephraim Chambers' *Cyclopaedia*," in *Notable Encyclopedias of the Seventeenth and Eighteenth Centuries: Nine Predecessors of the Encyclopédie*, ed. Frank Kafker, (Oxford: Voltaire Foundation, 1981), (hereafter *Nine Predecessors*) 123–39.

5. Annette Fröhner, *Technologie und Enzyklopädismus im Übergang vom 18. zum 19. Jahr-hundert: Johann Georg Krünitz (1728–1796) und seine Oeconomisch-technologische Enzyklopädie*, Mannheimer Historische Forschungen vol. 5 (Mannheim: Palatium Verlag, 1994), 24.

6. Sidney Landau, *Dictionaries: The Art and Craft of Lexicography* (New York: Scrib-ner's, 1984), 37–39; Georges Matoré, *Histoire des dictionnaires français* (Paris: Larousse, 1967), 67–68; James Augustus Henry Murray, *The Evolution of English Lexicography* (Ox-ford: Clarendon, 1900), 7–11, 23; DeWitt T. Starnes and Gertrude E. Noyes, *The English Dictionary from Cawdrey to Johnson* (Chapel Hill: University of North Carolina Press, 1946), 2–3, 197; Jonathan Green, *Chasing the Sun: Dictionary Makers and the Dictionaries They Made* (London: Jonathan Cape, 1996), 55–56.

7. Accademia della Crusca (Florence), *Vocabolario degli accademici della Crusca, con tre indici delle voce, locuzioni, e prouerbi latini, e greci, posti per entro l'opera* (Venice: G. Alberti, 1612); many editions as late as 1883–1884.

8. Académie française, *Le dictionnaire de l'Académie françoise, dédié au roy*. 4 vols. (Paris: Coignard, 1694); other editions have followed periodically to this day. The French Academy, in turn, inspired the founding in 1713 of the Academia Española, which published the *Diccionario de la lengua castellana* in six volumes in 1726–1739.

9. Pierre Richelet, *Dictionnaire de la langue françoise, contenant les mots et les matières, et plusieurs nouvelles remarques sur la langue françoise, ses expressions propres, figurées et burlesques, la prononciation des mots les plus difficiles, le genre des noms, le régime des verbes . . . avec les termes les plus connus des arts et des sciences: Le tout tiré de l'usage et des bons auteurs de la langue françoise*

(Geneva: Widerholt, 1680); later editions to 1706. Quotation from Bernard Quemada, *Les dictionnaires du français moderne 1539—1863: Etude sur leur histoire, leurs types et leurs
méthodes* (Paris: Didier, 1967), 209. See also Matoré, *Histoire des dictionnaires français*, 75—76.

10. Antoine Furetière, *Dictionnaire universel des arts et sciences contenant généralement
tous les mots françois, tant vieux que modernes et les termes des sciences et des arts*, 3 vols. (The
Hague: Leers, 1690); later editions to 1727. See Robert Lewis Collison, *A History of
Foreign-Language Dictionaries* (London: Deutsch, 1982), 86—94; Matoré, *Histoire des dictionnaires français*, 76—79; and Walter W. Ross, "Antoine Furetière's *Dictionnaire universel*,"
in Kafker, *Nine Predecessors*, 53—67.

11. Preface to *Dictionnaire de l'Académie françoise* (1694), 2.

12. Quoted in Quemada, *Les dictionnaires du français moderne*, 217 n. 134.

13. Thomas Corneille, *Le dictionnaire des arts et des sciences*, 2 vols. (Paris: Coignard,
1694); later editions to 1732.

14. Preface to *Dictionnaire de l'Académie françoise*, 4th ed. (1762), iii—iv.

15. Robert Cawdrey, *A Table Alphabeticall, conteyning and teaching the true writing, and
understanding of hard usuall English wordes, borrowed from the Hebrew, Greeke, Latine, or French, &c.*
(London: Edmund Weaver, 1604; subsequent editions in 1609, 1613, and 1617).

16. John Bullokar, *An English Expositor: Teaching the Interpretation of the Hardest Words
in Our Language* (London: Legatt, 1616), had five thousand entries; later editions followed until 1775.

17. Henry Cockeram, *An English Dictionarie: Or, An Interpreter of Hard English Words*
(London: Weaver, 1623); other editions until 1670.

18. Thomas Blount, *Glossographia: or, A Dictionary, interpreting all such hard words,
whether Hebrew, Greek, Latin, Italian, Spanish, French, Teutonick, Belgick, British or Saxon; as are
used in our refined English tongue. Also the terms of divinity, law, physick, mathematicks, heraldry,
anatomy, war, musick, architecture; and of several other arts and sciences explicated. With etymologies,
definitions, and historical observations on the same* (London: Humphrey Moseley, 1656); other
editions to 1681.

19. Edward Phillips, *The New World of English Words: or, A General Dictionary: Containing the Interpretations of Such Hard Words as are Derived from Other Languages* (London: Tyler,
1658), had eleven thousand entries; other editions followed until 1678.

20. Elisha Coles, *An English Dictionary: explaining the difficult terms that are used in divinity, husbandry, physick, phylosophy, law, navigation, mathematicks and other arts and sciences*
(London: Samuel Crouch, 1676); other editions to 1732.

21. Green, *Chasing the Sun*, 147—48.

22. John Kersey, *A New English Dictionary: or, A compleat collection of the most proper
and significant words commonly used in the language; with a short and clear exposition of difficult terms
and terms of art* (London: Bonwicke and Knaplock, 1702).

23. See Starnes and Noyes, *English Dictionary*, 69—73.

24. Edward Phillips and John Kersey, *The New World of English Words* (London,
1706). See Starnes and Noyes, *English Dictionary*, 48—57, 84—89.

25. John Kersey, *Dictionarium Anglo-Britannicum: or, A general English dictionary* (London: Phillips, 1708). See Starnes and Noyes, *English Dictionary*, 95—97.

26. Nathan Bailey, *An Universal Etymological English Dictionary* (London: Bell, 1721).
See Green, *Chasing the Sun*, 192—96; Starnes and Noyes, *English Dictionary*, 98—106; Landau, *Dictionaries*, 44—45; Murray, *Evolution of English Lexicography*, 35.

27. Thomas Dyche and William Pardon, *New General English Dictionary* (London: Ware, 1735). Among the French dictionaries it inspired, I might mention Antoine François Prévost, *Manuel lexique, ou Dictionnaire portatif des mots français dont la signification n'est pas familière à tout le monde*, 2 vols. (Paris: Didot, 1750). See Green, *Chasing the Sun*, 198–200; and Lael Ely Bradshaw, "Thomas Dyche's *New general English dictionary*," in Kafker, *Nine Predecessors*, 141–61.

28. Nathan Bailey, *Dictionarium Britannicum; or, A Complete etymological English dictionary, being also an interpreter of hard and technical words* (London: T. Cox, 1730); later editions to 1782. See Green, *Chasing the Sun*, 192–94.

29. Landau, *Dictionaries*, 47–48; see also Starnes and Noyes, *English Dictionary*, 117–25.

30. Read, "Dictionary," 390; John Wain, *Samuel Johnson* (New York: Viking, 1974), 137.

31. Samuel Johnson, *The Plan of a Dictionary of the English Language; Addressed to the Right Honourable Philip Dormer, Earl of Chesterfield* (London: Knapton, 1747). See Starnes and Noyes, *English Dictionary*, 160–61; Green, *Chasing the Sun*, 210–13; and Murray, *Evolution of English Lexicography*, 37–47.

32. "Preface" to *A Dictionary of the English Language* in *The Works of Samuel Johnson*, 16 vols. (Troy, N.Y.: Pafraets Press, 1903), 11:254–55. See also Starnes and Noyes, *English Dictionary*, 160–61, and Landau, *Dictionaries*, 50–54.

33. Abbé Jean-François Féraud, *Dictionnaire critique de la langue française*, 3 vols. (Marseille: Moissy, 1787–1788).

34. Quemada, *Les dictionnaires du français moderne*, 197; Matoré, *Histoire des dictionnaires français* 106–7.

35. Matoré, *Histoire des dictionnaires français* 106.

36. "Discours préliminaire," in Jean-Charles Thibault de Laveaux, *Dictionnaire de la langue française* (Paris, 1820), quoted in Quemada, *Les dictionnaires du français moderne*, 198.

37. Quoted in Quemada, *Les dictionnaires du français moderne*, 199.

38. Louis Moréri, *Le grand dictionnaire historique, ou le mélange curieux de l'histoire sacrée et profane* (Lyon: Jean Girin and Barthélémy Rivière, 1674). See also Arnold Miller, "Louis Moreri's *Grand dictionnaire historique*," in Kafker, *Nine Predecessors*, 13–52; and Lawrence E. Sullivan, "Circumscribing Knowledge: Encyclopedias in Historical Perspective," *Journal of Religion* 70 (1990): 319–31.

39. Ursula Paulsen and Gerda Grünewald, *Allgemeine Enzyklopädien und Konversationslexika aus 4 Jahrhunderten* (Bielefeld: Stadtbücherei, 1967), 9; Miller, "Louis Moréri's *Grand dictionnaire historique*," 13–52.

40. Pierre Bayle, *Dictionnaire historique et critique*, 2 vols. (Rotterdam: Reiner Leers, 1697). See also Paul Burrell, "Pierre Bayle's *Dictionnaire historique et critique*," in Kafker, *Nine Predecessors*, 83–103; and Matoré, *Histoire des dictionnaires français*, 97–98.

41. See Lael Ely Bradshaw, "John Harris's *Lexicon technicum*," in Kafker, *Nine Predecessors*, 107–21; and Alicia Perales Ojeda, *Las obras de consulta: Reseña histórico-crítica* (Mexico: Universidad Autónoma de México, 1962), 36.

42. Philip Shorr, "Science and Superstition in the Eighteenth Century: A Study of the Treatment of Science in Two Encyclopedias of 1725–1750: Chambers' *Cyclopaedia*: London (1728); Zedler's *Universal Lexicon*: Leipzig (1732–1750)" (Ph.D. dissertation, Columbia University, 1932), 7–34; Lael Ely Bradshaw, "Ephraim Chambers'

Cyclopaedia," in Kafker, *Nine Predecessors,* 123—31; Sullivan, "Circumscribing Knowledge," 328.

43. Ernst Herbert Lehmann, *Geschichte des Konversations-lexicons* (Leipzig: Brockhaus, 1934), 29.

44. Philipp Balthasar Sinold von Schütz, *Reales Staats- und Zeitungs-Lexicon* (Leipzig: Gleditsch, 1704); from the fourth edition on (1709), it was titled *Reales Staats-, Zeitungs- und Conversations-Lexicon.* See also Paulsen and Grünewald, *Allgemeine Enzyklopädien und Konversationslexika,* 11; Lehmann, 30—31; and Fröhner, *Technologie und Enzyklopädismus,* 18—19.

45. Paul Jakob Marperger, *Curieuses Natur-, Kunst-, Berg-, Gewerk- und Handlungs-Lexicon* (Leipzig: Gleditsch, 1712). See Lehmann, *Geschichte des Konversations-lexicons,* 33.

46. Johann Theodor Jablonski, *Allgemeines Lexicon der Künste und Wissenschaften* (Königsberg and Leipzig, 1721); later editions in 1748 and 1767.

47. Bernhard Kossmann, "Deutsche Universallexika des 18. Jahrhunderts. Ihr Wesen und Informationswert, dargestellt am Beispiel der Werke von Jablonski und Zedler," *Archiv für Geschichte des Buchwesens* 9 (1969): 1559—62; Lehmann, *Geschichte des Konversations-lexicons,* 34.

48. Johann Ferdinand Roth, *Gemeinnütziges Lexikon für Leser aller Klassen, besonders für Unstudierte* (Nürnberg: Ernst Christoph Grattenauer, 1791). See Lehmann, *Geschichte des Konversations-lexicons,* 35.

49. Friedrich Arnold Brockhaus, *Conversations-Lexicon oder kurzgefasstes Handwörterbuch für die in der gesellschaftlichen Unterhaltung aus den Wissenschaften und Künsten vorkommended Gegenstände, mit beständiger Rücksicht auf die Ereignisse der älteren und neueren Zeit,* 6 vols. (Leipzig and Amsterdam, 1809); 2-volume supplement (1809—1811). See Lehmann, *Geschichte des Konversations-lexicons,* 37—39.

50. "Konversations-lexikon," in *Der Grosse Brockhaus,* 16th ed. (Wiesbaden, 1952—1960), 6:547; Werner Lenz, *Kleine Geschichte Grosser Lexica: Ein Beitrag zum Internationalen Jahr des Buches* (Berlin: Bertelsmann, 1972), 54—55; Collison, *History of Foreign-Language Dictionaries,* 156—65; Paulsen and Grünewald, *Allgemeine Enzyklopädien und Konversationslexika,* 12—13; Lehmann, *Geschichte des Konversations-lexicons,* 40—41.

51. Lehmann, *Geschichte des Konversations-lexicons,* 44.

52. *Encyclopaedia Britannica; or, a Dictionary of Arts and Sciences, Compiled upon a New Plan. In Which the Different Sciences and Arts are Digested into Distinct Treaties or Systems; and the Various Technical Terms, &c. are explained as they Occur in the Order of the Alphabet. Illustrated with One Hundred and Sixty Copperplates. By a Society of Gentlemen in Scotland,* 3 vols. (Edinburgh: Macfarquhar and Bell, 1771). See also Frank Kafker, "William Smellie's Edition of the *Encyclopaedia Britannica,*" in *Notable Encyclopedias of the Late Eighteenth Century: Eleven Successors of the Encyclopédie,* ed. Frank Kafker (Oxford: Voltaire Foundation, 1994), (hereafter *Eleven Successors*), 145—82; Herman Kogan, *The Great EB: The Story of the* Encyclopaedia Britannica (Chicago: University of Chicago Press, 1958), 8—13; Paul Kruse, "The Story of the *Encyclopaedia Britannica,* 1768—1943" (Ph.D. dissertation, University of Chicago, 1958), 43—53; and Warren Preece, "The Organization of Knowledge and the Planning of Encyclopaedias: The Case of the *Encyclopaedia Britannica,*" *Journal of World History* 9 (1966): 801—10.

53. Kruse, "Story of the *Encyclopaedia Britannica,*" 56—68, 409—10; Kafker, "William Smellie's Edition," 178—79; Preece, "Organization of Knowledge," 803—7.

54. James Lawrence Fuchs, "Vincenzo Coronelli and the Organization of Knowledge: The Twilight of Seventeenth-Century Encyclopedism" (Ph.D. dissertation, University of Chicago, 1983).

55. Michel-Antoine Baudrand, *Geographia ordine litterarum disposita* (Paris: Michalet, 1682), translated into French as *Dictionnaire géographique universel* (Amsterdam and Utrecht, 1701); Guillaume Sanson, *In geographiam antiquam Michelis Antonii Baudrand disquisitiones geographicae* (Paris: Coignard, 1683).

56. Fuchs, "Vincenzo Coronelli and the Organization of Knowledge," 181.

57. Ibid., 188.

58. Vincenzo Marco Coronelli, *Biblioteca universale sacro-profana, antico-moderna, in cui si spiega con ordine alfabetico ogni voce, anco straniera, che puo avere significato nel nostro idioma italiano, appartenente a qualunque materia,* 7 vols. (Venice: A. Tiviani, 1701–1706).

59. Johann Heinrich Zedler, *Grosses vollständiges Universal-Lexicon aller Wissenschaften und Künste, welche bisshero durch menschlichen Verstand und Witz erfunden und verbessert worden,* 64 vols. (Halle and Leipzig: Zedler, 1732–1750); 4-volume supplement (Leipzig, 1751–1754). See also Peter E. Carels and Dan Flory, "Johann Heinrich Zedler's Universal-Lexicon," in Kafker, *Nine Predecessors,* 165–96; Shorr, "Science and Superstition," 35–77; and Kossmann, "Deutsche Universallexika," 1565–90.

60. Lehmann, *Geschichte des Konversations-lexicons,* 21.

61. On the *Encyclopédie* and the "tree of knowledge," see Robert Darnton, *The Great Cat Massacre and Other Episodes in French Cultural History* (New York: Basic Books, 1984), chap. 5.

62. Jean Le Rond d'Alembert, *Discours préliminaire de l'Encyclopédie,* (Picavet edition, Paris, 1894), III, quoted in Max Fuchs, "La langue des sciences," in *Histoire de la langue français des origines à 1900,* ed. Ferdinand Brunot (Paris: Colin, 1930), 6:600.

63. Among the works that emphasize the culture and politics of the *Encyclopédie* we might cite: John Morley, *Diderot and the Encyclopedists,* rev. ed. (London: Macmillan, 1923); Joseph Legras, *Diderot et l'Encyclopédie* (Amiens: Edgar Malfère, 1928); Jacques Proust, *Diderot et l'Encyclopédie,* 2d ed. (Paris: Colin, 1967); Jean Thomas, "Un moment du développement culturel de l'humanité: L'Encyclopédie," *Journal of World History* 9 (1966): 695–711; John Lough, *The Encyclopédie* (New York: McKay, 1971); Frank A. Kafker, "The Role of the *Encyclopédie* in the Making of the Modern Encyclopedia," in *The Encyclopédie and the Age of Reason,* ed. Clorinda Donato and Robert M. Maniquis (Boston: G. K. Hall, 1992), 19–25; Kafker, "The Influence of the *Encyclopédie* on the Eighteenth-Century Encyclopedic Tradition," in Kafker, *Eleven Successors,* 389–99. The *Encyclopédie* continues to arouse interest, even in the popular media; see Robert Wernick, "Declaring an Open Season on the Wisdom of the Ages," *Smithsonian* 28, no. 2 (May 1997): 72–83.

See also Robert Darnton, *The Business of Enlightenment: A Publishing History of the Encyclopédie, 1775–1800* (Cambridge, Mass.: Harvard University Press, 1979).

64. Ibid., 35.

65. Ibid., 524.

66. The original twenty-six divisions of knowledge were mathematics, physics, medicine, surgery, anatomy, chemistry, agriculture, natural history of animals, botany, natural history of the earth, mineralogy, geography, history, theology, philosophy, grammar and literature, law, finances, political economy,

commerce, navy, military science, fine arts, antiquities, and handicrafts. See George B. Watts, "The *Encyclopédie méthodique*," *PMLA* 73 (September 1958): 348–66.

67. Suzanne Tucoo-Chala, *Charles-Joseph Panckoucke et la librairie française, 1736–1798* (Pau: Marrimpouey jeune, 1977), 333; Jean Ehrard, "De Diderot à Panckoucke: Deux pratiques de l'alphabet," in *L'Encyclopédisme: Actes du Colloque de Caen, 12–16 Janvier 1987,* ed. Annie Becq (Paris: Klincksieck, 1991), 243–52.

68. Darnton, *Business of Enlightenment,* 420–21; Tucoo-Chala, *Panckoucke et la librairie française* 333.

69. Quoted in Tucoo-Chala, *Panckoucke et la librairie française* 328–29.

70. Panckoucke's prospectus to subscribers (1787), quoted in Darnton, *Business of Enlightenment,* 476.

71. Tucoo-Chala, *Panckoucke et la librairie française* 344; Darnton, *Business of Enlightenment,* 420–21.

72. Darnton, *Business of Enlightenment,* 421–36; Tucoo-Chala, *Panckoucke et la librairie française* 329–35.

73. Watts, "Encyclopédie méthodique," 362–65.

74. Quoted in Tucoo-Chala, *Panckoucke et la librairie française* 338.

75. The Chinese, however, published gigantic encyclopedias before the Europeans did: a 131-volume work in 1711, a 40-volume work in 1716, and a 130-volume work in 1726. See Collison, *History of Foreign-Language Dictionaries,* 96.

76. Johann Georg Krünitz, *Oeconomisch-technologische Enzyklopädie oder allgemeines System der Staat- Stadt- Haus- und Landwirtschaft und der Kunstgeschichte in alphabetisher Ordnung,* 242 vols. (Berlin: Pauli, 1773–1858).

77. J. Samuel Ersch and Johann Gottfried Gruber, eds., *Allgemeine Enzyklopädie der Wissenschaften und Künste in alphabetischer Folge von genannten Schriftstellern bearbeitet,* 167 vols. (1818–1889). See Lehmann, *Geschichte des Konversations-lexicons,* 25.

78. Lloyd William Daly, *Contributions to the History of Alphabetization in Antiquity and the Middle Ages* (Brussels: Latomus, 1967), 50; Mary A. Rouse and Richard H. Rouse, "Alphabetization, History of," in *Dictionary of the Middle Ages,* 13 vols. (New York: Scribner's, 1982–1989), 1:204.

79. Daly, *Contributions to the History of Alphabetization,* 35–36.

80. Jean-Louis Taffarelli, *Les systèmes de classification des ouvrages encyclopédiques* (Villeurbanne: Ecole Nationale Supérieure des Bibliothèques, 1980), 30–39.

81. Thomas Burns McArthur, *Worlds of Reference: Lexicography, Learning, and Language from the Clay Tablet to the Computer* (Cambridge: Cambridge University Press, 1986), 76; N. E. Osselton, *Chosen Words: Past and Present Problems for Dictionary Makers* (Exeter: University of Exeter Press, 1995), 117–18; Daly, *Contributions to the History of Alphabetization,* 69.

82. Quoted in Daly, *Contributions to the History of Alphabetization,* 71.

83. Quoted in Rouse and Rouse, "Alphabetization," 1:205.

84. Ibid., 204–7. For the reference to law books, I am indebted to François Velde of Northwestern University.

85. Quoted in Daly, *Contributions to the History of Alphabetization,* 72–73.

86. Robert K. Logan, *The Alphabet Effect* (New York: St. Martin's, 1987), 190–91.

87. Cawdrey, *Table Alphabeticall,* preface.

88. Lehmann, *Geschichte des Konversations-lexicons*, 12–13.

89. Göran Bornäs, *Ordre alphabétique et classement méthodique du lexique: Etude de quelques dictionnaires d'apprentissage français* (Malmö: Glerup, 1986), 6–7.

90. Kossmann, "Deutsche Universallexika," 1553–96; Quemada, *Les dictionnaires du français moderne*, 324–25. Alphabetizing problems persist to this day, of course: for example, in English, how to deal with *Mac* and *Mc*, German letters with umlauts and the letters *s* and ß; the French letter ç, the Spanish ñ and *ll*; and so on.

91. Osselton, *Chosen Words*, 118–21; Green, *Chasing the Sun*, 58.

92. Jacques Bernard Durey de Noinville, *Table alphabétique des dictionnaires, en toutes sortes de sciences et d'arts* (Paris: H. Chaubert, 1758).

93. Fuchs, "Vincenzo Coronelli and the Organization of Knowledge," 186–87.

94. Ibid., 214–15, 221.

95. Ephraim Chambers, *Cyclopedia*, xxii, quoted in Gunnar Broberg, "The Broken Circle," in *The Quantifying Spirit of the 18th Century*, ed. Tore Frängsmyr, J. L. Heilbron, and Robin E. Rider (Berkeley: University of California Press, 1990), 47.

96. Matoré, *Histoire des dictionnaires français*, 93.

97. Béatrice Didier, *Alphabet et raison: Le paradoxe des dictionnaires au XVIIIe siècle* (Paris: Presses universitaires de France, 1996), 1–6.

98. Ehrard, "De Diderot à Panchoucke," 243–52. See also Cynthia J. Koepp, "The Alphabetical Order: Work in Diderot's *Encyclopédie*," in *Work in France: Representations, Meaning, Organization, and Practice*, ed. Steven L. Kaplan and Cynthia J. Koepp (Ithaca, N.Y.: Cornell University Press, 1986), 229–57.

99. Denis Diderot and Jean Le Rond d'Alembert, "Discours préliminaire des Editeurs," *Encyclopédie* (Lausanne 1778 edition), 1: xxxi–xxxii.

100. Pierre Rétat, "L'âge des dictionnaires," in *Histoire de l'édition française*, vol. 2, *Le livre triomphant 1660–1830*, ed. Henri-Jean Martin and Roger Chartier (Paris: Promodis, 1984), 192–93; Ehrard, "De Diderot à Panckoucke," 249–50.

101. Pierre Mouchon, *Table analytique et raisonnée des matières contenues dans les XXXIII volumes in-folio du dictionnaire des sciences, des arts et des métiers et dans son supplément*, 2 vols. (Paris: Panckoucke, 1780).

102. Kafker, "The Role of the *Encyclopédie*," 20–21.

103. *Encyclopaedia Metropolitana; or Universal Dictionary of Knowledge, on an Original Plan: Comprising the Twofold Advantage of a Philosophical and an Alphabetical Arrangement*, 28 vols. ed. Edward Smedley, Hugh James Rose, and Henry John Rose (London: B. Fellowes, 1817–1845).

104. Samuel Taylor Coleridge, "On the Science of Method," *Encyclopaedia Metropolitana*, 1:42.

105. Quoted in Gunnar Broberg, "The Broken Circle," in *The Quantifying Spirit in the Eighteenth Century*, ed. Tore Frängsmyr, John L. Heilbron, and Robin E. Rider (Berkeley: University of California Press, 1990), 49 n. 12.

106. Quoted in Börnas, *Ordre alphabétique*, 7.

107. Robert Collison, "Samuel Taylor Coleridge and the *Encyclopaedia Metropolitana*," *Journal of World History* 9 (1966): 763.

108. Collison, "Samuel Taylor Coleridge," 764–65.

109. Rétat, "L'âge des dictionnaires," 186, criticizes Quemada's figures on the

grounds that they exclude subsequent editions of lesser works and many "portable" or "pocket" dictionaries; had they been included, the increase would have been even steeper.

110. Among the best-known textbooks were Thomas Dyche's *Guide to the English Tongue*, which ran over one hundred editions and sold some 275,000 copies between 1707 and 1799, and Noah Webster's *An American Spelling Book*, reprinted 260 times between 1783 and 1843.

111. See also Paulsen and Grünewald, *Allgemeine Enzyklopädien und Konversationslexika*, 11; and Fröhner, *Technologie und Enzyklopädismus*, 18—19.

112. Nathan Bailey, *A New Universal Etymological English Dictionary of Words, and of Arts and Sciences*, ed. Joseph Nicol Scott (London: Osborne and Shipton, 1755). See also Starnes and Noyes, *English Dictionary*, 98—106.

113. Heinrich Martin Gottfried Köster and Johann Friedrich Roos, eds., *Deutsche Encyclopädie oder allgemeines Real-Wörterbuch aller Künste und Wissenschaften von einer Gesellschaft Gelehrten*, 23 vols. (Frankfurt: Varrentrapp & Wenner, 1778—1807); David Brewster, ed., *Edinburgh Encyclopaedia; or, Dictionary of Arts, Sciences, and Miscellaneous Literature*, 18 vols. (Edinburgh: Balfour, 1808—1830); William Nicholson, ed., *The British Encyclopaedia, or Dictionary of Arts and Sciences, Comprising an Accurate and Popular View of the Present Improved State of Human Knowledge* (London: Longman, 1809). See also Uwe Decker, "Die Deutsche Encyclopädie (1778–1807)," *Das Achzehnte Jahrhundert. Mitteilungen der Deutschen Gesellschaft für die Erforschung des 18. Jahrhunderts* 14, no. 2 (1990): 147—51; Willi Goetschel, Catriona MacLeod, and Emery Snyder, "The Deutsche Encyclopädie and Encyclopedism in Eighteenth-Century Germany," in Donato and Maniquis, *The Encyclopédie*, 55—62; and Collison, *History of Foreign-Language Dictionaries*, 174—80.

114. Abraham Rees, *Cyclopaedia; or, An Universal Dictionary of Arts and Sciences . . . with the Supplement and Modern Improvments, Incorporated in one Alphabet*, 5 vols. (London: Strahan, 1778—1788).

115. Bradshaw, "John Harris's *Lexicon technicum*," 118—21.

116. Bradshaw, "Ephraim Chambers' *Cyclopaedia*," 138—39.

117. Burrell, "Pierre Bayle's *Dictionnaire historique et critique*," 98—99.

118. Carels and Flory, "Johann Heinrich Zedler's *Universal Lexicon*," 169—72; Kossmann, "Deutsche Universallexika," 1568.

119. Darnton, *Business of Enlightenment*, 33—35.

120. Rétat, "L'âge des dictionnaires," 188—89.

121. Kruse, "Story of the *Encyclopaedia Britannica*," 56, 67—68, 95—105; Kogan, *The Great EB*, 23—28; Collison, *History of Foreign-Language Dictionaries*, 140—41.

122. Collison, *History of Foreign-Language Dictionaries*, 158—65.

6

COMMUNICATING INFORMATION

Postal and Telegraphic Systems

Listen, my children, and you shall hear
Of the midnight ride of Paul Revere,
On the eighteenth of April, in Seventy-five;
Hardly a man is now alive
Who remembers that famous day and year.
He said to his friend, "If the British march
By land or sea from the town to-night,
Hang a lantern aloft in the belfry arch
Of the North Church tower as a signal light,—
One, if by land, and two, if by sea;
And I on the opposite shore will be,
Ready to ride and spread the alarm
Through every Middlesex village and farm,
For the country-folk to be up and to arm.

HENRY WADSWORTH LONGFELLOW,
"The Midnight Ride of Paul Revere"

PAUL REVERE, THE AMERICAN REVOLUTIONARY, REMEMBERED HIS MIDNIGHT ride of April 18, 1775, in these words: "I agreed with a Colonel Conant and some other gentlemen, that if the British went out by water, we should shew two lanthornes in the North Church steeple, and if by land, one, as a signal, for we were apprehensive it would be difficult to cross the Charles River, or git over Boston neck."[1] Eighteen years later, on July 12, 1793, Claude Chappe presented his semaphore telegraph to the Committee of Public Instruction of the French National Convention. At Saint-Fargeau, near Paris, Deputy Pierre Daunou sent a message to Deputy Joseph Lakanal at Saint-Martin-du-Tertre, thirty-five kilometers away: "Daunou has arrived here. He announces that the National Convention has just authorized its committee of general security to affix the seals to the papers of the representatives of the people." Nine minutes later, Lakanal replied: "The inhabitants of this beautiful country are worthy of liberty because of their love for it and their respect for the National Convention and its laws."[2]

Between these two dates there occurred a revolution in communication. Revere used a simple, prearranged, onetime signal containing only three potential messages: "by land," "by sea," or "no news." Chappe could communicate any message, in either direction, faster than a galloping horse. This was only one of several great changes in communication that occurred in the late eighteenth and early nineteenth centuries under the pressure of revolution and war.

Communication Systems

Humans are gifted, both naturally and culturally, at communicating face-to-face. Long-distance communications, however, require elaborate systems to convey information to its destination in a timely manner. Overcoming distances is but one of the functions of communication systems. We must also draw a distinction between the transmission of information from one person to another, for example, by speech, letter, telephone, telegram, or e-mail, and the dissemination of information from one point to many, by such means as newspapers, books, pamphlets, flyers, and posters, or by radio and television broadcasts and the World Wide Web.

The first characteristic of communication systems is the extent of their coverage. The most rudimentary communications systems involved sending a messenger whenever a message needed to be delivered. More elaborate were the methods devised to send a small number of prearranged messages over a prearranged course, usually in one direction only. Even more elaborate were permanent lines of communication, able to convey any message in either direction between two points, sometimes even keeping to a regular schedule. And the most elaborate systems involved a complete network of relay posts and messengers covering a large area, such as a kingdom.

An important characteristic of permanent systems is their ownership, control, and financing. Throughout history, governmental and nongovernmental communications systems coexisted, often in competition. Nongovernmental systems included those of business organizations, religious orders, and universities, as well as those run by private companies. Governments and private firms or organizations made various arrangements, ranging from contracting for stagecoaches to "farming" entire regions. The distinction between private and governmental was not always clear. Private firms needed to defray their expenses and sought to make a profit. Government networks, too, were often a source of income. At times, however, they required costly subsidies. Very occasionally, they broke even.

The first governmental networks were restricted to official messages, although by the seventeenth century, they also admitted private customers. Nongovernmental networks generally needed to spread their fixed costs (relay posts, horses, clerks) over many paying customers; given their high rates, theirs was largely an elite clientele. Access to the general public, so characteristic of today's communications networks, is a recent development.

A final characteristic is privacy and surveillance. Communicating messages has always been closely tied to the exercise of power, as is evident from the efforts of kingdoms and empires to create and maintain networks, often at tremendous cost. This link with power explains why governments worried about subversion and espionage—and what government wasn't?—sought to control access to such networks. When governments allowed public access to their official networks, they reserved the right to intercept and read messages, sometimes overtly, but more often in secret.

In this chapter, I will consider three long-distance communication systems: postal services, optical signaling systems on land, and naval flag-signaling systems at sea. Between them, they illustrate the characteristics just mentioned—coverage and organization, ownership, control, financing, access, and surveillance—and the impact of revolution and war on the transmission of information.

Postal Systems before the Eighteenth Century

Messengers were the first means of conveying information over long distances. Before the Battle of Marathon (490 B.C.), the Greek historian Herodotus informs us, Philippides, "by profession and practice a trained runner," ran to Sparta, 120 miles away, arriving "on the very next day after quitting the city of Athens."[3]

Runners and occasional travelers might suffice for city-states and isolated communities, but kings needed regular communications. To keep control of their far-flung domains, the Persians created a permanent postal system along the Royal Road that stretched 1,677 miles from Susa in western Iran to Ephesus on the Aegean Sea. Herodotus was amazed by its permanent posts that kept fresh horses for King Xerxes' messengers: "The first rider delivers his despatch to the second, and the second passes it on to the third; and so it is borne from hand to hand along the whole line, like the light in a torch-race."[4]

The Romans created a similar system of imperial messengers and relay posts along their major roads, the *cursus publicus;* so did the Chinese, the

Incas, the Mongols, and other empires. It is characteristic of these early imperial networks that they were reserved for official messages; anyone else
who had a message to send would have to find a traveler going in the right
direction and hope for the best.

During the Middle Ages, the governmental apparatus of classical
times disappeared, replaced by numerous unofficial channels of communication. The Benedictine monks of Cluny used pilgrims to carry messages
to and from other monasteries, from Spain to Poland. The mercantile cities
of the Hanseatic League shipped documents and messages along with mer-
chandise. Butchers, who traveled from place to place buying and slaugh-
tering livestock, carried messages for people. The most organized of these
nongovernmental networks was the one centered on the University of
Paris, whose students traveled between Paris and their homelands all over
Europe; though they were supposed to serve only the university community, they carried messages for the public as well.[5] These unofficial networks did not operate on a schedule, nor did they use relays of horses;
hence, they were slow and unreliable.

The first postal system that established permanent relays like the old
imperial networks, but offered its services to the general public, was
founded by Franz von Taxis, postmaster to the Holy Roman Emperor
Maximilian I. From 1489 until 1867, the Taxis (later Thurn und Taxis) family
provided a regular postal service not just in the lands of the Hapsburg dy-
nasty but throughout most of Europe. With its relays of horses on all the
main routes and up to twenty thousand messengers, the Thurn und Taxis
postal service was reliable and, by the standards of the day, fairly swift: from
Brussels to Paris in forty-four hours, to Innsbruck in six days, and to Toledo
in twelve days. It was, however, very costly.[6]

The Hapsburgs may have trusted the Thurn und Taxis family, but the
rising national monarchies of France and England did not, nor did they
trust any other private or nongovernmental message service. Their history,
until the end of the Old Regime, is one of constant tensions between royal
monopolies and private enterprises.

The first royal messenger service in France, founded in 1464, was reserved for official messages, although the royal couriers could be bribed to
carry private messages surreptitiously. Not until the early seventeenth century, under Louis XIII's chief minister, Cardinal de Richelieu, was the service opened to private messages. In 1622, regularly scheduled couriers
linked Paris with Lyon, Dijon, Bordeaux, and Toulouse. Five years later, the
postal service published rates for private letters but set them very high as a
means of subsidizing the official mail. Once the royal mail service was
opened to the public, the government attempted to suppress private messengers, in order to permit easier surveillance of potentially subversive

communications; the last nongovernmental service, that of the University of Paris, ended in 1719.[7]

The evolution of the English postal system paralleled that of France. There had long been royal messengers, but the first permanent service was founded in 1512 when King Henry VIII appointed Sir Brian Tuke as master of the posts. Tuke posted horses every ten to twelve miles along the main roads out of London. He personally received all letters addressed to the court and sent them on by messenger. Royal messages to and from foreign countries were hand delivered by special couriers.

Meanwhile, merchants had their own networks, in particular the Merchant Adventurers' Post for English merchants engaged in foreign trade, and the Foreigners' Post for foreign merchants in England. To Queen Elizabeth I, these channels represented a serious risk of subversion and espionage, in view of the wars and tensions with Catholic powers. Hence, she ordered all mail leaving or entering the country to be carried by the royal post. This decree would be repeated often by her successors but seldom fully enforced.

In 1635, during the reign of Charles I (1625–1649), the royal postal service was authorized to serve the public; two years later it included the foreign mails as well. As in France, "public service" was a euphemism, for postal rates were kept extremely high as a source of income for the treasury and various favorites of the king, and officials reserved the right to open and read private letters. Most people who needed to correspond preferred to send letters with a friend, a servant, a hired messenger, or a traveler.[8]

By the mid–seventeenth century, government-operated public networks served not one but two purposes, as the Act of Parliament of 1657 under Cromwell explained:

> not only to maintain certain intercourse of trade and commerce betwixt all the said places to the great benefit of the people of these nations, but also . . . to discover and prevent many dangerous and wicked designs, which have been and are daily continued against the peace and welfare of this Commonwealth.[9]

The dual purpose of a postal service was clearly revealed in the 1680s by the London Penny Post. Until 1680, there was no mail delivery within London or any other town. That year, a businessman named William Dockwra established the London Penny Post, promising to deliver any letter or package up to one pound in weight for one penny within the town, and for twopence to outlying areas. He designated 179 places where letters could be posted and promised four deliveries per day, and up to eight in the business district. To do so, he employed a hundred messengers; in comparison, the General Post Office employed forty-nine men in its inland department and another twelve in its foreign office.

Two years later, as soon as Dockwra's scheme began to show a profit, the government shut it down, alleging a violation of the official postal monopoly, then reopened it as a branch of the royal mail.[10]

European Postal Systems to 1840

The period from 1700 to the 1780s was one of slow change and small improvements in postal services. Gradually, the number of towns reached by the service increased. Better roads made the transport of mail faster and more reliable, especially after the 1780s.

Yet progress was much slower than it could have been. Governments had discovered that postage was a lucrative source of income, and they were reluctant to lower rates or invest in improved service. Another reason was political, for officials suspected all private letters to be part of some nefarious plot. A third reason was the organizational complexity and inefficiency of the postal systems. The cost of sending a letter, which varied not only by distance but also by the number of sheets it contained, had to be estimated at the beginning of its trip and registered at each stage along the way. Postage was usually paid by the addressee, for mailmen received a portion of the postage of each letter they delivered and had little incentive to deliver a prepaid letter. Since mailmen had to find the addressee and collect the postage on every letter they delivered, mail delivery was very slow.

In 1711, the English Parliament passed an act "for establishing a General Post Office for all Her Majesty's Dominions, and for settling a Weekly Sum out of the Revenues thereof, for the service of the War, and other Her Majesty's Occasions." The Post Office was required to contribute seven hundred pounds per week to the Exchequer. To generate the revenue, it raised postal rates by 50 percent and reduced the radius of the London Penny Post from twenty to ten miles. Not everyone paid, however; postal officials and, after 1763, members of Parliament enjoyed the franking privilege (free postage) not only for official business but also for their personal use and that of their friends. These abuses turned the postal service into a hidden tax and a burden on the economy.[11]

Under the Act of 1711, no letter could be detained or opened without a warrant from a secretary of state. Only one hundred such warrants were issued from that date until 1798. Yet the Committee of Secrecy, created in 1732 to practice covert surveillance of the mail, became so notorious that the House of Commons debated its activities among other "abuses of the Post Office" in 1735. Similarly, in France, a *cabinet noir*, or black chamber, operated throughout the century, as correspondents well knew and often remarked.[12] The most efficient postal espionage service was the Austrian Geheime Kabinets-Kanzlei, which could open, read, decrypt, translate, and reseal the letters to all the foreign embassies in Vienna between seven and nine-thirty every morning.[13]

The postal services increased their reach during the first three-quarters of the century. One improvement was the spread of byway posts and cross-posts. Until 1720, the English postal service carried the mail only to and from London; a letter going between two nearby towns, such as Bristol and Exeter, had to travel all the way to London and back, and pay double postage. That year, the postal clerk Ralph Allen purchased from the government the right to carry the mail between towns other than London (cross-posts) and between the main post roads and smaller towns not previously served (byway posts). By 1764, when Allen died, most of England and Wales received mail daily.[14] In France, however, no cross-posts were allowed before the Revolution, for fear of weakening the government's control; a letter from Toulouse to Marseille, for example, had to go through Paris.[15]

The impact of the French Revolution and the Napoleonic Wars on European postal systems was decidedly mixed, with advances in some areas and deterioration in others. The advances occurred primarily in the area of transportation technology. In particular, the quickening pace of business and political life led to the improvement of roads. Since the mid–eighteenth century, France had boasted the best roads in Europe, many of them built by graduates of the Ecole des ponts et chaussées, following the method developed by the engineer P. M. J. Trésaguet. By 1776, France had twenty-five thousand miles of all-weather highways under state control. Napoleon carried the French road-building tradition into the Low Countries, Germany, and Italy.

English roads were the responsibility of local parishes, not of the central government. On unimproved roads, carts traveled at two to three miles per hour, taking, for example, two days from London to Oxford. The General Turnpike Act of 1773 provided an incentive for turnpike trusts to build and maintain roads. New roads were built of crushed stone, following the system of Trésaguet as improved by Thomas Telford and John McAdam.

Better roads made it possible to substitute mail coaches for the postboys who previously had carried the mail on foot or on horseback. France was the first country to introduce mail coaches, called *diligences* for their greater speed or *turgotines* after the reformist minister of finance Robert Turgot, who inaugurated the system in 1776. In England, Comptroller-General of the Mails John Palmer introduced mail coaches in 1784. Mail coaches were much more reliable than postboys, for they carried an armed guard on the back to deter highway robbers, and they traveled day and night. Britain had forty-two mail coach routes by 1797 and fifty-nine by 1830.

As roads improved, the speed of mail coaches increased from three or four miles per hour at the beginning of the eighteenth century to six miles per hour in the 1780s, eight or nine miles per hour in 1800, and ten miles per hour in 1830. On long distances—from London to Edinburgh or Paris to Lyon—this faster speed shortened the trip by several days.[16] The European postal systems could finally boast speeds comparable to those of the Persians and the Romans.

There was a price to pay for the increase in speed, however. To defray the cost of the mail coach service, Palmer doubled the postage on intercity mails. In 1794, the London Penny Post began charging a second penny for letters sent from the suburbs to the city. In 1801, it charged twopence within the city, then added a third pence to the suburbs in 1805 and a fourth in 1812. The rise in postal rates reflected the rampant inflation of the war years and outpaced the rise in wages. A letter cost as much as a workingman's daily pay.

The rate structure also became increasingly complicated, with pennies added for crossing rivers or transferring from one system to another. People in positions of authority and their friends abused the franking privilege. Those without connections sent their letters, illegally, by post coaches, that is, by passenger vehicles that traveled on the post roads but were not supposed to carry mail.[17]

In France, the postal service, which had become fairly efficient by the end of the Old Regime, fell into chaos during the Revolution as employees were drafted into the army, fled for their lives, or were jailed or executed. In the early 1790s, roads fell into disrepair, banditry increased, and wars and rebellions disrupted the mails. Not until the Directory (1795–1799) did the postal service revive. It also served to disseminate thousands of copies of Parisian newspapers throughout the provinces.[18]

Postal surveillance became a serious issue during the French Revolution. In the *cahiers de doléances* (notebooks of grievances) presented to the Estates-General in 1789, one of the primary complaints against the royal postal service was that it violated the privacy of correspondence. In a debate on the postal system in the National Assembly on July 25, 1789, many delegates, led by Mirabeau, argued that the inviolability of the mail was a citizen's right. Article XI of the Declaration of the Rights of Man proclaimed the free communication of ideas and opinions. The penal code of 1791 guaranteed the inviolability of correspondence.

Yet the Revolution created reasons to break its own laws. By 1791, France was swept by conspiracies, and a year later the country was embroiled in the first of its many wars. In April 1793, the Committee of Public Safety, led by Robespierre, issued a decree:

> The Committee, considering that the Republic is being attacked, from outside and from within, by treason and perfidy and that the enemy

powers maintain contacts with the rebels . . . in the midst of such imminent danger, no citizen can expect the secrecy of his letters and correspondence.[19]

After Robespierre was overthrown and life returned to normal, the Directory and its successors reverted to the more sensible policy pursued by
most governments: strict laws protecting the privacy of correspondence—
along with a secret and hotly denied black chamber.[20]

Two Postal Revolutions

In superficial ways, the postal system of British North America and of the
United States followed the evolution of European postal systems. Yet, as
Richard R. John has shown, the postal system that emerged from the
American Revolution was itself revolutionary, both politically and organi-
zationally.[21]

The first attempts to establish postal service in the colonies date back
to the seventeenth century, but they were little more than offices in the
major East Coast ports where mail could be sent to or received from England. The first system of intercolonial mail began in the 1690s to carry mail
between Delaware and New Hampshire. After the midcentury, monthly
packet ships carried the mail between England and several East Coast ports.
By 1765, British North America had seventy-seven post offices from Canada
to Virginia, or one for every twenty-two thousand inhabitants, the same ratio as England and Wales.[22]

The British postal system in the colonies aroused the ire of the
colonists, for the rates were so high they constituted a heavy tax, and the
mail was often opened by postal officials. In 1774, the colonists established a
"constitutional post" to avoid the British; a year later it was taken over by
the Second Continental Congress.

In the port cities of the eastern seaboard, where men met daily in
coffeehouses and taverns, news spread quickly. Between towns, information moved on horseback or by ship at the same pace as in the days of King
Xerxes. News of the Battle of Lexington and Concord (April 19, 1775) reached
Connecticut the following day, New York City in four days, Philadelphia in
five, Charleston in twenty, and Savannah in forty-one.[23]

The postal system deteriorated during the American War of Independence (1775–1783). Deliveries were reduced from three times to once per
week. Because most of the mail was franked by members of Congress and
by soldiers and officers of the Continental Army, the service required heavy
subsidies, despite high rates for paying customers. Except for one route
westward from Philadelphia to Pittsburgh, the constitutional post served
only the major eastern seaboard towns, and the number of post offices was

almost the same in 1788 as it had been in 1765. Jefferson and Madison sent
their most important messages in cipher, knowing that postmasters routinely opened letters, as did innkeepers and postriders.[24]

After debating the postal situation for several years, in 1792 Congress passed
the Post Office Act, which created a national postal system and reserved for
itself the power to determine postal routes, establish post offices, and set
rates. Most important, it gave the postal system a radically new purpose.
Henceforth, its goal was not to carry official messages or to obtain revenue
but to disseminate, in the words of Benjamin Rush, "knowledge of every
kind . . . through every part of the United States."[25] Congressmen were
convinced that the government should keep the citizenry informed, especially of the debates in Congress, on the grounds that public access to political information would strengthen the union and the bonds between citizens and their elected officials. This revolutionary goal determined two
policies that Congress was to insist on. One was a vast and unprecedented
expansion of the postal network; the other was a plan to employ the network to distribute newspapers throughout the country.

   Having given itself the power to open new post roads, Congress now
did so with enthusiasm. Inhabitants of the smallest hamlets in the most remote regions of the South and the trans-Appalachian West petitioned their
congressmen for a post office of their own and a post road to bring them
news of the outside world. Their elected representatives were happy to
oblige, since the cost would be spread over the system as a whole, in particular over the more heavily used routes in the Northeast. Between 1792 and
1828, Congress opened 2,476 new postal routes and discontinued only 181.[26]

   The result was a phenomenal proliferation of post offices. In 1790, there
had been 75 post offices, or one for every 43,084 inhabitants and 3,492.7 square
miles; by 1840, there were 13,486 offices, each serving, on average, 1,087 inhabitants and 61.4 square miles.[27] By the 1830s, the United States boasted about
twice as many post offices as Great Britain and five times more than France.
The Post Office employed almost four out of every five federal employees.
It was the only contact most Americans had with the federal government.

   This enormous system was created mainly to carry newspapers. Before
1792, only two kinds of newspapers went as mail: those congressmen sent to
their constituents and those printers sent to one another—often the only
way news from one place could reach another. Other newspapers were carried at the pleasure of postmasters and postriders, not as regular mail.
When the printer Benjamin Franklin was appointed postmaster of Philadelphia in 1739, he used his office to distribute his newspaper and to prevent
his competitors from mailing theirs.[28] During the debates leading up to the
Act of 1792, Congress first considered admitting only selected newspapers
into the mail but finally settled on admitting them all. To realize this goal,

it set the rates very low: one cent for the first hundred miles, one and a half cents for over one hundred miles, and no charge for the papers printers exchanged with one another.[29]

This generous policy invigorated the press throughout the country. Publishers in remote places not only could obtain news from far away at no cost but also could now serve subscribers outside their own distribution area. As a result, the number of newspapers sent through the mail increased from half a million in 1790 (one for every five inhabitants) to thirty-nine million in 1840, or 2.7 newspapers per capita, a fourteenfold increase. The postal system became largely a newspaper delivery service. In 1832, newspapers constituted 95 percent of the weight of the mail but brought in only 15 percent of the revenue.[30] The postal service was the very foundation of American-style democracy, that system of government by elected politicians and by the media.

Besides carrying newspapers, the postal system provided two other services. Because banks and financial markets were still very primitive, the mail was the chief means by which merchants transmitted money in the form of checks, drafts, and banknotes.[31] It was also instrumental in developing intercity public transportation before the advent of the railroads. The Post Office contracted with stagecoach owners to carry the mail on a regular schedule. Stagecoaches also carried passengers, a service that was much appreciated by the general public and by congressmen who traveled regularly between Washington and their constituents. In the less populated southern and western regions of the country, federally mandated and subsidized stagecoaches were often the safest way to travel.[32] Stagecoach service often preceded and stimulated the construction of roads. As roads improved, stagecoaches increased their speed; for example, the trip from Philadelphia to Lexington, Kentucky—a distance of about six hundred miles—took sixteen days in 1789, eight days in 1810, and four in 1839.[33]

Although Congress was always eager to extend and increase postal service, it expected the Post Office to contribute to the Treasury or at least be self-supporting. The only way the Post Office could do so was by keeping high rates for ordinary mail. To send one sheet of paper from New York City to Troy, New York, 140 miles away, cost 18.5 cents, compared with 12.5 cents for a barrel of flour or 1.5 cents for a newspaper—this at a time when a workingman earned a dollar a day.[34] To avoid such high rates, people who lived in the densely populated Northeast turned to private courier services, to the detriment of both the postal system and interpersonal communications. By the 1840s, the American people, like those of Europe, were ready for the next revolution in postal service.

The 1830s and 1840s marked the great turning point in postal history, equivalent to the electric telegraph. It had two causes: the railways and the penny postage. The railways speeded the mails even more than mail coaches had a half century earlier. By 1838, railways connected London with Birmingham, Manchester, and Liverpool, replacing the mail coaches between these centers of population, trade, and industry. That year saw the introduction of the first railway postal car on which clerks sorted the mail. By the 1850s, as the rail network covered Britain, almost all mail coaches disappeared.[35]

Even more important was the introduction of cheap postage in the mid–nineteenth century. The originator of this change was Rowland Hill. In his pamphlet *Post Office Reform: Its Importance and Practicability*, first printed in 1837, Hill demonstrated that the true cause of high postage rates was the large and inefficient bureaucracy required to register every letter, calculate and collect postage on delivery, send the collected money back to the General Post Office, and keep track of it all. In comparison with these unnecessary expenses, the cost of transporting a letter from one city to another was insignificant. As a consequence of its excessive rates, postal service had stagnated since the end of the Napoleonic Wars, while the commerce, industry, and population of Britain had grown and all other public services had doubled. Meanwhile, private courier services were undercutting the government monopoly, illegally but effectively.

The solution, Hill argued, was a single prepaid postage rate for all of Britain, using stamped paper or postage stamps, thereby eliminating most of the work. No longer would postage depend on the number of sheets of paper a letter contained, requiring careful inspection; instead, it would be proportional to the weight, enabling senders to put their letters into an envelope for greater privacy. Postage could then be lowered to one penny for a half-ounce letter sent anywhere in the kingdom. This would transform the Post Office from a tax-collection agency into an instrument of popular communication, granting the working class access to the mails for the first time, thereby encouraging commerce and education. According to Hill, "The religious, moral, and intellectual progress of the people would be accelerated by the unobstructed circulation of letters and of the many cheap and excellent non-political publications of the present day."[36]

Postal officials rejected Hill's proposal, for they doubted that any increase in the amount of mail could possibly compensate for the sharp decline in revenue from each letter. The public, however, greeted the proposal with mass meetings and petitions boasting four million signatures. Under the pressure of public opinion, Parliament passed the reform in 1839, with inland penny postage to begin on January 1, 1840. That year, twice as many letters were sent as the year before, and by 1850 the number had doubled again.[37]

The British postal reform aroused a great deal of interest in other countries. In the United States, the demand for a similar reform was strongest in the northern and eastern states, where private entrepreneurs competed with the public postal service. Congressmen from the South and West resisted reform, for they feared that a loss of revenues would result in reduced service to their regions. Nonetheless, between 1845 and 1851, Congress lowered the postage to three cents for a prepaid half-ounce letter, and five cents for collect-on-delivery. Mandatory prepayment followed in 1854. The reform replaced the ideal of a self-supporting Post Office with that of a public service subsidized by the government.[38]

In France, a bill to introduce a uniform twenty-centime postage (equivalent to twopence) was narrowly defeated in 1844 but finally adopted in 1848. There, too, this change resulted in a surge of letter writing. Since letters were prepaid, they did not have to be registered or even carry a return address.

Interception of the mail and the use of black chambers to decrypt letters seem to have abated from the 1840s until World War I. Historian of cryptography David Kahn noted that the British government stopped intercepting diplomatic correspondence in 1844, as did the French and Austrian governments in 1848. He explained this change as a result of "the political gales of the 1840s which blew down most of Europe's remaining absolutism and the totalitarian agencies that propped it up."[39] Postal historian Yves Danan, however, has offered a different explanation. The decline in postal surveillance after the midcentury, he argued, was the result not of higher ethical standards but of the great increase in the volume of mail, which made it physically impossible for the authorities to inspect all the letters that came through.[40]

The Chappe Telegraph

Many scholars maintain that modern telecommunications began with the electric telegraph. One of the first books on telegraphy, George Sauer's *Telegraph in Europe* (Paris, 1869), discussed only electric telegraphs. A century later, the French historian Catherine Bertho wrote: "The Chappe telegraph . . . is not really part of the means of modern telecommunications. We must date the new age of information to the beginning of electric telegraphy."[41] More recently still, the Center for the History of Electrical Engineering had this to say: "Until the 1840s the speed of long-distance message transmission was limited to the speed of a galloping horse or the fastest sailing ship, much as it had been for the previous 2,000 years. Electricity, in the form of the telegraph, changed all that."[42]

Technologically, the advent of electricity was certainly revolutionary. From an information point of view, however, the revolution began half a century earlier, when Claude Chappe (1763–1805) devised a way to send any message whatsoever, in either direction, much faster than any horse could gallop. That, and not the technical means (electricity, radio waves, fiber optics, or any other), is the essence of telecommunication.

It was the demand for rapid communications that created the telecommunications systems, not the other way around. Before Chappe, people who needed to send a message used Paul Revere's method: they arranged a signal in advance and lit a fire to send it. Fire signals and chains of beacons are mentioned in Homer's *Iliad,* in Aeschylus's *Agamemnon,* and in the works of Thucydides and Herodotus.[43] The Bible says: "Oh ye children of Benjamin, . . . set up a sign of fire in Bethhaccerem: for evil appeareth out of the north, and great destruction" (Jer. 6:1).[44] The Romans, better organized, built 3,197 watchtowers along the Mediterranean and Atlantic coasts and used fire and smoke signals to warn of pirates or enemy ships.[45]

The tradition persisted right up to the French Revolution. Of the Scots, Geoffrey Wilson wrote: "An Act of the Scottish parliament in 1455 laid down that on the approach of English invaders one bale or faggot could be set ablaze. Two on fire would signify that the English were 'coming indeed' and four that they were 'in great force.'"[46] In 1588, when the Spanish Armada was sighted off the coast of Cornwall, fires relayed the news to the English fleet at Plymouth and to the rest of England.[47] France also had coastal watchtowers and prearranged fire signals.[48] And during the American Revolutionary War, General Lafayette used a variety of prearranged signals: shots from a heavy gun, flashes from torches or flares, even "the sun's rays, although no definite code for sending messages appears to have been in operation."[49]

It was not for lack of ideas that the system of one-way prearranged signals persisted as long as it did. In the second century B.C., the Greek historian Polybius proposed using a system of vases that could be seen at a distance and corresponded to the letters of the alphabet, but evidently nothing came of the idea.[50] In May 1684, the philosopher and physicist Robert Hooke spoke to the Royal Society of London on "how to communicate one's mind at distances in as short a time almost as a man can write what he would have sent."[51] He presented the results of experiments in which he represented the letters of the alphabet with boards of different shapes that were to be placed on hilltops so they could be seen at a distance with a telescope. Four years later, Guillaume Amontons demonstrated a similar system in the Luxembourg Gardens in Paris.[52] In the course of the eighteenth century, several other thinkers described clever methods of communicating at a distance, but they did not even get so far as to try them out.[53]

What can we conclude from these abortive attempts? By the late seventeenth century, the idea of an open-ended, bidirectional telecommunications system was in the air. But any serious experiments would have required a substantial investment, and for that, the demand was lacking. Until the 1790s, messengers and the postal system met the everyday needs of governments and merchants, and fire signals served for emergencies.

Claude Chappe was a persistent man.[54] Starting in 1790, he tried several methods of communicating at a distance. He experimented with electricity. He tried using gongs and synchronized clocks with hands that pointed to numbers. He tried shutters painted black on one side and white on the other. Finally, he adopted the "T," a post topped by a thirteen-foot-long board called a *régulateur,* at both ends of which were six-foot boards, or *indicateurs;* all three could be moved with the aid of ropes and pulleys. The *régulateur* could be placed in four positions: horizontal, vertical, oblique right, and oblique left; only the horizontal and vertical positions were used for signaling, however. Each *indicateur* could be placed in seven positions. Thus a total of ninety-eight positions of the arms could be used for signals. The arms were painted black and placed on top of towers, steeples, or high buildings. Silhouetted against the sky, the devices could be seen at a great distance.

Chappe first set up his devices in Paris, but they were torn down by crowds fearful of royalist intrigues. In March 1792, he approached the Legislative Assembly, where his older brother Ignace was a deputy, but was ignored. A year later, he tried again; this time the deputies Joseph Lakanal and Charles-Gilbert Romme supported his proposal, and he received funding to build an experimental line from Saint-Fargeau to Saint-Martin-du-Tertre.[55]

As noted earlier, the experiment was a technical success. More important, it succeeded politically, thanks to Lakanal. French politics were then at the height of their revolutionary fervor. Louis XVI was executed in January 1793, France was at war with the rest of Europe, the Vendée was in full revolt, and the Convention was split into warring factions and heading for the Terror. In August, amid an atmosphere of frenzied crisis, the deputies ordered the construction of fifteen telegraph stations from Paris to Lille in the north of France. They appointed Claude Chappe *ingénieur-télégraphe* under the Ministry of War; his brothers Abraham, Ignace, and Pierre-François became his deputies. When the line to Lille began operating in August 1794, the first official telegram, dated September 1, announced, "Condé is restored to the Republic. Surrender took place this morning at six o'clock."[56]

Chappe's optical telegraph was made of wood, iron, ropes, and stone. It involved no electricity or other scientific innovation—nothing that the ancient Greeks, Persians, or Chinese did not have. As Alexander Field has recently shown, what made it a technical success was not its hardware but its software. The positions of the arms indicated numbers, which in turn corresponded to words or phrases in a codebook. Of the ninety-eight positions, six were reserved for service instructions, leaving ninety-two for messages.

Chappe tried several different codes. His first codebook had 9,999 entries but required four positions for each signal, which made it very slow. In his second code of 1795, each signal consisted of two positions, the first one corresponding to the ninety-two pages in a codebook, the second one to the ninety-two words or phrases on each page. Hence, the device could send any of 8,464 (92 × 92) words or phrases. In 1799, Chappe added another book for geographic names, bringing the total number of signals to 25,392. Yet another code, issued in 1830, contained 45,050 words and phrases.

By using long codebooks and choosing the words and phrases carefully so as to equalize the probability of each position, Chappe was able to compensate for the slow rate of transmission inherent in the hardware.[57] As Claude's brother Ignace later wrote: "Its goal was not to find a language easy to learn without a dictionary . . . but to find the means to express many things with few signs."[58]

To operate such a system, with its complex codes and many stations, required a skilled and efficient administration. Each intermediary station had two *stationnaires,* one to watch the upstream station and call out its positions in a special vocabulary, the other to move the arms into the same position for the downstream station to see. These men, usually veterans, did not understand the signals they were transmitting, but they had to be diligent and accurate so that the message would not be garbled. At each end station was a *directeur* who translated outgoing messages into telegraphic style, then turned the telegrams into code, or who turned incoming codes into messages. In addition, each line had two *inspecteurs* to oversee the line and enforce the regulations. This administrative structure was created and supervised by the Chappe brothers. By the 1830s, it included a thousand *stationnaires,* twenty *directeurs,* and thirty-four *inspecteurs.*[59]

The optical telegraph had two weaknesses. One was human, for it relied on the punctilious performance of duty by every member of the organization. Efficient operation required quasi-military discipline, something that was never in short supply in Napoleonic and Restoration France. The other weakness was natural: the system could not operate at night or in rain or fog. On average, it worked six hours a day in summer, three in winter. A survey conducted in the early 1840s showed that 64 percent of dispatches arrived the day they were sent; in winter, the rate dropped to 33 percent.[60]

On good days, the optical telegraph was remarkably efficient. A line could transmit up to three signals (a number in the codebook or a letter of the alphabet) per minute, with an average of one per minute on a long line. A signal could travel the 225 kilometers between Paris and Lille in one or two minutes, or the 760 kilometers and 120 stations between Paris and Toulon in twelve minutes. In 1820, a hundred-signal telegram took fifty-six minutes to transmit to Lille, seventy-six to Strasbourg, and ninety-five to Bordeaux. By the 1840s, improvements in training and efficiency had doubled these speeds. In addition, it took fifteen to thirty minutes to encode and decode the message at each end. In other words, a line could handle four to six one-hundred-signal telegrams on an average clear day.

To twenty-first-century people, that sounds excruciatingly slow, but if we compare the Chappe system with its predecessors, the progress is striking: a message would have taken three days from Paris to Toulon on horseback, or over a week by stagecoach. The electric telegraph that eventually supplanted Chappe's system represented a less dramatic improvement.

Optical Telegraph Networks to 1815

Through all the changes of policies and ideologies, every French government expanded the telegraph network and supported the family that ran it. Under the Directory (1795–1799), the Chappe brothers built lines east to Strasbourg, west to Brest, and north to Dunkirk and Brussels. Napoleon extended the network south to Lyon and Marseilles. As his empire grew, lines radiated to Turin, Milan, and Venice, to Antwerp and Amsterdam, and to Mainz.[61]

In addition to the elaborate Chappe network, the Napoleonic government also created a network of coastal telegraphs to warn of enemy warships. At first they used flags and pennants; later they used a simple mechanism, called a *sémaphore,* and a simple codebook. By the end of Napoleon's reign, France had several hundred such stations.[62]

Neither hardware nor software can explain the success of the optical telegraph system, which was too complex and costly and too closely tied to the government to be anything but an expression of power and culture. Like the railroads and electric power of the later nineteenth century or the television networks and airlines of our own era, it was a social construction.[63] To what social forces, then, can we attribute the success of the optical telegraph?

The first and most obvious was military necessity. In his petition to the Legislative Assembly, Chappe promised that "the legislative body will be able to have its commands reach our borders and receive the answer in the course of a single session."[64] His system got its start at the peak of the French Revolution, when the National Convention desperately needed real-time information on the battles that would determine the fate of the nation and the revolution, and wanted to keep an eye on its generals, whom it did not fully trust. Napoleon, whose success was due, more than anything, to the superior speed at which he maneuvered his armies, was just as eager for timely information as were his revolutionary predecessors.

The optical telegraph was much more than a military necessity, however. From the beginning, it had a profound political, even ideological, significance. As Chappe wrote Lakanal in 1793, "The establishment of the telegraph is . . . the best response to the publicists who think that France is too large to form a Republic. The telegraph shortens distances and, in a way, brings an immense population together at a single point."[65] Bertrand Barère, prosecutor of Louis XVI and member of the Committee of Public Safety, put it even more succinctly: "By this invention, distances vanish. . . . this is a means to consolidate the unity of the Republic."[66] In other words, the telegraph was instrumental in the formation of the French nation-state.

The French government was so aware of the value of the telegraph as a means of consolidating and defending the unity of the nation that it placed the network under the Ministry of War, and later under the Ministry of the Interior (i.e., the police). The network was owned and operated by the government, and its use was restricted to government messages. When budget cuts threatened to close down several lines, Claude Chappe suggested that the network might increase its revenues by transmitting news dispatches, ships' arrivals and departures, stock and foreign exchange quotations, and other public information. Napoleon rejected all but one of these suggestions; the only news items allowed on the network were the results of the national lottery, to discourage speculation. Otherwise, the emperor reserved the network for military orders and reports and for official proclamations such as the announcement of the birth of his son in March 1811.[67]

Even though politics and war go a long way toward explaining the success of the optical telegraph in France, they are not sufficient. After all, there had been earlier wars and uprisings, yet governments before 1794 had not felt the need to build and maintain, at great expense, elaborate telecommunications lines. As Patrice Flichy has recently argued, what had changed was a new concept, the idea that humans could reorganize space and time through the use of reason.[68] The telegraph appeared at the same time that revolutionaries were restructuring the national territory into equal departments, imposing a homogeneous system of weights and measures, and reorganizing time itself through a new calendar. The same *mentalité* led them to seek a rational solution to the problem of communicating at a distance. The optical telegraph was not only a response to war but also a child of the Age of Reason. Revolutionary fervor ebbed after 1794, but the cult of reason never faltered.

If optical telegraphy was indeed a child of reason and war, and not a product of the genius of one man or one nation, it should have spread to other countries that combined the *mentalité* of the Enlightenment with the exigencies of war. And so it did.

In Britain, the outbreak of war and news of the Chappe telegraph inspired several amateurs to invent systems of their own. In 1794, Richard Edgeworth, an Irish landowner, suggested using fourteen-foot-high stands on hilltops fifteen to twenty miles apart. Each station would have two or three men armed with telescopes and triangular boards that could point in any of eight directions, representing the digits 0 through 7. He presented his plan to the Admiralty but was turned down.[69] A year later, two inventors presented the Admiralty with devices consisting of shutters that opened and closed. The Reverend John Gamble's system consisted of five shutters indicating the letters of the alphabet. Lord George Murray's had six shutters in two columns, with sixty-three combinations indicating letters, numerals, and a few code phrases such as "line-of-battleship" or "to sail, the first fair wind, to the northward."

The Admiralty picked Murray's method and erected stations linking London with Sheerness, Deal, and Portsmouth in 1796, at the height of the French revolutionary wars. When the Napoleonic Wars broke out in 1804, the Admiralty added lines to Plymouth in 1806 and Yarmouth in 1808. The system was dismantled in 1814, in the belief that peace had come.[70]

Sweden also built optical telegraphs. The first was the creation of Abraham Clewberg-Edelcrantz, a member of the Swedish Academy and private secretary to King Gustavus IV, who read about the Chappe system in the *Gentleman's Magazine* of September 1794. He demonstrated his first line on the king's birthday, November 1. Shortly thereafter, he erected three short lines connecting the royal castle in Stockholm to nearby fortresses and islands. By 1801, in anticipation of a British attack, a line was extended to Denmark. By 1809, the Swedish telegraph network had fifty stations covering two hundred kilometers, mainly along the coast to the north and south of Stockholm. It seems to have been used for local defense and under royal auspices. With no other commercial or naval purpose, it was largely abandoned after 1815.[71]

Spain also built a few local lines in the early years of the century between Madrid and the royal palace of Aranjuez and between the fortress of Cadiz and neighboring towns; but they were abandoned in the Napoleonic invasion and the turmoil that followed.[72]

Optical Telegraphy after 1815

In 1815, France lost its telegraph lines in Italy, Germany, and the Low Countries. Far from abandoning the network within France, however, the restored monarchy maintained existing lines and built new ones from Paris to Toulon (1821), Bordeaux and Bayonne (1823), Avignon and Montpellier (1832), and Dijon and Besançon (1842). By the 1840s, the optical network included over 530 stations and covered five thousand kilometers.[73]

The telegraph served Napoleon's successors as well as it had served him and his revolutionary predecessors, albeit in a different fashion. The governments of the Restoration (1815–1830) and the July Monarchy (1830–1848) lived in fear of conspiracies and uprisings and used the telegraph as a means of police control. As Abraham Chappe explained in 1832: "When the government must be ready to defend itself against the attacks of parties, when every minute must be put to use, . . . such a means can justly be considered one of the most powerful and worthwhile tools of administration. Telegraphy is an element of power and order."[74]

Politicians and military men were not the only ones who wanted more efficient communications. Businessmen did too, especially bankers and financiers, for whom time, even short intervals, had monetary value. Their demand for telecommunications produced two conflicting responses: liberalism in Britain and repression in France.

After 1815, financial activity quickened throughout western Europe, as interest in stock markets, bond issues, and foreign exchange quotations surged. The Rothschilds, with their pigeon post and private courier service, had shown what profits could be made from getting information quickly. It was not long before someone thought of using the telegraph to transmit business news. In 1831, Alexandre Ferrier proposed a commercial telegraph to connect London and Paris, and later other cities as well. The following year, encouraged by Prime Minister Casimir-Perier, the banker Laffitte, and other influential persons, Ferrier established a company to transmit commercial news by telegraph. His first line, from Paris to Rouen, opened in July 1833, but it lost money and closed a few months later.[75]

Other crude telegraphs appeared, some of them clandestine. Messages indicating the prime interest rate were transmitted once a day from Paris to Lyon by men standing on hilltops waving white cloths. Between Angoulême and Bordeaux, a line of windmills used the positions of their sails to transmit stock market quotations. Two bankers from Bordeaux—Joseph and François Blanc—conspired with government telegraph employees to slip a clandestine signal onto the end of official telegrams, indicating whether the Paris Bourse was up or down. Since the government did not allow such information on its lines and the mails took five days between Paris and Bordeaux, the Blancs quickly became rich. They were arrested, put on trial in March 1837, and acquitted because there was no law forbidding the private use of the telegraph. When a Belgian company proposed to signal stock market quotations using black rectangles and operators with telescopes, the interior minister advised prefects to observe but not interfere. Nonetheless, local authorities continued to harass the operators and forced the line to close after a year.

Meanwhile, political opposition to clandestine telegraphs was growing. Part of it came from policemen and provincial prefects, who saw conspiracies and subversion under every bush. On several occasions, the people who operated these "telegraphs" were arrested and harassed by local gendarmes, only to be released on orders from Paris.[76] In August 1836, Minister of the Interior Gasparin reprimanded the prefect of Angoulême for arresting clandestine telegraphers:

> I approve your solicitude regarding the clandestine telegraph.... In other places similar enterprises have aroused my attention; but I have ascertained that, at least so far, they only involve the stock market. In the absence of any law forbidding it, we must avoid using coercion and ordering confiscations which, if they were brought to court, would inevitably be overturned. Limit yourself to ordering a continuing surveillance and warn the principal agents of the enterprise ... that if they should favor partisan interests, they would incur grave sanctions.[77]

At no time in its history—not even in the 1830s—has France felt comfortable with capitalism. Many deputies believed that public access to the telegraph would favor wealthy speculators at the expense of impecunious ones. As Deputy Fulchiron put it: "Until now, I have not seen private individuals open telegraph lines with good intentions.... [It is] brigandage, designed to rob those who do not know the news from the Paris Bourse."[78] In its anxiety about the dangers of political and economic freedom, the Chamber of Deputies voted on May 3, 1837, to forbid anyone but the government to send information from one place to another. The public was allowed to use the postal service, but the telegraphs were reserved for the government alone.

Even after Waterloo, the British Admiralty remained worried. Rather than reopen its shutter telegraph lines, it built a new optical telegraph line from London to Sheerness at the mouth of the Thames in 1816 and another one to Portsmouth on the Channel in 1824. This system used a two-arm semaphore devised by Rear Admiral Sir Home Popham in imitation of the Chappe telegraph. It could transmit faster and be read more easily than Murray's, even without a telescope. It was costly, however, for it required a house with an officer and two men every five to ten miles. Such was the inertia of the Admiralty that this system lasted until 1847, long after the electric telegraph had proved its superiority.[79]

In addition to the Admiralty telegraph, Britain also had several commercial telegraphs that served shipowners and merchants. B. L. Watson erected the first of these between Holyhead and Liverpool in 1827 to announce the arrival of ships. It consisted of forty- to fifty-foot-high masts carrying three pairs of arms. The upper arms indicated a chapter in Watson's *Code of Signals,* covering letters of the alphabet, points of the compass, names of ships, place-names, common words, or sentences; all three pairs of arms then indicated an item within that chapter. The system was obviously derived from Chappe's. In 1839, the Liverpool-Holyhead line was taken over by Lieutenant William Lord of the Royal Navy, while Watson opened new lines near Hull, Southampton, Dartmouth, and other ports.[80]

The British optical telegraphs differed from the French in several important ways. First, no government agency other than the Admiralty seems to have been the least bit interested in telegraphy; no one suggested that telegraphy could build national unity, prevent uprisings and conspiracies, or play any other political role. Second, there was no opposition to privately owned commercial lines; this is not surprising, since Britain also had privately owned canals and turnpikes.[81] Finally, Britain's optical telegraphs did not form a network but only isolated lines.

There was a flurry of interest in optical telegraphy throughout Europe in the 1790s, but only a few short lines were built outside of Britain and the Napoleonic empire. Then, after a forty-year lull, interest in optical telegraphy revived in the 1830s.

In Hamburg, a private entrepreneur constructed a line to serve the local shippers and merchants. In Sweden, Carl Fredrik Akrell opened with a line from Karlskrona to Drottningskär in 1834; to defray its costs, this line accepted private messages, the first to do so. The Prussian government built a 550-kilometer-long line from Berlin to Cologne and Koblenz in 1832–1834, linking the two parts of the kingdom. The Russian government, after building local lines near Saint Petersburg in the 1820s and 1830s, built one in 1839 from Saint Petersburg to Warsaw, a distance of 830 kilometers. In both Prussia and Russia, national unity meant controlling distant provinces.[82]

In Spain, as Luis Enrique Otero Carvajal explains, "There is a clear connection between the development of the telegraph and the consolidation of the liberal State."[83] The difficulty of consolidating the liberal state (meaning one modeled on France) is reflected in the uses of telegraphy. The first short lines, reserved for the royal family, were built between Madrid and nearby royal palaces. Only in 1844 did the government decide to construct a national network linking the capital with San Sebastian in the north, Valencia and Barcelona in the west, and Cadiz in the south. In the codebook, seen only by high government officials and military commanders, 75 percent of the phrases referred to military matters or public order. The optical network, completed in the mid-1850s, was replaced within five years by an electric one.[84]

With few exceptions, these were government-owned systems reserved for official or military traffic. They consisted primarily of unconnected short lines and used a variety of structures and codes. Even when two systems met, as at the French-Spanish border, the rare message going from one system to the other had to be decoded, translated, hand carried across the gap, and encoded for further transmission. Public telecommunication had to await the introduction of the electric telegraph.[85]

Optical telegraphy also spread overseas, part of the expansion of European influence of the time. Under the Westernizing khedive Mehemet Ali, Egypt acquired a telegraph linking Cairo and Alexandria in the 1820s; it was the first non-Western country to build such a system. Algeria and Australia had very active systems, unlike South Africa and India, where telegraphy was little used before the advent of electricity.[86]

In the United States, the federal and state governments left telegraphs to private entrepreneurs. The first lines were harbor telegraphs. In 1801, Jonathan Grout opened a seventy-two-mile line between Boston and Martha's Vineyard to announce the arrival of ships; his line seems to have done poorly, for it folded in 1807. The next harbor telegraph connected Brooklyn and Staten Island, New York, during the War of 1812.

The most successful harbor telegraph was founded in Boston in 1820 by Samuel Topliff, the manager of the Exchange Coffee House. In 1822, it was taken over and expanded by John Rowe Parker, who adopted a code very similar to the one used on the Liverpool-Holyhead telegraph, established a few years later. This was no coincidence, for Boston and Liverpool had very close commercial ties at the time.

In the 1820s, speculators obtained market information before the general public by using mounted messengers who could outrun the postal coaches. Postmaster General John McLean considered creating a network of optical telegraphs for commercial information. Although Congress never authorized this project, the idea of a national telegraph system was to return a few years later when it took up Morse's electric telegraph.[87]

Not until 1840 did an optical line connect two cities, New York and Philadelphia, to convey stock prices and lottery numbers. Built by the Philadelphia stockbroker William Briggs, it was replaced five years later by the electric telegraph.[88]

The American experience shows that there existed a demand for real-time information, but only shippers and stockbrokers could afford the cost of optical telegraphy—hence the enthusiasm with which Americans adopted the much cheaper electric telegraph.

From Optical to Electric Telegraphy

Scholars have written volumes on the subject of the electric telegraph. Almost all of them describe its invention as the dawn of a new age. Thus, in his book *Emulation and Invention,* Brooke Hindle wrote:

The electromagnetic telegraph, like the steamboat, was something new under the sun. It was not an improvement within an existing technology, and it was not a combination of existing capabilities put together in answer to a clear social need. It appeared when it did because not until then had it been possible. The door was opened by the new knowledge of electricity developed by Ampère and Oersted and of electromagnetism by Sturgeon and Henry. This understanding was the precondition for the telegraph, and consequently it has been labeled the first science-based invention.[89]

Equating telegraphy with the electric telegraph is understandable if one thinks of the latter from the perspective of the devices it used or the science involved. As a means of communication, however, the electric telegraph most certainly *was* an "improvement within an existing technology." The question then arises: What elicited this improvement in the minds of its inventors?[90]

During the 1830s, Schilling, Gauss and Weber, Steinheil, and Wheatstone and Cooke all showed that electricity could be used to transmit messages. These inventors tried to create telegraphs in which the letters of the alphabet could be read directly off the receiver. Samuel Morse's contribution was not the electric telegraph but a code that allowed the use of only one wire, with the earth serving as a return; the cost savings more than compensated for the need for trained operators.

Morse deserves all the praise he has received, but he did not come up with his invention in a vacuum. Rather, he thought of it on board the *Sully* while returning from France. Before leaving Paris, he supposedly told his friend Richard Habersham: "The mails in our country are too slow, this French telegraph is better, and would do even better in our clear atmosphere than here, where half the time fogs obscure the skies. . . . But this will not be fast enough. *The lightning would serve us better.*"[91]

International interest in electric telegraphy had several causes. On the supply side, progress in physics made electric telegraphy possible. Science had provided the necessary theory in work by Oersted, Ampère, and Faraday's on the relationship between electricity and magnetism. More practically, experimenters were able to obtain reliable batteries. By 1838, the process of invention shifted from experiments to patents, including those of Wheatstone and Cooke, Edward Davy, William Alexander, and Samuel Morse.

The electric telegraph had a far greater capacity than the optical one because it could handle more information faster. An optical line could carry, on average, one or two signals per minute; since the average word or phrase in the codebook represented by one signal was ten characters long, this meant that an optical line could carry ten to twenty characters per minute. In comparison, a Cooke and Wheatstone needle telegraph of 1837 could handle twenty-five characters per minute, and a Morse telegraph, sixty. More important, the electric telegraph was not impeded by darkness or bad weather. Whereas the French optical lines operated, on average, six hours a day in summer and three in winter, an electric line could, if needed, operate day and night. In other words, from the beginning, the electric telegraph could handle at least ten times more information than the optical telegraph could after half a century of improvements and refinements.[92]

Electric telegraphy had become attractive on the demand side as well. By the 1830s, as we have seen, governments and entrepreneurs were setting up optical telegraph lines in most European countries, in the United States, and in other parts of the world. The optical telegraph proved useful in building nationhood, in maintaining public order, in preventing revolution, and in transmitting commercial information.

Inventors like Morse naturally turned to their government for support. The first electric telegraph in the United States, the Baltimore-Washington line, was operated by the Post Office from 1845 to 1847. Yet governments were technologically conservative; their demand was limited and did not justify investing in an electric telegraph network. In the United States, telegraphy became a private enterprise by default when Congress lost interest.

In Britain, William Cooke realized that the speed and capacity of the new device required new customers. The telegraph had long been valuable to shippers and shipowners in announcing ships' arrivals. News services, pigeon post, and the various attempts to set up alternative optical systems in France showed that there was a demand for rapid information among financiers and stockbrokers. On the new railways, information about trains had to precede the trains themselves, to prevent crashes. Cooke and Wheatstone's first operating electric telegraph was strung along the Great Western Railway in England. In countries that permitted private enterprise in telegraphy, the results were astonishing. By 1848, telegraph lines crisscrossed the British Isles and linked all the United States east of the Mississippi, except Florida.

France, which had pioneered the optical telegraph, resisted the electric one for political reasons. In 1842, the Chamber of Deputies voted to subsidize experiments with nighttime transmission on the optical lines, even though the physicist François Arago protested that the Chappe system was obsolete. Two years later, a commission found that Britain, the United States, and the German states were all forging ahead with electric telegraphs. In response, the electrician Louis Breguet and Alphonse Foy, director of the government's optical network, devised a two-needle telegraph that reproduced, on a small scale, the movements of the Chappe machine. This was not so much a case of technological conservatism as a rational desire to continue using the skills of existing telegraph personnel. Though slower than its neighbors, France gradually acquired electric lines. It soon became apparent that, unlike the optical lines, the electric ones could handle all conceivable official messages and still remain unused nine-tenths of the time. In 1850, under pressure from progressive Saint-Simonians, the business community, and the new president Louis-Napoleon Bonaparte (soon to be Napoleon III), the National Assembly finally allowed public access to its telegraph lines.[93]

If the electric telegraph was indeed revolutionary, it is not just because it was a child of electricity, "the first science-based invention." Rather, it represented a quantum leap in capacity and flexibility and a radical decline in cost compared with its optical predecessor. It opened up real-time information to railways, stockbrokers, capitalists, and merchants, to newspapers, and finally to the general public.

Naval Signaling

The combination of reason and war that led to the Chappe telegraph also produced a revolution in another form of communication: naval signaling. Before the eighteenth century, communication between ships was rudimentary, unidirectional, and prone to errors. According to the fourteenth-century "Black Book of the Admiralty," signals were used to identify the ships of the admiral and rear admiral, to note the presence of the enemy, and to call a council. Frobisher's fleet orders of 1578 declared: "Upon the sight of an Ensigne in the mast of the Admirall (a piece being shot off) the whole fleet shall repaire to the Admirall, to understand such conference as the Generall is to have with them." Any other message had to be transmitted orally, through "speaking trumpets" or by sending a boat.[94]

In 1649, the duke of York (later James II) began issuing "Fighting Instructions," a list of twenty-five signals made by displaying five flags at any of five different positions on the ship's rigging. New "Fighting Instructions" issued during the Dutch War of 1652–1654 used several more flags, along with miscellaneous other objects: a cask hoisted at the yardarm meant "need water," a hatchet meant "need wood," a tablecloth meant an invitation to dinner. By 1673, when the "Sailing and Fighting Instructions" were first printed, the number of flags had risen to fifteen and the number of positions to eighteen. With each edition, more and more new flags were needed until, by 1782, there were fifty flags, each one having several meanings, depending on its position.[95] The more elaborate the system of prearranged signals, the more rigid were the tactics it imposed, as naval historian John Keegan explains: "Unless the signals officers aboard accompanying ships had the hoists by heart, they could not decipher. . . . Admirals thus had to keep their orders simple, even though the changes of course and activity they wished, and ought to have been able, to order were complex and manifold."[96] The result was that, once a battle had started, "the natural tendency of individual ship captains was to seek out the nearest enemy ship and concentrate fire upon it."[97]

Naval communications were completely redesigned by three officers of the Royal Navy, Captain (later Rear Admiral) Richard Kempenfelt, Admiral Lord Howe, and Rear Admiral Sir Home Popham. The naval battles of the American Revolutionary War had convinced Kempenfelt that the "whole system of the 'Fighting Instructions' should be abolished because of their utter inefficiency." In 1779/80, he introduced a numerary system with three sets of ten flags each. This allowed a three-flag hoist to signify any number from 0 to 999, with each number referring to a sentence in a codebook.

Lord Howe began experimenting with a codebook during the American Revolutionary War. In 1790, he published both the *Signal Book for the Ships of War,* which listed numbers and sentences, and the *Instructions for the Conduct of Ships of War, Explanatory of, and Relative to the Signals Contained in the Signal Book.* This method divided the communications process into several parts: issuing the message, encoding it as flag signals, transmitting the signals, receiving them, decoding them with the *Signal Book,* and looking up the decoded message in the *Instructions.* During the French Revolution, Howe's books underwent many editions, the 1799 edition being officially issued by the Admiralty.[98]

Kempenfelt and Howe's system was not original. The French admiral Mahé de la Bourdonnais had proposed a numerary code as early as 1738, although it does not seem to have been used. Another French officer, Sébastian Francisco Bigot, published *Tactique navale ou traité des évolutions et des signaux* in 1763, which was translated into English in 1767.[99] Their contribution needed only the pressure of war to be implemented.

Howe and Kempenfelt's method, while an enormous improvement over previous systems, was still rigid. The 1799 edition, for instance, contained 340 signals, and only messages included among these signals could be sent. Popham remedied this defect in 1800 when he published his *Telegraphic Signals or Marine Vocabulary* as a supplement to Lord Howe's *Signal Book.* Using twenty-four different flags in hoists of two or three, Popham could transmit the numerals 0 to 9, the letters of the alphabet, or code numbers referring to words or sentences. Like Lord Howe's *Signal Book* before it, Popham's *Telegraphic Signals* went through several editions. The Admiralty adopted the 1803 edition, with its thousands of words and sentences, on an experimental basis, and made the 1813 edition the official code of the Royal Navy.[100]

Popham's system was both rapid and flexible, for it could transmit any message not only from the admiral to his fleet but also between any two ships. In Keegan's words, it "at last put a flexible, comprehensive and instantly communicable range of signals at a sea commander's disposal."[101] It was, in all respects, the naval equivalent of Chappe's land telegraph.

The commander who made the most spectacular use of Popham's code was Admiral Horatio Nelson. In 1803, it allowed him to blockade Toulon with a more distant and widespread line of frigates than had been possible earlier. Two years later, while blockading Admiral Villeneuve's combined French and Spanish fleet in Cadiz, he distributed copies of Popham's book to his fleet; this allowed him to engage in two-way conversations with his captains. On October 17, 1805, two days before the Battle of Trafalgar, Captain Blackwood of the frigate *Euryalus* wrote: "At this moment we are within four miles of the Enemy, and *talking to* Lord Nelson by means of Sir H. Popham's signals, though so distant, but repeated along by the rest of the frigates of this Squadron." On October 19, at 7:00 A.M., the frigate *Sirius* hoisted signal number 370: "Enemy ships are coming out of port"; it was retransmitted by the frigates *Euryalus, Phoebe, Naiad, Defence, Colossus,* and *Mars,* reaching Nelson on the *Victory,* forty-eight miles from the *Sirius,* at 9:30 A.M. Signals went up and down the line of frigates. Blackwood signaled: "The enemy appears to be determined to push to the westward, thirty ships." Nelson replied: "I rely on your keeping sight of the enemy." As the French and Spanish fleet came into sight, Nelson issued the most famous message in naval history: 253-269-863-261-471-958-220-370-4-21-19-24: "England expects that every man will do his d-u-t-y" (*duty* was spelled out because it was not in the codebook).[102]

What gave the Royal Navy the victory over the French and Spanish fleets was Nelson's tactic of "breaking the line," that is, driving his ships through the gaps between the ships in the enemy's line of battle. As Keegan remarks:

> Trafalgar, a "revolutionary" battle in its effects, owed its nature to revolutionary tactics; but those tactics . . . were chiefly the product of a revolution in control, brought about by the innovation of Home Popham's telegraphic signalling system. It was because Nelson had at his disposal the means to direct his ships wherever he wanted them to go at whichever moment he chose that he could risk the experiment of "breaking the line from to windward," and so encompass the destruction of the Combined Fleet.[103]

After Napoleon's final defeat at Waterloo on June 18, 1815, attention shifted from military to commercial activities. Signaling between warships, which had improved so dramatically in the previous twenty years, inspired a similar development among merchant vessels.

The man who brought the new signaling to the merchant marine was Captain Frederick Marryat (1792–1848), the son of Joseph Marryat, chairman of Lloyd's, the maritime insurance company. His *Code of Signals for the Use of Vessels Employed in the Merchant Service,* first published in 1817, was quickly adopted by British merchant ships, agents of Lloyd's, and coast guard stations. It was more complex and less rapid than Popham's *Telegraphic Signals,* for merchant ships had more time than warships. It used ten flags indicating the digits, of which up to four were hoisted at one time; in addition, pennants indicated one of six codebooks in which to look up the number indicated by the flags. These books referred to British warships, foreign warships and merchantmen, geographic locations, sentences, common expressions, words, and the alphabet.

Although competing French and American codes soon appeared, Marryat's code was gradually adopted by the merchant marines of France, the United States, and most other maritime countries; such was the influence of Britain in world trade. The most successful book of its kind, Marryat's *Code* went through nineteen editions between 1817 and 1879.[104] Unlike optical telegraphs, naval and maritime flag signaling persisted well into the twentieth century, when it was gradually superseded by radio-telegraphy.[105]

At the beginning of this chapter, I mentioned five characteristics of long-distance communications systems: their organization, ownership, financing, access, and surveillance. In the history of postal systems, I noted an evolution toward larger, denser, and more efficient permanent networks; toward broader access; from exclusively official messages to costly postage; and from costly to cheap postage.

The other three characteristics, however, do not follow a clear trend. In the period 1700–1850, governmental and private postal systems still competed, although the trend was toward public ownership, even in the United States. Likewise, financing went back and forth between profits for private firms and government subsidies or revenues. The privacy of communications, though vulnerable to wars and political upheavals, gained legal acceptance in the spirit of the liberal revolutions, forcing surveillance underground.

Given these changes, it is interesting to compare the evolution of postal and telegraph systems in the period 1700–1850. By the end of the Old Regime, postal service in France and England had become widespread, open to private customers, and fairly efficient, but it was still very costly and out of reach of most people. In the early nineteenth century, the United States introduced cheap postage, but only for newspapers. Then, in the mid–nineteenth century, Britain introduced the cheap postage that is now fairly universal.

The telegraph essentially recapitulated the evolution of the postal systems. In France, the optical telegraph was similar to the Roman *cursus pub-*

licus, a governmental network reserved for official messages; elsewhere it consisted only of short lines. The electric telegraph, in contrast, had both high fixed costs and much greater capacity. For financial reasons, therefore, governments everywhere allowed public access. To allay their security concerns, they switched from prohibition or censorship to covert surveillance.[106]

Two centuries later, the more advanced countries of the world have achieved mass mailings for everyone and telephones for the great majority, and they are moving toward universal access to cellular telephones and the Internet. The issue of ownership, however, is still being debated; witness the privatization of telecommunications and the resistance it has encountered. Likewise, the issue of subsidies is still in question: Should the Internet be subsidized by governments, or should it charge customers or carry advertisements?

Even the question of privacy versus surveillance is still alive. Two hundred years after the liberal revolutions, elected officials sworn to uphold the constitutional rights of citizens to privacy still propose to censor private communications in the name of protecting the public from hate speech, pornography, and terrorism. The instrumental progress of communications is obvious and irrefutable; whether this constitutes moral progress is very much in doubt.

Notes

1. Quoted in David Hackett Fischer, *Paul Revere's Ride, and the Battle of Lexington and Concord* (New York: Oxford University Press, 1994), 99. The poem "The Midnight Ride of Paul Revere" is from Henry Wadsworth Longfellow, *Poetical Works: Complete Edition* (Boston, J. R. Osgood, 1872), 290.

2. Geoffrey Wilson, *The Old Telegraphs* (Chichester: Phillimore, 1976), 122; see also Duane Koenig, "Telegraphs and Telegrams in Revolutionary France," *Scientific Monthly* 54 (December 1944): 433.

3. Herodotus, *The Persian Wars,* vol. VI, chaps. 105–6, in Francis R. B. Godolphin, *The Greek Historians* (New York: Random House, 1942), I:374–75.

4. Herodotus, *Persian Wars,* vol. VIII, chap. 98, in Godolphin, *Greek Historians,* I:499.

5. Alexis Belloc, *Les postes françaises; recherches historiques sur leur origine, leur développement, leur législation* (Paris: Fermin-Didot, 1886), 7–15; B. Laurent, *Poste et postiers* (Paris: Octave Doin, 1922), 7–15; and Wayne E. Fuller, *The American Mail: Enlarger of the Common Life* (Chicago: University of Chicago Press, 1972), 4–5.

6. Max Piendl, *Das Fürstliche Haus Thurn und Taxis: Zur Geschichte des Hauses und der Thurn und Taxis-Post* (Regensburg: Pustet, 1980), 7–83.

7. On the early French postal system, see Yves Maxime Danan, *Histoire postale et libertés publiques: Le droit de libre communication des idées et opinions par voie de correspondance*

(Paris: Pichon & Durand-Auzias, 1965), 18–24; Eugène Vaillé, *Histoire générale des postes françaises* (Paris: Presses Universitaires de France, 1947), vols. 3 and 4; Belloc, *Les postes françaises*, 16–17, 59–63; and Laurent, *Poste et postiers*, 7–10.

8. Joseph C. Hemmeon, *The History of the British Post Office* (Cambridge, Mass.: Harvard University Press, 1912), 4–14; Frank Staff, *The Penny Post* (London: Lutterworth, 1964), 20–28.

9. Hemmeon, *History of the British Post Office*, 23–24.

10. Howard Robinson, *The British Post Office: A History* (Princeton, N.J.: Princeton University Press, 1948), 70; Hemmeon, *History of the British Post Office*, 28–30; Staff, *Penny Post*, 37–48.

11. Staff, *Penny Post*, 54; Hemmeon, *History of the British Post Office*, 34–35, 48; Robinson, 96–98.

12. Hemmeon, *History of the British Post Office*, 46; Robinson, *British Post Office*, 120. On the connections between the postal systems and the secret intelligence services, see Eugène Vaillé, *Le cabinet noir* (Paris: Presses universitaires de France, 1950), and Kenneth Ellis, *The Post Office in the Eighteenth Century: A Study in Administrative History* (London: and New York: Oxford University Press, 1958).

13. David Kahn, *The Codebreakers: The Story of Secret Writing* (New York: Macmillan, 1967), 163–64.

14. Staff, *Penny Post*, 57; Robinson, *British Post Office*, 100–110; Hemmeon, *History of the British Post Office*, 36–38.

15. Vaillé, *Histoire générale*, VI, pt. 1, p. 275.

16. Belloc, *Les postes françaises*, 220–33; Hemmeon, *History of the British Post Office*, 40, 100–105; Robinson, *British Post Office*, 125–27, 139–42, 223–38.

17. Staff, *Penny Post*, 64–73; Robinson, *British Post Office*, 192–93; Hemmeon, *History of the British Post Office*, 52–53.

18. Laurent, *Post et postiers*, 11–17.

19. Danan, *Histoire postale*, 61.

20. Ibid., 29, 53–63; Laurent, *Post et postiers*, 12; Belloc, *Les postes françaises* 252–57.

21. Richard R. John, *Spreading the News: The American Postal System from Franklin to Morse* (Cambridge, Mass.: Harvard University Press, 1995), chaps. 1–3.

22. Ibid., 26, 293 n. 8; Fuller, *American Mail*, 13–29.

23. Richard D. Brown, *Knowledge Is Power: The Diffusion of Information in Early America, 1700–1865* (New York: Oxford University Press, 1989), 247–49.

24. Fuller, *American Mail*, 31–40; John, *Spreading the News*, 25–27.

25. Benjamin Rush, "Address to the People of the United States" (1787), quoted in John, *Spreading the News*, 29–30.

26. John, *Spreading the News*, 49–50.

27. Ibid., 51.

28. Fuller, *American Mail*, 24–25.

29. John, *Spreading the News*, 36.

30. Ibid., 4, 38.

31. Ibid., 53–55.

32. Ibid., 91–110.

33. Ibid., 17–18.

34. Ibid., 159; Fuller, *American Mail*, 61.

35. Robinson, *British Post Office*, 241.

36. Rowland Hill, *Post Office Reform: Its Importance and Practicability*, 4th ed. (London: Charles Knight, 1838), 6.

37. On Hill's reform, see Staff, *Penny Post*, 76–95; Robinson, *British Post Office*, 244–57; and Danan, *Histoire postale*, 22–43.

38. Fuller, *American Mail*, 64–66; John, *Spreading the News*, 160; Staff, *Penny Post*, 97–98.

39. Kahn, *Codebreakers*, 188.

40. Danan, *Histoire postale*, 66–73.

41. Catherine Bertho, *Télégraphes et téléphones de Valmy au microprocesseur* (Paris: Livre de Poche, 1981), 9.

42. Center for the History of Electrical Engineering, *Newsletter*, no. 38 (spring 1995): 1.

43. George Dyson, *Darwin among the Machines: The Evolution of Global Intelligence* (Reading, Mass.: Addison-Wesley, 1997), 131–38.

44. Capt. L. S. Howeth, USN, *History of Communications-Electronics in the United States Navy* (Washington, D.C.: Office of Naval History, 1963), 3.

45. Yves Lecouturier, "Les sémaphores de la Marine," in Fédération Nationale des Associations de personnel des Postes et Télécommunications pour la Recherche Historique, *La Télégraphie Chappe* (Jarville-la-Malgrange: Editions de l'Est, 1993), 306; Wolfgang Riepl, *Das Nachrichtenwesen des Altertums, mit besonderer Rücksicht auf die Römer* (Leipzig, 1913), 74–78; Gerald J. Holzmann and Björn Pehrson, *The Early History of Data Networks* (Los Alamitos, Calif.: IEEE Computer Society Press, 1994), 15–23.

46. Geoffrey Wilson, *The Old Telegraphs*, 2–4.

47. Colin Martin and Geoffrey Parker, *The Spanish Armada* (London: Hamilton, 1988), 23.

48. Alexis Belloc, *La télégraphie historique, depuis les temps les plus reculés jusqu'à nos jours* (Paris: Fermin-Didot, 1888), 1–21.

49. Major D. B. Sanger, "General La Fayette: Some Notes on His Contribution to Signal Communications," *Signal Corps Bulletin* 78 (May–June 1934): 49.

50. Holzmann and Pehrson, *Early History of Data Networks*, 23–29.

51. Robert Hooke, "Discourse Shewing a Way to communicate one's Mind at great Distances" (speech to the Royal Society, May 21, 1684), in *Philosophical Experiments and Observations of the late Eminent Dr. Robert Hooke*, ed. W. Derham (London: W. Derham, 1726), 142–43.

52. Edouard Gerspach, "Histoire administrative de la Télégraphie aérienne en France," *Annales Télégraphiques* 3 (1860): 48–49; Belloc, *La télégraphie historique*, 58–59; Geoffrey Wilson, *The Old Telegraphs*, 5, 120; Holzmann and Pehrson, *Early History of Data Networks*, 31–39.

53. Geoffrey Wilson, *The Old Telegraphs*, 112–19.

54. Although Claude Chappe has been a hero in France for two hundred years, his telegraph has only recently begun to interest scholars in other countries. See, in particular, Alexander J. Field, "French Optical Telegraphy, 1793–1855: Hardware, Software, Administration," *Technology and Culture* 35 (April 1994): 315–47;

Holzmann and Pehrson, *Early History of Data Networks*, 51–55; and Holzmann and Pehrson, "The First Data Networks," *Scientific American*, January 1994, 124–29.

55. On the beginnings of the Chappe telegraph, see Ignace Urbain Jean Chappe, *Histoire de la télégraphie* (Paris, 1824), 123–28; Henri Gachot, *La télégraphie optique de Claude Chappe, Strasbourg, Metz, Paris, et ses embranchements* (Saverne, 1967), 1–5; John Charles Dawson, *Lakanal, the Regicide: A Biographical and Historical Study of the Career of Joseph Lakanal* (Alabama: University of Alabama Press, 1948), 33; Gerspach, "Histoire administrative de la Télégraphie aérienne," 3:56–65; Holzmann and Pehrson, *Early History of Data Networks*, 55–61; and Geoffrey Wilson, *The Old Telegraphs*, 120–22.

56. Gerspach, "Histoire administrative de la Télégraphie aérienne," 3:53–66; Holzmann and Pehrson, *Early History of Data Networks*, 64.

57. In contrast, the Morse code used only four elements (dot, dash, short space, long space), and modern digital codes use only two bits (on and off); each element transmits very little information—several elements are needed to transmit one number or one letter of the alphabet—but, since the hardware can handle many elements per second, the efficiency of the hardware compensates for the inefficiency of the codes. The best explanation of these matters can be found in Field; but see also Holzmann and Pehrson, *Early History of Data Networks*, 66, 81–85; Gachot, *La télégraphie optique de Claude Chappe*, 30–36; G. Contant, "Vocabulaires," and E. P. Lhospital, "Signaux," in *Télégraphie Chappe*, 201–20.

58. Chappe, *Histoire de la télégraphie*, 135–36.

59. Gérard Contant, "L'administration centrale," Jean Michel Boubault, "Directeurs et inspecteurs," and Guy De Saint Denis, "Les stationnaires," all in *Télégraphie Chappe*, 257–97.

60. Patrice Flichy, *Une histoire de la communication moderne: Espace public et vie privée* (Paris: La Découverte, 1991), 41; for an English translation of chapter 1, see Flichy, "The Birth of Long Distance Communication: Semaphore Telegraphs in Europe (1790–1840)," *Réseaux: French Journal of Communication* 1, no. 1 (spring 1993): 81–101.

61. P. Charbon, "Histoire générale et formation du réseau," in *Télégraphie Chappe*, 18–62; Chappe, *Histoire de la Télégraphie*, 129–31; Gachot, *La télégraphie optique de Claude Chappe*, 38–39; Gerspach, "Histoire administrative de la Télégraphie aérienne," 3:526–46, 4:32–36; Holzmann and Pehrson, *Early History of Data Networks*, 67–68; and Geoffrey Wilson, *The Old Telegraphs*, 127–30.

62. Yves Lecouturier, "Les sémaphores de la Marine," in *Télégraphie Chappe*, 306–16; Geoffrey Wilson, *The Old Telegraphs*, 130–32.

63. On this concept, see Wiebe Bijker, Thomas P. Hughes, and Trevor Pinch, eds., *The Social Construction of Technological Systems: New Directions in the Sociology and History of Technology* (Cambridge, Mass.: MIT Press, 1987). An impressive example of this approach is Thomas P. Hughes, *Networks of Power: Electrification in Western Society, 1880–1930* (Baltimore: Johns Hopkins University Press, 1983).

64. Flichy, *Une histoire de la communication moderne*, 19.

65. Ibid., 21.

66. *Le Moniteur Universel*, August 18, 1794, 516.

67. Gérard Contant, "L'administration centrale," in *Télégraphie Chappe*, 258–62;

Geoffrey Wilson, *The Old Telegraphs,* 132—35; and Gerspach, "Histoire administrative de la Télégraphie aérienne," 3:543.

68. Flichy, *Une histoire de la communicaton moderne,* 21—30.

69. Geoffrey Wilson, *The Old Telegraphs,* 102—4.

70. David L. Woods, *A History of Tactical Communication Techniques* (New York: Arno, 1974), 18—19; Capt. Barrie Kent, R.N., *Signal! A History of Signalling in the Royal Navy* (Clanfield, Hampshire: Hyden House, 1993), 13—15; Holzmann and Pehrson, *Early History of Data Networks,* 190—92; and Geoffrey Wilson, *The Old Telegraphs,* 12—31. Like the French, the British also had a coastal semaphore system during the Napoleonic Wars; see Geoffrey Wilson, *The Old Telegraphs,* 64—65.

71. Holzmann and Pehrson, *Early History of Data Networks,* 101—26.

72. Luis Enrique Otero Carvajal, "La evolución del telégrafo en España, 1800—1936," in *Las comunicaciones en la construcción del Estado contemporáneo en España: 1700—1936,* ed. Angel Bahamonde Magro, Gaspar Martínez Lorente, and Luis Enrique Otero Carvajal (Madrid: Ministerio de Obras Públicas, Transportes y Medio Ambiente, 1993), 127—28.

73. Gerspach, "Histoire administrative de la Télégraphie aérienne, *Annales télégraphiques,* 4 (1861), 236—37.

74. Quoted in Flichy, *Une histoire de la communication moderne,* 33.

75. Paul Charbon, "Projects et réalisations télégraphiques de Ferrier," in *Télégraphie Chappe,* 349—55.

76. André Muset, "Les techniques clandestines," in *Télégraphie Chappe,* 356—71.

77. Quoted in ibid., 364.

78. Quoted in Flichy, *Une histoire de la communication moderne,* 39—40.

79. Kent, *Signal!* 15—17; Geoffrey Wilson, *The Old Telegraphs,* 33—42, 59—60; Holzmann and Pehrson, *Early History of Data Networks,* 195.

80. On the Liverpool-Holyhead line, see Geoffrey Wilson, *The Old Telegraphs,* 68—80; on other commercial lines, see 81—93.

81. Two centuries later, Britain has many privately owned telephone companies, while in France the public utilities are branches of the government. Plus ça change . . .

82. On the various European optical telegraphs, see Geoffrey Wilson, *The Old Telegraphs,* 159—85. On the telegraphs in Germany, see also Horst Drogge, "Die Entwicklung der optischen Telegraphie in Preussen under ihre Wegbereiter," *Archiv für Deutsche Postgeschichte* 30 (1982): 5—26.

83. Otero Carvajal, "La evolución del telégrafo en España," 123.

84. Ibid., 129—31.

85. Daniel R. Headrick, *The Invisible Weapon: Telecommunications and International Politics, 1851—1945* (New York: Oxford University Press, 1988).

86. Ibid., 188—206. On Algeria, see Alfred Jamaux, "Le réseau algérien," in *Télégraphie Chappe,* 152—61; and Gerspach, "Histoire administrative de la Télégraphie aérienne," 4:238—47.

87. John, *Spreading the News,* 86—87.

88. John R. Parker, *A Treatise upon the Semaphoric System of Telegraphy* (Boston: Pendelton's, 1838); John Pickering, *Lecture on Telegraphic Language; delivered before the Boston Marine Society, February 5, 1833* (Boston: Hiliard Gray, 1833); William Upham Swan,

"Early Visual Telegraphs in Massachusetts," Bostonian Society (Boston), *Proceedings* 10 (1933): 31–47; Robert L. Thompson, *Wiring a Continent: The History of the Telegraph Industry in the United States, 1832–1866* (Princeton, N.J.: Princeton University Press, 1947), 11; Geoffrey Wilson, *The Old Telegraphs,* 210–17.

89. Brooke Hindle, *Emulation and Invention* (New York: Norton, 1983), 85.

90. For the British story of the telegraph, see Geoffrey Hubbard, *Cooke and Wheatstone and the Invention of the Electric Telegraph* (London: Routledge, 1965). Russophiles may prefer Baron Shilling, who demonstrated "an operational electromagnetic telegraph" in 1832, according to A. V. Yarotsky, "150th Anniversary of the Electromagnetic Telegraph," *Telecommunication Journal* 49 (October 1982): 709. Spain can also boast an inventor of the electric telegraph, Dr. Francisco Salvá y Campillo; see Otero Carvajal, "La evolución del telégrafo en España," 135–36.

91. Quoted in Carleton Mabee, *The American Leonardo: A Life of Samuel F. B. Morse* (New York: Knopf, 1943), 145.

92. On the speed and efficiency of optical and electric telegraphic systems, see Holzmann and Pehrson, *Early History,* 89–90; Holzmann and Pehrson, "The First Data Networks," 127–28; Gerspach, "Histoire administrative de la Télégraphie aérienne," 4:244–45; Field, 343; "French Optical Telegraphy," and Lhospital, "Signaux," 218. The electric telegraph was quickly improved; the Wheatstone Automatic Telegraph of 1858 took messages prepared on punched paper tape and transmitted them at a rate of two thousand characters per minute, eight hundred times faster than the optical telegraph.

93. Michel Siméon, "Les débuts de la télégraphie électrique," in *Télégraphie Chappe,* 372–96; Flichy, *Une histoire de la communication moderne,* 63–67; Gerspach, "Histoire administrative de la Télégraphie aérienne," 4:253–58; Gachot, *La télégraphie optique de Claude Chappe,* 117.

94. Kent, *Signal!* 1–2; Timothy Wilson, *Flags at Sea: A Guide to the Flags Flown at Sea by British and Some Foreign Ships, from the 16th Century to the Present Day* (London: HMSO, 1986), 77.

95. Commander Hilary P. Mead, "Naval Signalling. I. Historical," in *Brassey's Annual* (London, 1953), 177–78; Julian S. Corbett, ed., *Fighting Instructions, 1530–1816* (London: Navy Records Society, 1905), 152–63, 195–232; L. E. Holland, "The Development of Signalling in the Royal Navy," *Mariner's Mirror* 39 (1953): 5–7; Timothy Wilson, *Flags at Sea,* 77–78; Woods, *History of Tactical Communication Techniques,* 35; Kent, *Signal!* 3.

96. John Keegan, *The Price of Admiralty* (New York: Penguin, 1988), 50–51.

97. Ibid., 45.

98. Howeth, *History of Communications,* 6; Mead, "Naval Signalling," 178–79; Kent, *Signal!* 3–5; Woods, *History of Tactical Communication Techniques,* 36–39; Holland, "Development of Signalling in the Royal Navy," 7–13; Corbett, *Fighting Instructions,* 233–52.

99. Kent, *Signal!* 4; Woods, *History of Tactical Communication Techniques,* 36–37; Howeth, *History of Communications,* 6.

100. Hugh Popham, *A Damned Cunning Fellow: The Eventful Life of Rear-Admiral Sir Home Popham KCB, KCH, KM, FRS, 1762–1820* (Twyardreath: Old Ferry Press, 1991), 125–30; Kent, *Signal!* 5; Timothy Wilson, *Flags at Sea,* 81–82; Holland, "Development of signalling in the Royal Navy," 14–18. Popham's system found imitators in other coun-

tries, in particular Barron's signal book in the U.S. Navy and Ramatuelle's in the French navy; see Howeth, *History of Communications,* 6; and Woods, *History of Tactical Communication Techniques,* 39.

101. Keegan, *Price of Admiralty,* 51.

102. Hilary P. Mead, *Trafalgar Signals* (London, 1936), 42–43; Keegan, *Price of Admiralty,* 51–56; Kent, *Signal!* 6; Popham, *Damned Cunning Fellow,* 127.

103. Keegan, *Price of Admiralty,* 98.

104. Capt. Frederick Marryat, *A Code of Signals for the Use of Vessels Employed in the Merchant Service* (London: Richardson, various editions, 1817–1879); Christopher Lloyd, *Captain Marryat and the Old Navy* (London: Longmans, 1939), 176–81; Mead, "Naval Signalling," 180–81.

105. See Keegan, *Price of Admiralty,* 122–23.

106. On the electric telegraph and its security aspects, see Kahn, *Codebreakers,* chap. 6; and Headrick, *Invisible Weapon,* chaps. 5, 6.

7

INFORMATION AGES

Past and Present

Upon my word, I have been speaking prose these forty years
without realizing it.

MOLIÈRE, *Le bourgeois gentilhomme*

POLITICIANS MAY HARK BACK TO OUR FOUNDING FATHERS, THE FALL OF THE
Bastille, the Battle of Trafalgar, and other such historical events to legitimize their actions, but the pundits who bombard us with hype would
have us think the information age was born yesterday, the product of the
latest machines. Ours is not the first information age in history, for humans have always needed and used information. Yet in certain periods the
methods used to handle information changed dramatically. We live in such
an age, but it is not the first. The appearance of spoken languages must have
been a momentous event, although we can only guess at it. Writing is a
method we know much more about, as we do about other innovations like
the alphabet, geometry, and Arabic numerals. We can also identify information machines in ancient times (e.g., the sundial and clepsydra) and
even more so in the Middle Ages (the mechanical clock and the printing
press).

The purpose of this book is to argue that the information revolution
in which we live is the result of a cultural change that began roughly three
centuries ago, a change as important as the political and industrial revolutions for which the eighteenth and early nineteenth centuries are so well
known. The cultural change, itself closely intertwined with the demographic, economic, and social transformations of the period, manifested itself in an increasing interest in information of all sorts—about nature,
people, events, business, and other secular and practical topics. Public
officials and private citizens alike not only demanded more information
but also wanted it more readily accessible and easier to understand and
apply—hence the development of information systems that the Age of

Reason and Revolution produced in such profusion. It is these information systems that are the basis for today's information age.

Consider the links between the systems described in this book and those we use today. Systems of classification, nomenclature, and measurement have spread from the sciences to everything else. The products we buy are standardized into grades. Groceries, clothes, and household objects carry bar codes and other mysterious symbols that identify them to specialists (and their computers) as readily as *Pisum sativum* means "garden pea" to the followers of Linnaeus. Social status, political opinions, intelligence, and every other kind of information that comes in series are measured, categorized, classified, and identified in one system or another.

Statistics and numbers do not merely surround us; they have become part of everyday discourse. We know the weather by its probability of precipitation, its windchill factor, its temperature-humidity index. We judge people by their net worth, their grade point average, their SAT scores. Upon opening the morning paper, we turn to the sports scores, the Dow-Jones Industrial Averages, the Consumer Price Index. We are becoming a "calculating people," swept up in a vast statistical movement.

The visual display of information is, if anything, more ubiquitous than its statistical presentation. Thanks to television and computers, almost any kind of information can be displayed in a graphical form, and what cannot be displayed graphically is deemed unimportant. Computerized maps are now appearing on the dashboards of automobiles, changing as one drives along. Global satellite positioning devices guide not just ships and missiles but even hikers and drivers of late-model cars.

Encyclopedias and dictionaries still exist, but computers are transforming them beyond recognition. Spell-checkers, CD-ROMs, and on-line encyclopedias are new bottles for old wine. Databases, updated daily, are today's answer to annual supplements and new editions every few years. And beyond databases, browsers and search engines find and retrieve all sorts of information, even if it is not in alphabetical order.

Nowhere has change been as dramatic and thorough as in communication systems. Postal service still exists, if mainly to deliver advertisements. Newspapers have survived the competition from television but not without a struggle. The telegraph has faded away, replaced by telexes, pagers, and computer networks. The telephone is spreading and will continue to do so until every person, every computer, and every car is wired. And the Internet, still in its infancy, is likely to overshadow them all, although we cannot guess how.

If Europeans and North Americans created and improved elaborate systems for handling information in the eighteenth and early nineteenth centuries, does that allow us to call those systems an information revolution, or are we simply forcing a late-twentieth-century concept upon our ancestors? Is the historian's job to recount the events of the past as people experienced them at the time, or is it to use hindsight to find the origins of today's world?

I prefer history as hindsight, for it is a historian's job to interpret the past in light of the present and the present in light of the past. The Industrial Revolution was only "discovered" (i.e., named) in the 1840s; social history dates from the 1930s; feminist and gender history from the 1970s; environmental history from the 1980s. Since we now live in an age of information, we need to understand how we got here. Our ancestors, as Molière might have said, also lived in an age of information, without realizing it.

SELECTED BIBLIOGRAPHY

There is an enormous literature on the cultural history of the eighteenth and early nineteenth centuries. Notable works on specific information systems are listed in the notes to each chapter. The following list contains works that I found especially interesting and valuable.

Three books deal with information systems in the periods preceding and following the Age of Reason and Revolution. For an earlier period, see Elizabeth Eisenstein, *The Printing Revolution in Early Modern Europe* (Cambridge: Cambridge University Press, 1983); and Alfred W. Crosby, *The Measure of Reality: Quantification and Western Society, 1250–1600* (Cambridge: Cambridge University Press, 1997). For the later nineteenth and twentieth centuries, see Steven Lubar, *InfoCulture: The Smithsonian Book of Information Age Inventions* (Boston: Houghton Mifflin, 1993).

In the large literature on Linnaeus, see especially Frans Antonie Stafleu, *Linnaeus and the Linnaeans: The Spreading of Their Ideas in Systematic Botany, 1735–1789* (Utrecht: Oosthoek, 1971). On Lavoisier and his chemical nomenclature, see Marco Beretta, *The Enlightenment of Matter: The Definition of Chemistry from Agricola to Lavoisier* (Canton, Mass.: Watson, 1993); and Maurice P. Crosland, *Historical Studies in the Language of Chemistry* (Cambridge, Mass.: Harvard University Press, 1962). The best work on the metric system is Ronald E. Zupko, *Revolution in Measurement: Western European Weights and Measures since the Age of Science* (Philadelphia: American Philosophical Society, 1990).

The history of statistics and quantification is a new field. I found the following four books especially valuable: Tore Frängsmyr, J. L. Heilbron, and Robin E. Rider, eds., *The Quantifying Spirit in the Eighteenth Century* (Berkeley: University of California Press, 1990); Theodore Porter, *The Rise of Statistical Thinking, 1820–1900* (Princeton, N.J.: Princeton University Press, 1986); Patricia Cline Cohen, *A Calculating People: Numeracy in Early America* (Chicago: University of Chicago Press, 1982); and James Cassedy, *American Medicine and Statistical Thinking, 1800–1860* (Cambridge, Mass.: Harvard University Press, 1984).

In the large literature on maps, there are only a few outstanding books on this period: Josef W. Konvitz, *Cartography in France, 1660–1848: Science, Engineering, and Statecraft* (Chicago: University of Chicago Press, 1987); Adrian Robinson, *Marine Cartography in Britain: A History of the Sea Chart to 1855* (Leicester: Leicester University Press, 1962); and Arthur H. Robinson, *Early Thematic Mapping in the History of Cartography* (Chicago: University of Chicago Press, 1982). The story of John Harrison has been told several times, most recently in the charming best-seller by Dava Sobel, *Longitude: The True Story of a Lone Genius Who Solved the Greatest Scientific Problem of His Time* (New York:

Penguin, 1996). The history of graphs is told, and shown, in a wonderful book by Edward R. Tufte, *The Visual Display of Quantitative Information* (Cheshire, Conn.: Graphics Press, 1983). A very special aspect of graphic display is described by Martin Rudwick in "The Emergence of a Visual Language of Geology, 1760–1840," *History of Science* 14 (1976): 149–95.

Two books on the history of dictionaries were especially valuable in this study: Sidney Landau, *Dictionaries: The Art and Craft of Lexicography* (New York: Scribner's, 1984); and Bernard Quemada, *Les Dictionnaires du français moderne, 1539–1863: Etude sur leur histoire, leurs types, et leurs méthodes* (Paris: Didier, 1967). There is a voluminous literature on the *Encyclopédie*, most of it philosophical; but see Robert Darnton, *The Business of Enlightenment: A Publishing History of the Encyclopédie, 1775–1800* (Cambridge: Harvard University Press, 1979). In contrast, there are very few works on other encyclopedias of that era; see Frank A. Kafker, ed., *Notable Encyclopedias of the Seventeenth and Eighteenth Centuries: Nine Predecessors of the Encyclopédie* (Oxford: Voltaire Foundation, 1981); and Kafker, ed., *Notable Encyclopedias of the Late Eighteenth Century: Eleven Successors of the Encyclopédie* (Oxford: Voltaire Foundation, 1994).

The postal history of three countries can be found in Howard Robinson, *The British Post Office: A History* (Westwood, Conn.: Greenwood, 1970); Yves Maxime Danan, *Histoire postale et libertés publiques: Le droit de libre communication des idées et opinions par voie de correspondance* (Paris: Pichon et Durand-Auzias, 1965); and especially Richard R. John, *Spreading the News: The American Postal System from Franklin to Morse* (Cambridge, Mass.: Harvard University Press, 1996). Telegraphy before Morse is the subject of Gerald J. Holzmann and Björn Pehrson, *The Early History of Data Networks* (Los Alamitos, Calif.: IEEE Publications, 1994).

CREDITS

Figure 1. Académie des Sciences. "Carte de France corrigée par Ordre du Roy sur les Observations de Messieurs de l'Académie des Sciences" (1682). In *Mémoires de l'Académie royale des Sciences*, vol. 7, pt. 1. Paris, 1729. Department of Special Collections, the University of Chicago Library.

Figure 2. César-François Cassini de Thury. "Planche X: Paris-Dunkerque." In *La Méridienne de l'Observatoire*. Paris, 1744. Photo courtesy of The Newberry Library, Chicago.

Figure 3. César-François Cassini de Thury. "Compiègne." In *Carte de France levée par ordre du Roy*, sec. 2. Paris 1756. Map Department, the University of Chicago Library.

Figure 4. Colonel Jacotin, "Acre, Nazareth, le Jourdain" (detail). In *Carte topographique de l'Egypte* (n.d.), map 46. Published with *Description de l'Egypte*. Paris, 1809–1828. Photo courtesy of The Newberry Library, Chicago.

Figure 5. Murdoch MacKenzie Sr. "The Channel between Sky I. and the Lewis" (detail). In *Orcades: or, a Geographic and Hydrographic Survey of the Orkney and Lewis Islands in Eight Maps*. 3rd ed. London, 1776. Map Department, the University of Chicago Library.

Figure 6. John Walker. "Mouth of the Thames" (detail). In *Map of the Inland Navigation, Canals, and Rail Roads, with the Situation of the Various Mineral Production throughout Great Britain*. Wakefield, 1830.

Map Department, the University of Chicago Library.

Figure 7. Alexis Jaillot. *Les montagnes de Alpes, où sont remarquées des passages de France en Italie* (detail). Paris, 1692. Photo courtesy of The Newberry Library, Chicago.

Figure 8. Jean-Louis Dupain-Triel. *La France considerée dans les différentes hauteurs des ses plaines*. Paris, 1791. Photo courtesy of The Newberry Library, Chicago.

Figure 9. John Whitehurst, "A Section of the Strata near Black-Brook." In *An Inquiry into the Original State and Formation of the Earth; deduced from Facts and the Laws of Nature*, pl. 3. London, 1778. Department of Special Collections, the University of Chicago.

Figure 10. William Playfair. "Chart of the National Debt of England." In *The Commercial and Political Atlas*. London, 1801. Department of Special Collections, the University of Chicago.

Figure 11. William Playfair. "Statistical Chart shewing the Extent, the Population & Revenues of the Principal Nations of Europe in the order of their Magnitude." In *Statistical Breviary*. London, 1801. Department of Special Collections, the University of Chicago.

Figure 12. Heinrich Berghaus. "Geistige Bildung." In *Dr. Heinrich Berghaus' Physikalischer Atlas*, vol. 2. Gotha, 1848. Photo courtesy of The Newberry Library, Chicago.

INDEX